WHEN THE
church
BECOMES YOUR
party

African American Life Series

*A complete listing of the books in this series can be found
online at wsupress.wayne.edu*

Series Editors

MELBA JOYCE BOYD

Department of Africana Studies, Wayne State University

RONALD BROWN

Department of Political Science, Wayne State University

Deborah Smith Pollard

CONTEMPORARY
GOSPEL MUSIC

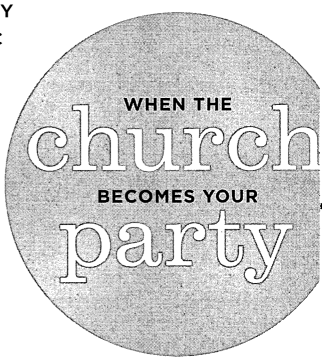

WHEN THE church BECOMES YOUR party

WAYNE STATE UNIVERSITY PRESS

Detroit

© 2008 by Wayne State University Press, Detroit, Michigan
48201. All rights reserved. No part of this book may be reproduced
without formal permission. Manufactured in the United States
of America.

12 11 10 09 08   5 4 3 2 1

Library of Congress Cataloging-in-Publication Data

Pollard, Deborah Smith.
When the church becomes your party : contemporary gospel music /
Deborah Smith Pollard.
p. cm. — (African American life series)
Includes bibliographical references (p. 181) and index.
ISBN-13: 978-0-8143-3218-4 (pbk. : alk. paper)
ISBN-10: 0-8143-3218-8 (pbk. : alk. paper)
1. Gospel music—History and criticism. 2. African Americans—
Music—History and criticism. 3. African American churches.
4. African Americans—Social life and customs. I. Title.
ML3187.S53 2008
782.25'4—dc22
2007036533

An earlier version of chapter 2 was published as "The Phenomenon
Known as the Gospel Music Stage Play" in *CEA Critic 62*, no. 3
(Summer 2000): 1–17. Reprinted by permission.

∞ The paper used in this publication meets the minimum
requirements of the American National Standard for Information
Sciences—Permanence of Paper for Printed Library Materials,
ANSI Z39.48–1984.

Designed by Isaac Tobin
Typeset by The Composing Room of Michigan, Inc.
Composed in Adobe Caslon Pro & Gotham

CONTENTS

PREFACE

This book is titled *When the Church Becomes Your Party*, but not because
I deliberately aim to be provocative. Instead, with this title and within
the chapters, my goal is to reflect the sacred yet celebratory intentions
that exist throughout the gospel music community despite the wide variety of sounds, performance styles, and controversies that often sur-
round them.

The phrase first surfaced in 1995 while I was conducting research on
gospel attire as part of a project for the Michigan State University Museum. One of those I interviewed, Claudette Manners, was a designer
who had created garments for many well-known gospel divas. When I
asked her why there had often been so much beading and glitter on their
outfits in the early 1990s, she responded this way: "When the church becomes your party . . . within moderation, you have to transfer your party
clothes from there, from the clubs, to the church. So they [the performers and audiences] *dress; I dress.* There's never too much glitter, too many
rhinestones. . . . And even for the women that are conservative dressers,
there's never too much tailoring." She did not mean to suggest that *no one*
who comes to Jesus and joins the church ever goes into nightclubs there-

after. Rather, she was describing what church and gospel fans have said among themselves for years: "When I found Christ, I didn't stop dancing; I just changed partners." Her dressmaker's interpretation was that the ladies did not stop partying or give up their party clothes; they just started partying a little differently, in a new, more sacred space.

Whether I am in a praise and worship service, at a holy hip hop event, at a Saturday night musical with ten or more performers, or in an auditorium enjoying a gospel musical stage play with two thousand others, at some point I will hear someone—an emcee, a character, or a singer—talk about "the praise party," "gettin' your praise on," or "the Holy Ghost party." Someone else might exhort the congregation or crowd to chant, "Ain't no party like a Holy Ghost party 'cause a Holy Ghost party don't stop," an adaptation of a secular refrain that can be found throughout black culture. These and similar phrases refer to the highly charged, spirit-filled connections that can occur when believers come together. When that happens, congregant connects with congregant and the faithful encounter the Almighty. Whether dressed up, dressed down, performing "old school" gospel or something edgy and controversial, they all seem to agree that there "ain't no party" that can compare with that which believers can create wherever they "touch and agree" that God is in their midst.

I know about the Holy Ghost party from several perspectives: scholar, gospel announcer, concert producer, churchgoer, former church and community choir member, and fan. I am the oldest of four children born to a piano accompanist and to a baritone/choral conductor. My father, the Reverend Elmer W. Smith, eventually became the pastor of the Elyton Baptist Church in Detroit, where he remained for twenty-five years until his death in 1981. My mother, Rosa Lee Smith, has served as the minister of music at that church for more than five decades. Because these two formally trained musicians introduced my siblings and me to all kinds of music, I appreciate a range of musical sounds and styles. But gospel music is my heart; it is what I listen to most often in my own house and car and what I have gleefully offered to my listeners on FM 98 WJLB.com–Detroit on Sundays, 6–10 AM, since October 1994, even though I am not a morning person.

With this collection, I aim to provide a look inside some of the emerging trends within the gospel music world at the turn of the twenty-first century, a world some may not know is as diverse, complex, and exciting as it is. Whether you are a scholar, a gospel music insider, or someone simply curious about all forms of great music, my hope is that you will enjoy reading about the more contemporary music, its history, and the people who keep the Holy Ghost party going!

ACKNOWLEDGMENTS

This book would never have come to fruition had it not been for the following individuals and institutions. Thank you to:

University of Michigan–Dearborn (UM-D) Office of Research and Sponsored Programs and Dr. Drew Buchanan, director, for providing support for my research

University of Michigan–Ann Arbor Office of the Vice President for Research for providing me with a publication subvention award

My colleagues in the African and African American Studies Program at UM-D, especially Claude Jacobs, Gloria House, Joe Lunn, and Ahmad Rahman, who listened to an early draft of the holy hip hop chapter; Humanities colleagues Sheryl Pearson and Randy Woodland, for their early feedback on gospel attire; and Mardigian Library librarian Carla Brooks and Bob Fraser for their research assistance

Michigan State University Museum and Francie Freese, who transcribed many recorded interviews for me

My gospel music industry colleagues: Tracey Artis, Lisa Collins, Neily Dickerson, B. Jeff Grant, Teresa Hairston, Al "the Bishop" Hobbs, Jamillah

Muhammad, Jackie Patillo, George Stewart, Telisa Stinson, Carla Williams, and Bishop Sam Williams

The members of the church community who were part of my research: Greater Christ Temple Church—Bishop Carl Holland, Elder Carl B. Phillips, Evangelist Consuella Smith, and the praise and worship team; Perfecting Church—Pastor Marvin L. Winans, Kasey Shepard, Randy Short, April Green, and the praise and worship team; St. James Baptist Church (now known as Shield of Faith Ministries)—Pastor James Jennings Jr., Min. Marcus D. Jennings, Felicia Jennings, and the praise and worship team; Rosedale Park Church—Pastor Haman Cross, Pastor Dennis Talbert, and Sister Sonya; the founders of the Detroit Musicians' Fellowship, Carolyn Cole and Alvin Waddles, for allowing me to distribute my survey; and the musicians and choir directors who completed my praise and worship survey

The feedback panel for my research on the changing dress code: Portia Dye, Timothy Dye, Kyra Edwards, Sean Mosley, Carl Phillips, Consuella Smith, and DeRonae Smith

The members of the Christian rap/holy hip hop community: Kiwi (Kimberly Williams), the Cross Movement, Corey Red, the Qwest (Reginald and Ebony Dockery), Kia Jones-Glenn, Maji, Nana Dansoa Paintse, Dr. D., and Shannon Gaston (Vessel)

Those who assisted me in securing the photographs found in this book, including: Jelani Jones; Bill Carpenter; Romie Minor, curator of the E. Azalia Hackley Collection at the Detroit Public Library; the family of the late Ron Milner; Vy Higginsen and the Mama Foundation for the Arts; Rogers William Foster; Michael Lavine; Mark Mann; Steve Holsey and the *Michigan Chronicle*; Irene Johnson Ware; Diane Steinberg Lewis; Barton Lessin, Wayne State University Library System, African American Literature Special Collection; Faith Entertainment; Tyscot Records; Integrity Music; Cross Movement Records; Spirit Rising Music/Music World Entertainment; Faith Entertainment; Damon Williams, Kieron Goring of Zomba Gospel, LLC (including the Verity, Fo Yo Soul, and GospoCentric labels)

Bill McNeece who stepped in to shoot, evaluate, and consolidate photos for me

The members of the writing group to which I belong: Professors Aneb Kgositsile, Esther M. Coleman, and Penny Godboldo

My friends—especially Gail, Linda, Connie, Marsha, Teresa, Maggie, Larry, Lorraine T., Pat, Rosemary, Elnora, and The Other Deborah—who allowed me to talk, and talk, and talk about what I was doing and why I thought it mattered

My longtime mentor, Larry Berkove, for his advice on the praise and worship and clothing chapters and for his immortal words about writing with clarity: "Just say it, Deb!"

Wayne State University Press, especially Acquiring Editor Kathy Wildfong and editorial board member and friend Professor Melba Boyd

Claudette Manners, who in 1995 uttered a phrase that never left me, a phrase that became the title for this book

My mother, Rosa Lee Smith; my husband, Basil Pollard; my brothers, DeRoy and DeLyle; my pastor, Dr. Charles G. Adams; and my prayer partner, Marilynn Bell, who believed I could get this book into print even on the days I just couldn't see it

And all not named here who shared their time, information, resources, and words of support along my journey.

INTRODUCTION

WHEN THE CHURCH BECOMES YOUR PARTY

When the initial chords of gospel music were being created at the turn of the twentieth century, places to experience the new sounds were few, usually the storefront Primitive Baptist and Pentecostal churches where gospel music was born. Early challenges to this music arose because it included blues and jazz elements, which some viewed as incompatible with praising the Creator. The singers and musicians were denounced for "jazzin' God," and with the addition of each new instrument, such as the Hammond organ in the 1930s, or a new performance style, including contemporary gospel in the late 1960s, the outcry was always the same: "That's the devil's music."[1]

Despite, or perhaps because of, the controversies, gospel music slowly began to infiltrate the world beyond the walls of the Black Church. Radio programs showcased gospel quartets and soloists; gospel publishing houses began turning out the new, sought-after sheet music; and vinyl recordings captured the attention of the "churched" and the "unchurched," who stood in line together to purchase the first big sellers in gospel released by Mahalia Jackson and the Clara Ward Singers in the mid-1940s.[2] These early marketplace victories hinted that gospel music could be viewed as a vital expression of black culture, even when detached from the formal worship experience. Six decades later, gospel music comprises a significant part of the soundtrack of American life, and not merely because it is the form through which pop music stars, including Aretha Franklin and Whitney Houston and, more recently, Kelly Price and Fantasia have honed their vocal talents.

In the twenty-first century, gospel artists who choose to incorporate the latest musical trends in their music ministries are still frequently able to attract nonbelievers and then share the message of Jesus Christ, even as they express their own creativity and connection to the black community. The responses to the new subgenres created by these innovators are mixed: they are applauded by some, derided by others, and eyed with a level of bewilderment by yet another group. And what exactly are the most pointed questions being raised about this sacred form that outsells the likes of jazz and classical music?[3] Are sales proof that the gospel is in fact reaching the masses? Is today's gospel music capable of being used as an evangelistic tool just as more traditional forms were in the past? Or, as one critic has charged, is this music "opiate for the masses of African American people," all praise singing and ecstasy without the social and political power of its predecessor, the Negro spiritual?[4]

No matter what answers any one scholar or practitioner offers in response to these questions, someone will undoubtedly be dissatisfied. For as long as human beings are the singers and consumers of gospel music, there will always be conflicting ideas about how gospel music should sound, how its performers should look, and what new configurations it should and should not take if it is to be considered authentic, pure, and untainted.

In the five chapters of this collection, I do not define authenticity, sigh about the presence of secular elements, or issue a plea for a return to the traditional performances of days past. For despite the unconventional packaging, a historically based, close reading of testimonies, lyrics, and interviews by the artists who create such controversial forms as holy hip hop, praise and worship, and gospel musical stage plays reveals that their ministries rest on the same time-honored principles as more traditional gospel music forms. At the core of all these diverse, new subgenres is the gospel message: God's love demonstrated through the life, death, and resurrection of Jesus Christ for the salvation of humankind. Gospel music at the beginning of the twenty-first century, then, is very much in line with the most basic doctrinal teachings of the Christian Church and its cultural counterpart, the Black Church.

Each form or issue investigated in this collection—praise and worship music, gospel musical stage plays, the changing dress code, women gospel announcers, and holy hip hop—has roots in African, Black Church, and Christian traditions. And each, because of how its artists deviate from these traditions, has its share of detractors. While I expected to encounter the anti–holy hip hop discussions in some quarters, I was initially caught off guard when the phrase "I hate praise and worship music" was spoken by a young Detroit-area musician. In fact, I actually laughed out loud, not at his discomfort, but at the realization that the praise team and the Christian rappers have more in common than most would think.

Instead of dwelling on the controversies that have emerged around these forms, I use them as a point from which to begin the examination of these subgenres, each of which, I assert, is a reflection of two factors: the timelessness of several elements within black sacred music and the dynamic transformations that continually occur within black culture. Each chapter incorporates a number of examples and illustrations, a substantial percentage of which involve gospel music and artists with Detroit connections.

There are personal reasons why this predominately black city is in the spotlight in this volume: it is where I live and worship as well as the base from which I conduct my research and host my gospel radio program on Sundays (FM 98 WJLB.com). For eight years, I produced an Emmy Award–winning gospel television show on WDIV, Detroit's NBC affiliate. Since 1983 I have produced outdoor gospel events, specifically, the McDonald's GospelFest (1983–2004), the first in the country created and underwritten by the fast food company, and the Motor City PraiseFest (founded in 1991). Hundreds of thousands have reportedly attended these two festivals that were combined in 1999, resulting in one of the biggest free gospel events in the country.[5]

Of course, there are substantial historical and musical reasons for Detroit-based artists to be featured in this volume. The Motor City has been a major hub, some have even said "the capital," for gospel music for several generations, a complete history and analysis of which have yet to be fully presented.[6] Some of the city's earliest steps into gospel history

3

Minister Sheila Vann directs the Second Ebenezer Choir during the McDonald's GospelFest in Detroit 1984. Collection of author.

were taken when it hosted the National Convention of Gospel Choirs and Choruses (NCGCC), the first convention of its kind, in 1936, just three years after the organization was founded by Thomas A. Dorsey, the father of gospel music. The convention subsequently returned to Detroit in 1945, 1956, and 1970. The NCGCC continues to thrive, with forty-eight nationwide choral unions, that is, affiliated chapters, including one in Detroit.[7]

In 1968 the Motor City became the launching site for the Gospel Music Workshop of America, Inc. (GMWA), reportedly the largest convention focused on the genre. The GMWA, founded by the late Reverend James Cleveland, held its first week-long meeting at the King Solomon Baptist Church, which was already a civic and cultural center. By hosting the GMWA, the church enhanced its decades-long reputation as a venue for performances by gospel greats like the Clara Ward Singers, Sister Rosetta Tharpe, and the Reverend James Cleveland. For a number of years, King Solomon was where quartet lovers could hear their favorite national groups, including the Mighty Clouds of Joy and the Dixie Hummingbirds as well as some of the finest locally based singers.[8]

Detroit is the city from which the Reverend C. L. Franklin became a nationally revered preacher, singer, civil rights activist, and recording artist, with almost eighty sermons, including a million-seller, placed on vinyl. In the sanctuary of the New Bethel Baptist Church, one of his daughters, Aretha, among the most celebrated vocalists in American history, recorded two historic gospel albums, one in 1956 when she was a mere teenager and the other in 1986. She continues to make her presence known in the city's church and gospel music worlds through highly anticipated sacred events featuring nationally known preachers and singers.[9]

Some of gospel music's most influential families have called Detroit their home. The late Bill Moss and one of his sisters, Mattie Moss Clark, who migrated to Detroit from their home in Selma, Alabama, created intertwining musical dynasties that extend for several generations. Singer/composer Moss recorded and traveled the world with his group, the Celestials, consisting of his wife, Essie, and one of their daughters, Theresa, as well as with Leviticus and the Bill Moss Singers. Among the other talented family members is Bill Jr., a keyboardist, composer, recording artist, and minister of music at Christian Tabernacle Church in Detroit. Another son, Jimmy, now known as J. Moss, is a Stellar Award–winning, Grammy-nominated composer and singer dubbed "the Voice." J. Moss also functions as one-third of the acclaimed production team PAJAM, sought after by secular and gospel recording artists alike.[10]

The other side of that family's dynasty begins with Moss's sister, the late singer/composer/arranger Mattie Moss Clark, whose classic gospel songs include "Salvation Is Free" and "Climbing up the Mountain." She first came to prominence as the director of the Southeast Michigan State Choir of the Church of God in Christ (COGIC) and later served as president of the international music department for COGIC, the denomination that produced such gospel superstars as Andrae and Sandra Crouch, the Rance Allen Group, and the Hawkins Family. Among the most popular singers to have been directly influenced by Clark are her daughters, the Clark Sisters. Jacky, Twinkie, Dorinda, and Karen have earned numerous industry music citations, including Stellar and Dove awards and the President's Award of Merit during the 2007 Grammy Salute to

Dr. Mattie Moss Clark. Photograph by Glynn Chisholm. Courtesy of KCS Productions.

Gospel. Several grandsons have performed as the Clark Brothers, and a granddaughter, Kierra "KiKi" Sheard, an award-winning vocalist, released her critically and popularly acclaimed solo project *I Owe You* while still in high school in 2004. Her second release earned her a Grammy nomination.[11]

Elder David Winans Sr. and Delores Winans, aka Mom and Pop Winans, and their children brought international attention to the city beginning in the early 1980s with the award-winning brothers Marvin, Carvin, Michael, and Ronald, known as the Winans. They were followed by BeBe and CeCe, Angie and Debbie, and Daniel. Among the Winans,

The Clark Sisters (*left to right*): Dorinda Clark Cole, Twinkie Clark, Jacky Clark Chisholm, and Karen Clark Sheard. Photograph by Michael Gomez. Courtesy of KCS Productions.

often called "the first family of gospel," are Grammy and Stellar award–winning singers, composers, arrangers, and record label owners. They, along with Commissioned, Vanessa Bell Armstrong, Minister Thomas Whitfield and the Thomas Whitfield Company, Witness, and other Detroiters, helped to shape the contemporary and urban contemporary gospel sounds of the 1980s and 1990s and paved the way for today's praise and worship movement.

Native New Yorker Donnie McClurkin, one of gospel music's most acclaimed artists, earned a place in Detroit's gospel music history having served as assistant to Pastor Marvin L. Winans at Perfecting Church in the Motor City from 1989 to 2001. The award-winning singer now pastors Perfected Faith in his home state. Photograph by Rogers Wm. Foster. Courtesy of Perfecting Church.

The city has also been the proving ground for generations of great church- and community-based groups and choirs, among them the Meditation Singers (which originally included Della Reese), Lucylle Lemon and the Lemon Gospel Chorus, the Voices of Tabernacle, the Harold Smith Majestics, the Donald Vails Choraleers, Elma Lois Hendrix and the Community Youth Ensemble, the Michael Fletcher Chorale,

In 1971 the Rance Allen Group of Monroe, Michigan, signed with the Gospel Truth/Stax label after winning a talent contest sponsored by Detroit radio station WCHB. Since that time, Pastor Allen (*left*), who performs with his brothers Steve and Tom, has been revered as a show-stopping vocalist and contemporary gospel music icon. Photograph by Reggie Anderson. Courtesy of Tyscot Records.

Deitrick Haddon and the Voices of Unity, and Fred Hammond and Radical for Christ. Similarly, the Flying Clouds, the Violinaires, the Evereadys, and Evelyn Turrentine Agee and the Gospel Warriors are a few of the Detroit-based names that have given the city a national place within the quartet world. Of course, a city where half of the people can sing and the other half can really sing would naturally be the place where the International Gospel Music Hall of Fame and Museum would be sit-

Pastor Rance Allen. Photograph by Rogers Wm. Foster. Courtesy of Perfecting Church.

uated. With such a rich and varied history in gospel music, Detroit has understandably produced several of the current leaders in almost every area of gospel music covered in the five chapters of this book.

Chapter 1, "Praise Is What We Do," focuses on one of the fastest growing aspects of the Black Church experience and the gospel music industry: praise and worship music. In fact, this music can be found in thousands of churches around the world. While some have insisted that it is a "new thing," there are biblical as well as African and African American cultural forms that predate, gave rise to, and can often be identified within it. I also examine the extent to which several leading gospel artists as well as three diverse churches in the metropolitan Detroit area have adapted this form that originated in the White Evangelical Church.

The chapter reveals that instead of turning away completely from traditional music, which is what the anti–praise and worship crowd argues has happened, a majority of churches and many artists use an "inclusive" model. So, while the devotional period may be referred to as praise and worship, traditional songs are usually performed within it for various reasons, including satisfying older members of the congregation and maintaining the musical heritage of a church or denomination.

Among those highlighted because of their inclusive praise and worship practices are acclaimed artists Fred Hammond, Israel and New Breed, Byron Cage, Judith Christie McAllister, and William Murphy III. The section on how praise and worship is executed within local churches builds on my observations of praise and worship music and services around the country over the last fifteen years. Here, however, the focus is on three Motor City churches, chosen because of their differences in size, musical traditions, and denominational affiliations: Perfecting Church, headed by Pastor Marvin L. Winans, a member of the Winans family; St. James Baptist Church, a leader in the 1960s–80s in recording the sound of the Baptist Church tradition, where the Reverend James A. Jennings Jr. is the pastor; and Greater Christ Temple Church, where Bishop Carl Holland, founder of the Pentecostal Assembly of Believers, Inc., is the pastor.[12]

I have been part of praise and worship services in Detroit-area churches since the early 1990s. At Hartford Memorial, the church to which I belong, the praise team led by Marc Ivory begins the Saturday night service each week. My exposure to this form also continues to come through serving as emcee for or as an invited guest or congregant at scores of gatherings where praise and worship music is performed, including musicals, recording sessions, and regular services at churches like Greater Grace Temple, Greater Emmanuel Institutional COGIC, and Triumph Baptist Church.

Chapter 2 focuses on gospel musical stage plays. Its title, "Right under Our (Upturned) Noses: The Phenomenon Known as the Gospel Musical Stage Play," initially referred to my own rather myopic response to them. In the mid-1990s, I told one of my former instructors, Dr. Bill Wiggins, professor emeritus from Indiana University, that the plays were all

Perfecting congregation in praise at Calihan Hall, University of Detroit, during Holy Convocation. Photograph by Rogers Wm. Foster. Courtesy of Perfecting Church.

the same and, therefore, if you had seen one, you had seen them all. His response was, "You know how Beethoven's Fifth ends, but you go to a performance to see how that conductor will get you there." That was the impetus for me to view the plays not as inferior versions of the work of August Wilson but as a continuation of the black sacred dramas that, since the time of enslavement, have attempted to convey an *anticipated* spiritual message and outcome (Jesus *always* wins in the end!) in an engaging and entertaining manner. Within the chapter, I discuss the elements that have allowed the most popular plays of this genre, written by such names as Tyler Perry, David E. Talbert, Angela Barrow-Dunlap, and Mike Matthews, to out-earn most Broadway plays, usually without the knowledge or attendance of mainstream America.

Chapter 3, "Muscle T-shirts, Tight Jeans, and Cleavage: (W)rapping the Gospel for a New Generation," examines the changing dress code among gospel performers and their audience members and is the culmination of research I began over a decade ago. I began making note, both as a scholar and as a participant, of how difficult it was becoming to get dressed to go to a gospel music event. My friends and I found ourselves acting like twelve-year-olds, the kind who call one another and ask, "What are you wearing?" "Is this a pants program?" "Are you going to glitter?" Instead of dressing up for every church or gospel occasion, which had been the tradition for generations, increasingly people were "freestyling," as GospoCentric vice president Tracey Artis has described it, wearing casual, funky attire to various events.

This chapter was formally begun in 1999, when Dottie Peoples, Vickie Winans, CeCe Winans, and Helen Baylor were the headliners for my event, the Motor City PraiseFest featuring the McDonald's Gospel-Fest.[13] That year was memorable because, with the exception of Peoples, these women artists wore pants during their performances. My friend and radio idol the late missionary Bertha Harris made some rather startling remarks as we talked the next day. "If they had really been set free, they wouldn't have had those pants on," she said as she discussed Vickie and CeCe Winans and their spiritual "freedom." "Helen wasn't raised in the church," she continued. "She'll do better as she grows in Christ." When I explained that what the performers had worn were women's, not men's, pants, she replied, "It was too close to disobedience," referring to the Old Testament prohibition about women wearing "that which pertaineth to a man." Her strong opinions made me ask if I could type while she talked; as I did, I thought I might be close to a topic worth investigating.

Later, I called Vickie Winans to thank her again for her performance and asked about the pants she wore without ever alluding to what Missionary Harris had said. Vickie explained that she had only begun wearing trousers when she entered her thirties, that she always checks to see if pants are appropriate for the venue, and that she never wears them in a sanctuary. Then, most memorably, she added, "I've been shown a freer way, and I am walking therein." That the two women, Missionary Harris and Vickie Winans, had used "free" in such completely different ways put me in full research mode; the result is chapter 3.

Here, I begin with some of the earliest known proscriptions regarding clothing in the Christian Church, many of which were adapted by various denominations within the Black Church. After investigating how and why the church or gospel dress code has changed in recent years, I conclude that the challenges to the tradition can be attributed in part to a more casual American culture. However, a major factor is the desire by many artists to connect with their younger audiences with clothing that declares that one can be young, hip, and Christian. The chapter also raises the question of whether the changing silhouette of gospel—from the full-figured shape of Mahalia Jackson to the more streamlined image of Yolanda Adams—can be used to draw individuals to the message of the gospel or whether it merely draws their roving eyes to the messenger.

Chapter 4, "From Princess Premium Stuff and Miss Mandy to Holy Boldness: The Influence of Women Gospel Announcers," is the continuation of the research I conducted for my doctoral dissertation, "The Gospel Announcer and the Black Gospel Music Tradition" (Michigan State University, 1994). Although I had been a gospel radio announcer (disc jockey) for a while, it did not occur to me to research gospel announcers until Dr. Marsha MacDowell (Michigan State University) and Dr. Mellonee Burnim (Indiana University) made the suggestion. For my dissertation, I interviewed more than thirty fellow announcers, both male and female, most of them members of the Gospel Announcers Guild of the GMWA. But when I decided to concentrate solely on women gospel announcers and search for print resources for this project, I was startled to find how infrequently they are mentioned in the existing historical literature, and that when they are the information is often incomplete, even when they have been major figures.

Chapter 4 looks at the history and roles of women gospel announcers beginning with their forerunner Rosalie Latimer Wood, who sat behind a microphone in the 1920s as cohost to the first black radio announcer in the United States, Jack L. Cooper. After establishing the early history of women in gospel announcing, I devote most of the chapter to examining the careers of Martha Jean "the Queen" Steinberg and Irene Johnson Ware, two dynamic women who became iconic and sometimes controversial figures in radio and barrier breakers within the industry with their music, informed, inspirational talk, business acumen, and expansive personalities. They serve as examples of the influence women have had and can continue to have within gospel radio.

My late friend Tim Smith was the first to compel me to listen closely to holy hip hop, the subject of chapter 5, "Preachers in Disguise: Bringing the Holy to Hip Hop." A noted gospel music reviewer and Stellar Award winner for Announcer of the Year, Tim played holy hip hop on his radio program, which aired on WDTR FM–Detroit for fifteen years until his passing in 2004. I would hear him introduce on Sunday morning songs that often sounded like what my colleagues play on FM 98 WJLB.com, which has eighteen- to thirty-four-year-olds as its target audience. Rather than turning Tim's music off, I kept listening because he often told me of the calls he received thanking him for being able to share the gospel in a way that hip hop fans could understand. The more I listened, the more I recognized that the message of the gospel was in fact clearly in place; it was just the presentational style that was different. Before long, holy hip hop became part of my radio play list also, and certain artists became favorites because of the deft way they used language while extolling biblical principles.

After a recap of the vital oral tradition that runs from Africa through the Black Church, I present a historical overview of holy hip hop followed by a textual analysis of several songs that demonstrate what I discovered: Christian rappers cover everything from praise and worship and the plan of salvation to eschatology, the study of the end times. Special attention is given to the Cross Movement, one of the most successful groups within the genre.

The epilogue is actually a bird's-eye view of newer settings and formats associated with gospel not covered in this collection, including movies, the Internet, television, outdoor festivals, and print outlets.

Before closing, I need to comment on the number of references that come from Internet sources, some of which are academic but many of which are not. In the case of the former, I join with researchers in every field who have applauded the ease with which we can now access scholarly articles, dissertations, abstracts, and educational websites as we pursue our various interests. What I have found extremely relevant to my own study of contemporary aspects of gospel music is a range of websites, including online gospel magazines, artist webpages, fan sites, and message boards that have information on personalities, many of whom have not been written about in any mainstream publications, academic journals, or books. While researchers may look skeptically at such sites, I have found using them has greatly enhanced my ability to tap into what credentialed writers as well as record labels, artists, and fans are discussing in terms of the music and the range of topics that are a part of contemporary gospel music. As is the case with any online research that includes nonacademic sites, I always seek other forms of corroboration through my interviews with various practitioners when published academic sources are not available. But because so much of contemporary gospel is sold, discussed, and displayed through electronic sources, the Internet is becoming an important resource for this research.

The chapters in this collection can be read front to back or in whatever order the reader chooses, since they have been written to stand alone. My hope is that those who read this collection will better appreciate the diverse modes of performance chosen by gospel artists and that there are biblical as well as Black Church, cultural, and community traditions that run through them all. Finally, I hope that the readers will accept that, based on their testimonies and lyrics, the holy hip hopper and the praise and worship team member, the artist in the tight leather pants and the one making us laugh and cry in the gospel musical play, all are trying to introduce others to the same God, to invite outsiders to see the church as a site for spiritual celebrations, and to make gospel music, in one form or another, their party music of choice.

"PRAISE IS WHAT WE DO"

THE RISE OF PRAISE AND WORSHIP MUSIC IN THE URBAN CHURCH

If the young people were allowed to ... take over the church, we would lose Devotion. They think Devotion is a waste of time.

SISTER ROSIE SIMS, in Walter F. Pitts, *Old Ship of Zion*

Judith Christie McAllister is great ... because she is tied to her past. If you listen to what she does, incorporated in her new stuff, you can hear the sound of old gospel.

PASTOR MARVIN L. WINANS, January 14, 2004

They can be found standing before a few or before thousands in churches and auditoriums across the country. With microphones in hand, they speak and sing words of praise with musical accompaniment that might be provided by a commercially produced music track, a single keyboardist, or an eight-piece band. Their lyrics are given to the congregation in call-and-response style, projected on a screen, or printed in the church bulletin. Individually, they are called praise and worship leaders, while collectively—as few as two or as many as a dozen in number—they are referred to as praise teams. Their mission: through example and exhortation, to move congregants from passive observation to active participation in the worship experience so that they might usher in and experience the presence of God.

The label "praise and worship" is used within the Christian Church in reference to a particular musical repertoire and mode of performance that emerged during the last decades of the twentieth century. Generally, praise and worship music is used during the opening period of a worship service, gospel musical, or concert; however, its rising popularity has led to its use at other times as well. In some instances, entire services and events are built around praise and worship music.

While it would seem to be a benign set of rituals, especially since it is a church-oriented musical form, praise and worship has created its share of controversies. Many of its supporters view it as a "move of God" as well as a welcome break from the traditional devotional service that preceded it, thanks in large measure to its perceived and actual innovations. Others ask whether the rise of praise and worship is a case of "bandwagoning," or possibly a situation in which an older tradition that was never fully understood is being replaced by "a phenomenon that has been copied without spiritual insight."[1] Some charge that praise and worship has sidelined age-old musical repertoires and, in some denominations, middle-aged and elderly deacons. These have been replaced, the critics argue, by the under-forty praise team with its new sounds and terminology.

In reality praise and worship is neither as completely new as some would suggest nor as destructive to traditions as others assert. An examination of the music presented and the intentions expressed by those involved in praise and worship in Detroit's black churches as well as within the national gospel industry reveals that the perception that there has been a complete generational shift is incorrect. As this study reveals, praise and worship leaders and teams frequently incorporate this genre as a "new layer" that enhances rather than replaces the African, African American, and mainstream Christian rituals that already exist within the Black Church.[2] The result is a devotional mode that meets the spiritual demands and musical needs of many contemporary black congregations.

Praise and Worship: Definitions, Form, and Function

Although the individual words "praise" and "worship" are often spoken as if they are interchangeable, many who teach the concepts of praise and worship or who are acknowledged worship leaders differentiate between the two. Pastor and author Myles Munroe writes that praise means commending, glorifying, and otherwise "putting God in first place"; however, he writes later that "worship is what praise is all about: seeking God until He graces us with His presence."[3] The act of praise can include speaking of God's attributes in a loud voice, singing, dancing, waving the hands, or clapping.[4] Marcus Jennings, minister of praise and worship at Detroit's St. James Baptist Church as well as a minister of the gospel, explains that praise is offered to God "for what He's done, for how He's blessed us. . . . He woke you up this morning. He's given you life." In contrast, he explains, worship is offered "just because He's God."[5]

Many pastors and praise leaders describe praise as a pathway to worship. Author Terry Law outlines the progression: "First we will to praise God, then we sanctify our minds through the power of the Spirit, then our emotions take over and bring us through the veil into the presence of God in worship."[6] Munroe writes that the purpose of worship is to render adoration and devotion to God because of who He is and is the sole domain of those who have a personal relationship with Him.[7]

As for the function of praise and worship music, Consuella Smith, an evangelist and a praise and worship leader at Greater Christ Temple Church in Detroit, explains that this particular music form is usually found at the start of the worship service so that the Spirit of the Lord can be ushered in. At the same time, worshippers can prepare themselves to experience the presence of God.[8] Despite its association with the opening segment of the worship service, praise and worship can occur whenever and wherever believers seek to reach beyond their current situation. Byron Cage, a native Detroiter who has become an award-winning praise and worship leader and recording artist, views praise and worship as an experience that benefits the congregants while it simultaneously glorifies God: "In order to maximize who we are and our potential we have to maximize who God is. The only way we can really do that is to get into His presence. We need to allow His presence to saturate us. The Bible says that He dwells in the midst of our praise. Where He dwells there is freedom and liberation to do whatever it is that we need to do."[9]

Ancient and Biblical Antecedents

While the contemporary Christian Church has applied the inclusive label "praise and worship" to a specific set of devotional rituals, the Old and

New Testaments are filled with instances of God's people performing acts of praise and worship.[10] There are a number of other words from the Old Testament/Hebrew Bible that have also found their way into the vocabulary of those involved in praise and worship, such as *barak, halal, shabach, tehillah, towdah, yadah, and zamar.*[11]

These terms, which Munroe calls "the seven dimensions or portraits of praise," are often alluded to in the instructions the praise and worship leader gives to the congregation ("Let's bless the Lord with a sacrifice of praise").[12] But almost as frequently, the Hebrew words themselves are included ("Now, let's *shabach* the Lord!"). Some of the most popular praise and worship songs, such as the one titled "Shabach," include several Hebrew terms, including *shabach, barak, yadah,* and others.[13]

The hyphenated names of Jehovah found in the Bible as God revealed Himself to His people, including Jehovah-Jireh (provider), Jehovah-Shalom (peace and unity), and Jehovah-Nissi (banner), can also be found in praise and worship songs, such as "Because of Who You Are" composed by Martha Munizzi.[14] They are also used during the worship service to remind participants of the various attributes believers ascribe to God.

The use of these ancient terms from the Old Testament/Hebrew Bible means, among other things, that this movement within the Christian Church, thought by some practitioners to be the domain of those rebels perceived as bringing something brand new to the worship experience, has in reality pulled terminology to the forefront that is older than Christianity itself.[15]

The Traditional Devotional Service

We cannot look at how praise and worship is practiced within the contemporary Black Church without examining its African and African American predecessors.[16] Multiple generations of Africans had been sold and born into slavery before large numbers of slave owners decided to introduce them to Christianity in North America. It was also well into the 1700s before the enslaved Africans embraced Christianity in significant numbers. This slow acceptance was due in part to the fact that many practiced the beliefs and rituals that had made the journey with them or their ancestors through the Middle Passage, much to the consternation of the missionaries and evangelists who had tried to lure them with the gospel for decades. The ring shout, spirit possession, and ecstatic/religious dance, rituals that existed before the founding of the Black Church, were valued links to a West African heritage that placed these expressive cultural elements at the very center of life.[17]

Once Africans in America began to accept Christianity, they adapted the religion using their own spiritual and cultural values. This adaptation included giving birth to new musical forms, such as the Negro spiritual, through which they addressed a range of earthly and heavenly concerns while praising God. While some might have difficulty connecting this part of black America's past to today's contemporary sacred music practices, there are others who see linkages between these periods. Jackie Patillo, Zomba Gospel's vice president of A&R and artist development, an industry leader in gospel music, says the roots of the genre were within the enslaved Africans: "Though we have contemporary choruses that people define as praise and worship, I would say that our ancestors had praise and worship in the fields; we call that music 'spirituals.' Some were prayers asking for help. Some were moans. And some were songs worshipping God and acknowledging His greatness."[18]

The cultural and religious rituals of these Africans in America persisted, not only during slavery, but long after, as they were carried into the establishment of the Black Church, a term which, according to C. Eric Lincoln and Lawrence Mamiya, is sociological and theological shorthand regarding the pluralism of black Christian churches in the United States.[19] While the line is blurry that separates some of the practices of the White Church from that of the Black Church, certain behaviors and performances are widely viewed as synonymous with the traditional black worship experience, even if not all branches of the Black Church practice them. Among them is the devotional service, sometimes called "devotion," which has been the opening segment of the traditional worship in several denominations of the Black Church.

Arthur Paris categorizes the major subsegments of the typical opening service he observed for his study of the black Pentecostal worship as opening song(s), scripture reading, requests for prayer, prayer, song service, and testimony service.[20] Similarly, Walter F. Pitts Jr. writes that within the Afro-Baptist Church tradition there are two ritual "frames," or segments, the first of which is the devotional service; it consists of prayers, lined hymns, congregational songs, and spirituals that precede the main frame of the service, in which the preaching and ecstatic elements of the Black Church ritual are to be found. He has identified these components throughout the African diaspora and views them as tying disparate black cultures to the African continent.[21] No matter which combination of building blocks is included, devotion not only signals the start of the service in the churches that practice these rituals but it also prepares the worshippers for the apex of the experience: the sermon, or "The Service of the Word," as Paris has labeled it.[22]

Among the opening music generally found within the devotional service can be congregational songs ("I'm a Soldier in the Army of the Lord" or "Woke Up This Morning with My Mind Stayed on Jesus," e.g.), well-known, easily sung gospel songs ("He's Sweet I Know"), and centuries-old hymns led, or "lined out," in a call-and-response mode ("A Charge to Keep I Have" or "I Love the Lord"). This service within the Baptist Church has traditionally been conducted by the all-male or predominately male board of deacons. They lead the songs, read the scripture, offer the prayers, as well as solicit prayer requests and testimonies; within a number of progressive churches, however, women have been added to this auxiliary and also lead these services. Within Apostolic/Pentecostal churches, these services are often conducted by the ministers or evangelists. The devotional service is not, however, part of the regular worship structure of the Methodist Church.

Congregants are expected to participate by singing, listening, testifying, and praying silently along with the individuals leading the devotional service. At certain times, the congregation is directed to stand, sit, or kneel, and they may be told to perform two or more of these actions during a single song. For example, the congregation may begin singing while seated, but after a verse or two, the person leading the song can signal them to stand. If that individual segues from a song to a prayer, he or she may direct those standing to sit or may gesture for them to kneel; either position is acceptable at that point.[23]

Though the gospel and congregational songs that are performed during devotional service can be spirited and fast-paced, the lined hymns, part of the Baptist tradition, are generally sung in a manner that is anything but jubilant-sounding.[24] Lining out involves one individual, usually a deacon during a regular service or perhaps a layperson during a testimonial meeting, chanting a line or two of a hymn and ending on a

pitch. The congregation follows by singing that same passage
ne variation on the tune. Practiced in North America by early
s, lining out later became a hallmark of hymn singing in black
s, perhaps because of its similarities to call and response found
out the African diaspora.[25] Pitts describes the practice as he ob-
it in the Afro-Baptist churches he documented:

ve the Lord, He heard my cry," Deacon cries out. The newly gathered con-
ation, now seated in their pews, echoes his words in a plaintive tune. They
this without the support of piano, organ or hymnal. . . . "And pitied every
an!" The deacon, not waiting for his chorus to finish the first line, bellows
the second from a hymn composed by Dr. Isaac Watts at the beginning of the
eighteenth century. Again the congregation resumes their mournful melody,
overlapping the deacon's last verse with their chorus. . . . As the interaction between deacon and congregation unfolds, mothers wrestle with their smaller children to sit still while beckoning to their older ones to come into the sanctuary.[26]

While such singing resonates with many older congregants, and with
younger ones who have come to appreciate the tradition, it is usually not
the music of choice for many under a certain age, as Pitts indicates. This
is probably due to the tempo, the fluctuations between major and minor
keys, and the unaccompanied nature of the singing. Marcus Jennings
shared what he saw as the signs that the older devotional form was passing in many contemporary churches: "In the traditional devotion, people
would almost purposely come late, just to avoid it, and quite frankly, it became really boring. People didn't enjoy it. They would sit there and you
could just see on their face, 'As soon as this is over, the better it would
be.'"[27]

Another reason many of a certain age group may have not gravitated
toward these songs is offered by Dorgan Needom, minister of music at
Detroit's Unity Baptist Church: "Today's twenty-first-century churchgoer doesn't understand its relevance. Deacons don't take time to explain
it; they just [start singing] and expect people to join in."[28] Not only were
many ignorant of the significance of the rituals, there were probably as
many who could not understand the actual lyrics as they were being sung.
The melismatic, elongated vowels couched in often somber tones ("I-I
lo-ove the Lo-o-ord, He heard my cry-e-y-ee") for years have been

fodder for Christian comedians, who have commented on being amused and puzzled by much of the devotional ritual.[29]

Ironically, the old devotional service and the contemporary praise and worship service parallel one another in this area. For just as there were those younger congregants who felt left out of devotion because they did not understand the words being spoken and sung and were not drawn to the traditional music, today there are congregants who have not been schooled in the Hebrew terms or the new lyrics and music and thus may not be fully engaged by the contemporary praise and worship songs and behaviors. Fortunately, the most skillful and sensitive praise and worship leaders have learned to accommodate these congregants, as will be discussed later in this chapter.

The Emergence of Praise and Worship Music

In the 1970s, a time during which many younger Black Church members were not actively involved in the traditional devotional service, a similar level of disengagement was running through the White Protestant Church. For many on each side of the Christian Church's racial divide, the praise and worship movement would be the sound that drew them back.

Praise and worship music arose within the White Evangelical Church because of a unique set of circumstances. According to Robert L. Redman, two major influences shaped what he calls the "sweeping changes in Christian worship" during the latter part of the twentieth century. The first, the evangelical seeker service movement, was launched by those who, after reviewing research on the habits of the baby boomer generation, "set to create a 'nonreligious' environment for services, an alternative setting for presenting the gospel that suggests church without its supposedly negative connotations."[30] What resulted were services that included sermons with themes about domestic life and personal development, multimedia presentations, dramatic skits that set the stage for the message, and inspirational, sometimes secular, songs whose text matched the sermon's theme.[31]

The second influence Redman names is the charismatic praise and worship movement. He outlines the worship experience: "A typical service begins with twenty to thirty minutes or more of congregational singing, led by a worship leader, a band with a small ensemble of singers, and often a choir as well, modeled on the gospel choir in African-

American churches. Leaders encourage a wide range of physical expressions through clapping, raising hands, swaying and even dancing."[32] The praise and worship services include "participatory" sermons and contemporary worship music, which is a considerable departure from traditional multiverse hymns in that the songs are shorter and more focused on single themes or images. This allows the congregation to create a spiritual and emotional bond with God. Another feature of this service may be "singing in the Spirit," which the leader may encourage at the end of a quiet song if he or she wishes the congregation to focus on God's presence.[33]

From these seeker service and praise and worship service movements emerged the popular praise and worship musical genre that not only reflects these influences but also mirrors the fact that a generation that defined itself in its youth by music—rock and roll and Motown—seeks to do so during its religious life as well.[34] As a result, Michael S. Hamilton writes, thousands of individuals select their churches, or at least the services they attend within a given church, not on the doctrine preached, but on the music that is performed.[35] Such is the case with praise and worship music; many are drawn to those churches that offer it as a contemporary prelude to the sermon, which is still considered by most to be the high point of the worship experience.

Before the phrase "praise and worship" became widely used within the Christian Church, contemporary Christian recording artists such as Twila Paris ("Lamb of God") and Keith Green ("Rushing Wind") performed songs that could be easily categorized within that genre today. Gospel singer and composer Pastor Marvin Winans also names music recorded in the late 1960s and early 1970s by Andrae Crouch, the 2nd Chapter of Acts, and Danny Lee and the Children of Truth as having opened the door for today's praise and worship explosion.[36] By 1981 there was a large enough pool of recording artists producing praise and worship music that the Gospel Music Association (GMA), whose artists primarily sing contemporary Christian music (CCM), presented its first Dove Awards in that category.[37]

Praise and Worship Movement Grows

At the time the GMA initially created this category, most of those who were being nominated were white artists who performed for white congregations and consumers. Eventually there would be black singers, such as Alvin Slaughter, Ron Kenoly, Bob Bailey, and Larnelle Harris, who would also perform in that style for predominately white audiences. But it would take a merging of several different factors for most black audiences to be exposed to praise and worship music.

Broadcast television and cable television outlets and programs that regularly allowed artists to interact with and be exposed to audiences who were not from their own racial or ethnic community included Black Entertainment Television (BET), Trinity Broadcast Network (TBN), and, much later, the Word Network; shows like *PTL* before the Jim Bakker scandal; and music award shows, including, the GMA (Dove), Stellar, American Music, and Grammy award programs. As for radio, the AM and FM bands have been a meeting place for racially mixed gospel music loving audiences since the advent of the medium. Because of these outlets, what was a tiny number in the late 1970s is today an impressive and growing roster of black and white artists with multicultural audiences.[38]

Also priming the black community for praise and worship were several black artists who performed and recorded praise and worship music before most members of their core audience were familiar with that designation. That list includes the late minister Thomas Whitfield, whose commercial recordings for the Sound of Gospel, Onyx, and Benson labels beginning in the 1970s included a number of songs, such as "We Need a Word from the Lord" and "Lift Those Hands," that were performed in the praise and worship style. For that reason, several of today's most prominent worship leaders and composers, among them Byron Cage, cite him as a forerunner in the genre for the black community.[39]

Another name on that list of black artists recording praise and worship for black audiences is the West Angeles Church of God in Christ, which recorded a series called Saints in Praise beginning in the late 1980s. Volume 1 of the series was an early, if not the first, praise and worship project purchased by a large segment of the black gospel music community, thus opening the door for the platinum sales of Fred Hammond, often called the "architect of urban praise and worship," at the turn of the twenty-first century to that same constituency. Judith Christie McAllister, one of the praise leaders for that series and congregation, remains one of the premier female voices of the genre today. Composer, arranger, and singer Richard

Minister Thomas Whitfield. Courtesy of David Whitfield.

Smallwood has recorded songs since the early 1980s that are now considered classics of the genre, including "Total Praise" and "Anthem of Praise."
    Another catalyst for the overall expansion of praise and worship mu-
sic was the emergence of several record labels whose sole or primary interest is praise and worship music, including Maranatha! Music, Integrity,
Vineyard Music, Hillsong, and Hosanna! Two of the best known are
Maranatha! Music and Integrity. Maranatha! Music emerged during the
"Jesus movement" of the early 1970s, which found thousands of young

Fred Hammond CD cover, 2006. Photograph by Michael Lavine. Courtesy of
Zomba Gospel, LLC.

people converting to Christianity and enjoying what was being called
"Jesus music." The company flourished. Today Maranatha is an award-
winning company that focuses exclusively on worship music including
special series.[40]

Emerging approximately fifteen years after the founding of Maranatha
was Integrity Media, known as "the largest company in the Christian music industry that specializes exclusively in the praise and worship genre."
Integrity produces, publishes, and distributes praise and worship recordings, books, including Bibles and related materials.[41] Initially, Integrity
was to be a Christian magazine, but a plan to send an audio cassette of
music to subscribers brought an avalanche of requests from recipients for

Judith Christie McAllister. Photograph by Carl McKnight Enterprises. Courtesy of Judah Music, Inc.

more music. The company now exists to fill that need, according to Jackie Patillo, who was Integrity's general manager before moving to Zomba Gospel. Integrity has promoted and recorded some of the most recognized and respected names in that genre, among them Ron Kenoly, Joe Pace, Don Moen, and Israel and New Breed.[42]

Today, praise and worship recordings are available worldwide and are produced by artists of every ethnic and racial background, who perform in virtually every gospel subgenre, from traditional to holy hip hop. Among the recordings are individual praise and worship songs, whole

CDs devoted to praise and worship, and repackaged songs from previous projects, either from one artist's catalog or from the repertoires of many.[43]

The consumer response to praise and worship—whether it is a trend, a move of God, or a combination of the two—has been noteworthy. The *New York Times* reported in 2004 that the sales of praise and worship albums had doubled between 2000 and 2003 to about twelve million units. While music sales overall had slumped in 2003, including that of other Christian music, worship music sales were up by 5 percent the following year.[44] And sales are not all that attest to the genre's popularity. Howard Rachinski, president of Christian Copyright Licensing International (CCLI), which tracks the music sung by congregations in 137,000 churches across America, estimated in 2004 that praise and worship music made up 75 percent of the repertoire in half of the churches in the United States. In 2006 Paul Herman, marketing manager for CCLI, updated the company's coverage to 138,000 churches in the United States and estimated that 15 to 20 percent of that number are African American Baptist or Church of God in Christ congregations.[45]

One possible key to understanding why this musical genre has found such broad acceptance in a relatively short period is to view it as another example of the complex generational behavioral transformations that have occurred throughout history. Using that perspective calls to mind a familiar interpretation of Judaism that centers on the Bible verse "I am the God of Abraham, the God of Isaac, and the God of Jacob" (Exodus 3:6). Many understand this to mean that God remained the same over time, but each of the patriarchs saw, experienced, and responded to God uniquely and therefore loved and showed reverenced for God in his own way.[46]

The same could be said of praise and worship music: several key national performers and scores of black congregations in the metropolitan Detroit area praise God in a way that seems appropriate to them for today using praise and worship music that is reflective of this generation's aesthetics, language, and viewpoints. What their detractors may find surprising, however, is that a great deal of room and respect is still being given to older musical forms within the Black Church. A majority of the artists and churches reviewed for this study use an inclusive model. They combine the traditional devotional songs with the contemporary praise and worship music, as I have documented after observing several Detroit area praise and worship services, analyzing the responses to a praise and worship survey, and listening to recordings by key artists of the genre.

Bridging the Cultural Divide

One question loomed as I was conducting my research: why do the detractors of praise and worship see it as having decimated earlier devotional forms? The answer may lie in the fact that some praise and worship music, despite often presenting lyrics taken straight from the Bible, is markedly different from its predecessors in sound and instrumentation. Exposure to the forms that fall outside of the Black Church tradition can be troubling to some musicians. As one younger musician, who asked for anonymity, explained, "It's just too hard to play because it's not the music I know." There are actually sub-subgenres within the subgenre, that is, different forms of praise and worship music. Artists and composers such as Shekinah Glory Ministry (Kingdom Records) and Joe Pace II (Integrity Gospel Records) produce what Patillo describes as "more gospel influenced praise and worship." Paul Allen of PAJAM explains how that combination occurs: "We make it our own by changing a little bit here, making it a little bit more soulful there, so it's praise and worship with a little Black Church soul. . . . You add a little extra drums here when they [in the White Church] just have strings and piano. We add some drums, and we add some bass and some guitar, and we add some climaxes, some key changes."[47]

In contrast to the "gospel influenced" style, there are also artists whose approach is more eclectic. The songs these musicians create can combine world music, rhythm and praise, hip hop, rock, and other contemporary styles.[48] Composer and producer Kurt Carr's 2005 release *One Church* contains several songs that could easily place the CD in the eclectic category, including the infectious "If I Tell God" with its South African influences. He explains to Rene Williams that after his composition "In the Sanctuary" from his *Awesome Wonder* collection (2000) was translated into nine languages, he felt led to reach out to a global community:

> Though I never want to forsake my base—which is the black church, the Pentecostal movement, the Charismatic movement—this time, it's time for Kurt Carr to reach out to the world. Whether or not they embrace it, it's my mandate to present music and a sound that would appeal to people around the

world. That's what I've done on this project. I've always tried to be broad, but this time I went further. I got African drummers and percussionists; I have an accordion player from Armenia; I have a violinist from China; I have a bagpiper from Scotland; I have a sitar on the album. So I have lots of different sounds and lots of different influences from around the world with the same message. It still has the Kurt Carr production style, but I've made it more world-appealing.[49]

The music of singer, composer, and producer Israel Houghton's music is described by one publication as "an eclectic, almost un-classifiable blend of Christian pop, gospel, worship, and other influences."[50] Similarly, Christie McAllister's CD *In His Presence Live* is characterized this way: "One of the album's unquestionable highlights is the 'Expressions From My Soul' mini-mix (Bless Thou the Lord Oh My Soul). Leading it off is an anthem of high worship, transitioning into a moment of contemporary call and response, soaring with harmonic modulations and ending with a 'Praise Jam'—an all out jamboree of dancing, shouting and high praise."[51] Carr, Christie McAllister, and Houghton are just a few on a long list who have included the sounds of the Caribbean and the African and Asian continents within their repertoires.[52] The resulting songs are an attraction for some but can be a repellent for others, especially those for whom Sunday morning connotes a very specific "Black Church" sound.

There are at least two observations to be made regarding this musical form, particularly the kind that steps beyond the borders of the Black Church sound. First, this sonic fusion has become welcoming to fans of various ethnic and racial backgrounds and thus has expanded the range of musical forms and artists many are willing to accept and enjoy. So while black artists still perform primarily for black audiences and white artists for white audiences, unprecedented numbers of black consumers are buying music recorded by white praise and worship leaders, such as Vicki Yohe, Judy Jacobs, Mary Alessi, and Martha Munizzi, each of whom has a soulful style of delivery, much like the so-called blue-eyed soul singers of a generation ago, such as Hall and Oates and the Righteous Brothers, who found themselves embraced by black audiences.[53]

That style of delivery, along with the praise and worship songs they perform and compose, makes Yohe and Munizzi bestselling favorites

Israel Houghton at Perfecting Church's Holy Convocation at Calihan Hall in Detroit. Photograph by Rogers Wm. Foster. Courtesy of Perfecting Church.

among thousands of consumers, black and white. Munizzi is the first white artist to win a Stellar Award (2005), widely heralded as the "Grammy of gospel" for performers of black gospel music. Her 2003 CD, *The Best Is Yet to Come*, remained on the *Billboard* magazine Top Gospel Chart—where the sales of black gospel artists are normally tracked—for seventy-two straight weeks and reached the number 2 slot on the chart. A frequent collaborator of Israel Houghton, she has written songs that are considered classics of the praise and worship genre, including "Glorious," also recorded by Karen Clark Sheard, and the previously mentioned "Because of Who You Are." Munizzi explains one of the key motivators behind her music ministry: "My deepest desire is to transcend cultural, generational, and denominational boundaries, and to bring all people together through worship."[54] Her twin sister, Mary Alessi, has more recently been embraced by the same audiences.

Before Yohe signed with Pure Springs Records, owned by Detroit-born CeCe Winans, her music had not been marketed to black audiences. Still, they had embraced her after hearing and seeing her presented in huge auditoriums by such Black Church favorites as Bishop T. D. Jakes and Prophetess Juanita Bynum. Known for her sense of humor, Yohe has been heard to say, "I just feel like I should be on gospel radio even though I'm a white girl."[55] Apparently, a number of others agree with her. *I Just Want You* (2003), Yohe's first CD for Winans's label, enjoyed popularity on black radio and was on the gospel chart for more than eighteen months, achieving the number 7 slot at its height. The composer of such notable songs as "Mercy Seat," "Comforter," and "Under the Blood," Yohe has been described as "powerful, passionate, sincere and, above all, anointed."[56] Her second CD, *He's Been Faithful* (2005) has also found wide acceptance; the song "Deliverance Is Available" was listed as one of the ten most frequently played singles in gospel radio during the week of March 31, 2006.[57]

The second observation is that whether or not one is a devotee of praise and worship music, this genre with its world music sounds and accompanying "vertical texts," that is, lyrics that are directed to God and not to other human beings, is helping to replicate the multiethnic listening and, to some extent, the mingling that occurred in the worship practices during the Second Great Awakening and the Azusa Street movement that occurred at the turn of the nineteenth and twentieth centuries, respectively. While Anthony Heilbut writes that throughout the twentieth century there were white religious songs that became staples in the Black Church and vice versa, during the Second Great Awakening and Azusa Street movement something different occurred in that thousands of worshippers stepped beyond their natural boundaries to experience God with individuals from other cultural backgrounds.[58] Not only are today's praise and worship artists crossing the boundaries to perform, but audiences are crossing boundaries to experience this music together, sometimes in performance settings, sometimes in church settings and arenas, but more frequently in virtual togetherness as they buy the same music and then listen to it in their individual cars, homes, or on their desktops and iPods.[59]

Straight Gate International Church exemplifies those predominately black churches that have welcomed a full array of multicultural artists who perform praise and worship and that have made a name for themselves by inviting others to do the same. Founded in a storefront in 1978 by Bishop Andrew Merritt, Straight Gate, with a reported five thousand members, has incorporated praise and worship in its own services for years. Some of the best-known praise and worship artists, including Fred Hammond and Richard Smallwood, have performed and recorded in the church's westside Detroit edifice.

But it is the event called One in Worship, also billed as "the spiritual Super Bowl," that represents Straight Gate's most expansive efforts to bring praise and worship to the world. In 2004 and 2005 the church rented Ford Field, home of the Detroit Lions, with a seating capacity of seventy thousand, to accommodate the tens of thousands the pastor and membership invited to hear a roster of black and white praise leaders and ministers, such as Houghton, Hammond, Yohe, Jacobs, Munizzi, Phil Driscoll, David and Nicole Binion, and Morris Chapman.[60]

Certainly, many churches around the city and country host events at which dynamic praise leaders are presented. What sets One in Worship apart from most is that Bishop Merritt and Straight Gate have agreements with Total Christian Television, Christian Television Network, Daystar, the Miracle Network, and Trinity Broadcasting, which means that there is a potential international television audience of four hundred million people. Bishop Merritt explained the reasons behind the event to the *Detroit Free Press:* "Diversity is a reflection of the core of Christ, out of one blood made He all nations," Merritt said. "Arabs will participate, Greek, French, Hispanics. But no cultural names, no denomination will get in the way of what people are coming here to do, and that is to worship as one body."[61]

The Sound of a New Breed of Worshipper

Israel and New Breed are among those whose music and lyrics embody the multicultural mission expressed by Bishop Merritt and others of like mind. They were recipients of many awards in 2005, including two Stellar Awards (CD of the Year and Male Vocalist of the Year) and two Dove Awards (Contemporary Gospel Album of the Year and Contemporary Gospel Recorded Song of the Year), as well as a Soul Train Award. A worship leader at the Lakewood Church in Houston, Texas, Israel Houghton, is a self-described "black kid who grew up in a white family in a Hispanic church."[62] He writes and produces in a way that reflects his upbringing as well as the existence of a growing multicultural audience that is accepting of sounds beyond those traditionally found in their own communities. He explains: "As far as leading worship goes (which is my passion and calling), I now realize that there have been demands put on me from every part of my experience since day one—culturally, emotionally, musically, and more. So things tend to sound cross-cultural, cross-denominational, and cross-generational. I like to call it, 'The Sound of New Breed Worship.'"[63] Veteran music director and producer Aaron Lindsey discussed in a 2003 interview why he and Houghton used multicultural influences on two of their projects, *Kids Praise* and *Kids Praise 2:*

> Our kids aren't really listening to very much other than secular music most of the time. They're not listening to older versions of gospel stuff; they're listening to the new stuff, which is not that cultural.
>
> When you think of producers like the Neptunes, one guy is Black and one guy Asian ... they're very successful in getting our kids' ears. So our objective is to make sure that what we did is relevant.... The way we do that is include basically every generation, every culture and every tribe.[64]

Though their music is culturally expansive, Israel and New Breed point out in the song called "I Hear the Sound" that trying to categorize what they do is difficult since it goes beyond racial musical profiling:

> It ain't a black thing
> It ain't a white thing
> It ain't a colored thing
> It's a kingdom thing.

Here, they sing, is music that is so reflective of diverse cultural influences that it defies easy classification.

While Israel and New Breed and many of their contemporaries create and present music through which they do not consciously strive to reflect racial aesthetics, they clearly project their desire to focus on "kingdom business" in a way that they believe separates them from earlier generations:

> I hear the sound of a new breed
> Marching toward the gates of the enemy
> We're armed and dangerous
> Strong and serious
> Clothed in righteousness
> It's a new breed, a new breed.[65]

They declare themselves to be "a new breed" of worshipper and Christian warrior, thus invoking the Abraham/Isaac/Jacob distinction mentioned earlier. The Reverend Edgar L. Vann Jr., pastor of Detroit's Second Ebenezer Church, summarized the reason he had embraced praise and worship music so readily: "Some of us have always been the 'uncola'" [a reference to a past commercial for 7Up that emphasized its distinctive place among other soft drinks].[66] Israel and New Breed project a similar message that defines their identity in the chant found in "Come in from the Outside":

> We're the generation
> That will give You praise and adoration
> Let Your kingdom come
> Let Your will be done
> Establish now Your throne, oh my Lord.

With these lyrics, they appear to draw a generational line in the proverbial sand—"We're going to praise God in a way our forefathers did not." That is what they appear to do, until we listen and look carefully at the refrain that follows:

> O my Lord
> Lord, Lord, Lord
>
> Praise You Lord
> Lord, Lord, Lord

We love You Lord
Lord, Lord, Lord
O my Lord.

The refrain, "Oh my Lord, Lord, Lord," one of thousands of communally
created phrases and refrains within the black sacred repertoire, came to
the attention of movie fans in the 1989 release *Glory*, which is set in the
1860s during the Civil War. The scene in which the refrain is heard features the soldiers enlisted in one of the country's first all-black regiments
singing together the night before going into one of the bloodiest battles
of the war, one in which many of them lost their lives. In the film, the refrain serves as a bridge between spoken testimonies. However, it can also
be viewed as a plea to the Almighty as the men willingly face possible an-
nihilation to be seen by society as black men fighting for their own freedom.

As Israel and New Breed repeat the refrain, its melody, which they initially sing as simply as the black soldiers perform it in the movie, takes on
the complexity that is a hallmark of their contemporary sound. But their
stacked, intricate harmonies in no way negate the fact that a centuries-old
refrain is embedded within it. On the same CD, the infectious "Friend of
God" praise and worship song and chant leads to a "Friend" medley that
includes two of the venerable hymns of Christianity, "No Not One" and
"What a Friend We Have in Jesus." That medley flows into several minutes of singing in the Spirit, in which audience and artists eventually move
into spontaneous sounds of adoration that can often arise during a successful praise and worship experience. Equally noteworthy is that the
combination of the so-called old school and new school brings this audience to a moment of high worship.

Fred Hammond, the acclaimed Detroit-based composer, musician,
singer, and producer, does something similar as he juxtaposes traditional
devotional songs and contemporary praise and worship music on CDs
and in live performance settings. One of his most popular recordings of
the last decade is "Jesus Be a Fence," a traditional gospel song composed
and performed by Sam Cooke in the days when he was with the gospel
quartet the Soul Stirrers. Hammond first recorded it on Bishop Carlton
Pearson's *Live at Azusa III*, which was released in 1999, though relatively

few took note of it at the time. He re-recorded it for Verity Records in 2000 on his own CD titled *Purpose by Design,* where it is listed among songs more readily placed within the praise and worship category, such as "When You Praise" and "You Are the Living Word."

A similar mix of the traditional gospel and the contemporary praise and worship forms reportedly moved the audience that attended Hammond's performance October 4, 2004. In a review of that evening, Dwayne Lacy comments on how seamlessly and effectively Hammond brought together the past and the present:

> Fred called on guitarist Joey Woolfalk to kick some old school riffs, and then he sang a variety of old church songs such as "God Is a Good God," "I'm a Soldier in the Army of the Lord," and "I Know It Was the Blood." As he slowed things down, he sang some old COGIC favorites (such as "Yes Lord") and the Baptist devotion song "I Love the Lord, He Heard My Cry." . . . Hammond then went into a worship set with such songs as "Give Me a Clean Heart," "Please Don't Pass Me By" . . . [and] into an acoustic version of "I Will Find a Way." . . . People were worshipping and singing along. . . . What a night! Fred Hammond was the worship leader, and we were the worshippers.[67]

Lacy acknowledges Hammond's deft interweaving of both devotional songs and praise and worship tunes during that evening; presented together by Hammond, they equaled a memorable worship experience for those involved in the service.

As Pastor Winans mentions in the epigraph to this chapter, Judith Christie McAllister incorporates "the sound of old gospel" during her live and recorded performances. The CD titled *Raise the Praise,* for example, includes her popular praise and worship songs "Hallelujah, You're Worthy" and "Lift Him High," but it also features a medley called "Jubilation" with such traditional congregational songs and hymns as "Praise Him," "Let All the People Praise Thee," and "Glory to His Name."

Similar descriptions of inclusiveness have been made about Detroit native Byron Cage. Reviewer LaTonya Taylor applauds him for including a full-out traditional gospel song, "Still Say Yes," on his award-winning self-titled CD for GospoCentric Records. She writes, "That participatory, 'inclusive' element—and the fact that there's just a touch of 'old time' church in this sound—will aid this genre's entree into churches where older members are more likely to listen to traditional gospel than CCM."[68]

Praise and Worship in Detroit's Churches

That "old time" touch is being incorporated in a number of Detroit's black churches that use praise and worship music, based on what I have witnessed personally and have documented for this study. That the traditional devotional and congregational music is usually intertwined with the contemporary sounds of praise and worship is also reflected in the responses provided by thirty-seven Detroit-area church musicians and ministers of music who completed my informal survey.[69] Almost 86 percent of those reported that praise and worship music is performed during their worship services; 70 percent use it during all their worship services, and 16 percent use it during most of them. That is close to the percentage (87 percent) that reported that traditional music is used at every service (72 percent) or at most services (15 percent).

This combination of the old and the new is also being duplicated in the churches specifically monitored for this research, Greater Christ Temple, St. James Missionary Baptist Church, and Perfecting Church.[70]

PRAISE AND WORSHIP AT GREATER CHRIST TEMPLE CHURCH

Greater Christ Temple Church, located on Hilton in Ferndale, Michigan, is led by Bishop Carl E. Holland, who became the congregation's pastor in 1969, five years after it was founded. For most of its existence, the church had been affiliated with the Pentecostal Assemblies of the World (PAW). However, in 2000 Bishop Holland founded the Pentecostal Assembly of Believers, Inc. The organization consists of churches in Michigan, Alabama, Georgia, and Tennessee, with others scheduled to be added soon in Texas and California.

Greater Christ Temple's reported current membership is three hundred. Its core congregation, with a median age between thirty and forty, comprises those with high school diplomas, those who have had some college course, and those with college degrees. Their occupations are split between blue collar work and various professional fields.

Greater Christ Temple praise team, 2006 (*left to right*): Darron Donaldson, Carl B. Phillips, and Barbara Butler. Photograph by Bill McNeece.

Carl B. Phillips, the church's minister of music, has been involved in music since he was twelve and a member of the Baptist Church. His background also includes participation in high school and community gospel choirs, including singing with Savoy recording artists the Reverend Donald Vails and the Voices of Deliverance. He joined Christ Temple in 1976 and was director of the Christ Temple Inspirational Choir before assuming his current duties. His activities in the Detroit gospel music community also include serving as coordinator of local artists for the Motor City PraiseFest and as a gospel radio announcer. He served as cohost of DetroitGospel.com on the Air, heard for two years on 1340 WEXL AM, and is an international minister of music for the Pentecostal Assembly of Believers.[71]

Phillips brought the idea of praise and worship to Bishop Holland around 1998. He describes the moment that gave him the impetus to approach his pastor: "The choir was singing Kirk Franklin's 'Now Behold the Lamb' and a spirit of praise and worship was created."[72] Phillips wanted to see that spirit envelop the church regularly, so he asked the pastor's permission to slowly bring praise and worship to the church. He began with gospel songs, such as "God Is" and "Can't Stop Praising His Name," as well as the music of Fred Hammond and Thomas Whitfield.

Today, the church has five praise and worship leaders, each assigned to a different Sunday. According to Phillips, the two female worship leaders, who are also ministers, use more hymns and gospel songs; he and evangelist Consuella Smith use a combination of contemporary praise and worship songs and traditional gospel music on their respective Sundays; while the fifth and youngest leader uses almost all contemporary praise and worship songs.

The church holds Sunday morning worship at 11:30 AM and Bible study Wednesday at 7:30 PM, as well as choir rehearsals on Tuesday and Thursday evenings. The praise and worship team rehearses monthly. The Sunday morning and evening services begin with praise and worship, as do revival services. Sunday night differs slightly, however, in that the opening period includes testimony service as well. All other church meetings and rehearsals begin with prayer.[73]

To ensure that the entire membership understands praise and worship, its concepts and terminology are taught to the new converts who join Greater Christ Temple by Evangelist Smith; she is, besides being one of the praise and worship leaders and an ordained evangelist, the administrative assistant to the bishop within the church and within the Pentecostal Assembly of Believers.

The Sunday, December 12, 2002, morning worship I documented is an excellent example of how praise and worship is conducted at Greater Christ Temple.[74] The service began at 11:30 AM with prayer by one of the church's ministers; it has been the custom at Greater Christ for the ministers, not the deacons, to handle the opening devotional services. This particular prayer included petitions for the worship service, the congregation, and the pastor. The five-person praise and worship team for that Sunday began their portion of the service at 11:42. The worship leader, Evangelist Smith, began with an adapted Christmas carol, "O Come All Ye Faithful," with additional verses that have been sung in the Black Church for decades ("For He alone is worthy," "O come and lift Him higher").

This seasonal song was followed by several praise and worship songs—"With My Hands Lifted Up (and My Mouth Filled with Praise)," "None Like You," and "Lord, I Lift Your Name on High," one of the most popular songs of the genre—along with the devotional songs "Jesus, I'll Never Forget" and "There's a Storm Out on the Ocean" and the traditional gospel song "Can't (Cain't) Nobody Do Me Like Jesus."

Evangelist Smith selected music that conveyed a sense of the holiday season while simultaneously involving the congregation in the worship experience by including something for the varied musical tastes represented within the congregation: praise and worship music, traditional devotional music, and gospel songs. She explains, "Our congregation is in transition. Therefore your praise and worship has to be inclusive of music for a variety of ages and tastes."[75] Her selections also coincide with the desires of Bishop Holland that the congregation maintain the hymns and apostolic music traditions.[76] Consequently, not only are they interwoven into most of the praise and worship segments, but they constitute most what the congregation sings during the balance of the service.

PRAISE AND WORSHIP AT SAINT JAMES MISSIONARY BAPTIST CHURCH

The St. James Baptist Church was officially incorporated in 1921, but it was under the leadership of their third pastor, the Reverend W. C. Barnett (1938–72), that the church, then located at the intersection of Mt. Elliott and Pulford streets, earned its national reputation as its St. James Young Adult Choir (later the St. James Adult Choir) released recordings that captured the sound and feel of the black Baptist gospel choir.

The church's organist at that time, Charles H. Nicks Jr., later became its fifth pastor (1972–89). He and minister of music Jimmy "J. D." Dowell led the choir through their popular "O Give Thanks" Thanksgiving week concerts, standing-room-only Sunday night musicals, appearances before and with national and international figures, and recordings that were embraced throughout the gospel music community.[77] The current pastor, the Reverend Dr. James A. Jennings Jr., who was installed in 1990, moved the church to its present location on Van Dyke in Detroit. The reported membership at the time of my fieldwork was three thousand.

Marcus Jennings, the son of Reverend Jennings, introduced the praise and worship concept to St. James Baptist around 1999. He holds the positions of minister of praise and worship and director of the young adult choir. Minister Jennings is part of a family of preachers and pastors that stretches back to his paternal great-grandfather and includes five uncles, several cousins, and his late brother. The singing tradition comes from both sides of his family but more strongly from his mother, maternal grandparents, and siblings. A former youth drummer, he has been a singer since he was fourteen.

Jennings first heard praise and worship in a local Detroit church in the late 1990s, and he talked with both Pastor Jennings and Dowell, then minister of music, about bringing it to St. James. They gave their blessing without hesitation. In fact, Dowell initially worked with him to pick out sixteen vocalists they felt would serve well as praise and worship team members. Within three months, the number was ten and remained there through the time of our interview. The team often performed songs Jennings had composed, but they also sang music from many of his favorite praise and worship artists, including Kurt Carr, Judith Christie McAllister, Richard Smallwood, and Israel and New Breed.

He summarized his views on the differences between praise and worship and the traditional devotional service this way:

> I believe the focus [of devotional service] is getting to the emotions of the people, whereas praise and worship, to me, is and should be, not about people's emotions, but [about] how can we get the people into God's presence? How can we get God to come where we are? How can we set the atmosphere to where the Holy Spirit feels welcome, to where He feels at home, where He can manifest Himself and He won't have to feel awkward when He's there? . . . So He wants to be where His praise is. So, if you want to pursue His presence, you're going to have to pursue it through praise.[78]

The service I analyzed at the St. James Missionary Baptist Church was their annual Watch Night service of December 31, 2002–January 1, 2003.[79] That evening was filled with a mix of traditional gospel, congregational songs, and contemporary praise and worship music. The praise and worship service, which began at 9:07 PM, was led by praise and worship leader Marcus Jennings and a praise team of six. Two musicians, an organist and a drummer, provided accompaniment for the three praise and worship songs that followed: "He Is Good," "Let Jesus Fill This Place," and "Wonderful (Yes He Is)."

Next, the minister of music greeted the audience and introduced a children's liturgical dance troupe of six that performed to Fred Hammond's version of the traditional gospel song "Jesus Be a Fence." Two adult liturgical dancers followed the children and used a gospel-influenced version of the hymn "O, To Be Kept" for their performance. The praise and worship segment ended with an upbeat congregational song, "This Morning When I Rose," introduced and directed by the minister of music.

As was the case with the other two spotlighted churches, both long-standing traditional songs and praise and worship songs were performed; the congregation was exhorted to offer praises to God orally and physically, regardless of the type of music being introduced at the time. The combination reflects the church's historic musical roots, the contemporary leanings of its young minister of praise, the support he has received in launching praise and worship at St. James, and, perhaps most important, his willingness to accommodate various segments of his congregation.

Minister Jennings recalls that in his early days of introducing the form, there were senior members of the congregation who asked him to teach the praise and worship team specific traditional devotional songs they loved and missed. He admits that his first response was a silent but emphatic "no." But after listening to pastor and recording artist Bishop Carlton Pearson explain that some of the older saints will never become fans of praise and worship and that they need to be reached where they are, he began to include more traditional songs.[80]

Praise and Worship at Perfecting Church

Perfecting Church is perhaps the best known of the three churches in the study because of the fame and popularity of its founder and pastor, Marvin L. Winans. The fourth of ten children born to David Sr. ("Pop") and Delores ("Mom") of the internationally acclaimed Winans family of Detroit, he was raised within the preaching and musical traditions of the Church of God in Christ. He and his family members have collected many awards, including Grammys, Stellars, and Doves, and he and three of his brothers, Ronald, Michael, and twin Carvin, known collectively as the Winans, were pacesetters in urban contemporary gospel music.[81]

Pastor Marvin L. Winans at Perfecting Church, 2006. Photograph by Bill McNeece.

Pastor Winans, who has recorded two projects with his church choir, *Marvin L. Winans Presents Perfected Praise and Friends,* is still actively involved in recording as a guest with many of his colleagues and released his own solo project, *Alone but Not Alone,* in September 2007 on the Pure Springs label. His weekly activities also include hosting *Rhythm and Praise,* a Sunday morning gospel music program on Detroit's 92.3 FM WMXD.

Pastor Winans held the initial meeting for Perfecting Church in the basement of his home with eight individuals, but the first official service for the church occurred at the Michigan Inn in Southfield, Michigan, on

May 27, 1989. Because of the church's rapid growth, the congregation moved several times before settling into their present edifice on East Nevada Street in Detroit in March of 1996. Under the Perfecting Community Development Corporation, the church in 2003 began a $100 million building project to create an expansive church and business complex that will better house its members, ministries, and activities.

The congregation's reported membership is four thousand, a sizeable percentage of whom have taken some college courses or have earned college degrees. Like Greater Christ, theirs too is a fairly young membership with a median age falling between thirty and forty. Perfecting Church is nondenominational.[82]

Praise and worship was instituted at Perfecting Church by Pastor Winans after a trip he took to Holland in 1990. There he heard a multicultural, multiracial congregation perform "Lord, I Lift Your Name on High," a popular praise and worship song, for the first time. He knew immediately upon hearing it that he was going to bring it to Perfecting Church.

Although pastoral duties are his primary focus, Pastor Winans continues not only to set policy for what music will be sung, but he participates in praise and worship, often playing the electric piano and introducing a variety of songs during that part of the service just as he does throughout the rest of the worship experience. Perfecting Church has embraced praise and worship extensively as exemplified by the fact that virtually every church service as well as the Bible studies begin with it. The church has also devoted entire weekends to exploring praise and worship and related topics, with invited speakers, classes on praise and worship, and a master songwriting course taught by Pastor Winans.[83]

Randy Short is the director of the Department of Praise and Worship; she oversees fifty individuals whose backgrounds range from having traveled the world as professional gospel singers to having served solely in the local church. There are two praise and worship leaders; the rest of the singers serve on six teams consisting of three sopranos, three altos, and three tenors. The six-piece band that accompanies them includes an organist, a keyboardist, a drummer, a percussionist, and bass and lead guitarists.

Short, who hails from a family of singers, is the niece of a former New York City district choir director for the Church of Our Lord Jesus Christ.

Perfecting Church praise team led by Randy Short (*front*), 2006. *Back row, left to right:* Kim Reed, Latonia Hardy, and Twoney Brewster. Photograph by Bill McNeece.

Classically trained in elementary and middle school, Short remembers hearing praise and worship music for the first time in the 1980s: "I was a new mom, at home, and would listen to a radio program that played Hosanna! and Integrity music all through the night. Waking up to it at 3:00 AM is an incredible experience. Your sleep is broken by your own voice saying, 'Hallelujah!'" Her attendance at a praise and worship conference in Houston during that same time period completely transformed her into a worshipper: "I went home and got on my face, determined to get in God's presence. . . . My job as the director of Praise and Worship is to lead the congregation into the presence of God, show them how to linger in His presence until He blesses them, and how to worship Him for who He is, not what they can get from Him."[84]

Perfecting Church's Tuesday evening Bible study is conducted with virtually the same elements as their Sunday morning worship, which is why a description of the Bible study held on Tuesday, August 12, 2003, is indicative of how praise and worship music is used there. A praise and worship team of nine opens the service, Pastor Winans delivers the lesson/sermon, an invitation is made to Christian discipleship, tithes and offerings are received, and announcements are made before the benediction. Before the music from the praise and worship team begins, the members of the congregation meditate or pray individually. That night, Pastor Winans came to the podium at 8 PM and led the congregation in the praise and worship song "I Love You Lord," after which the praise team and leader took over with two more praise and worship songs, "Hallelujah You're Worthy" and "Shout unto God with the Voices of Triumph (Clap Those Hands, O Ye People)." The exhortations from the praise and worship leader were placed between songs, just as they would be during the traditional devotional service.

Just before Pastor Winans began the lesson for the evening, he led the congregation in the hymn "Great Is Thy Faithfulness." Because it contains lyrics that are as reverential as those of the more contemporary songs that came before it ("Thou changest not, Thy compassions, they fail not"), the placement of this hymn at the beginning of the most sacred moment of the worship experience is testament to the pastor's knowledge of and appreciation for a wide range of musical genres, from the traditional to the contemporary, and his determination to make that eclectic mix a hallmark of the church he pastors. Short elaborates: "Pastor Winans has set an order for worship service. Our worship leaders incorporate hymns, praise and worship music in our services. We know what is expected in terms of musical content, so we choose music that edifies, speaks the truth, exhorts, and worships God."[85] Pastor Winans summarized the inclusive nature of the music that is offered: "Again Perfecting is different in that we'll go from 'The Lord Is My Light' to 'Halle, halle, hallelou.' I mean, we'll go from the islands to slavery to Holland without missing a beat."[86]

Closing Comments on Praise and Worship in the Black Church

Clearly, this model in which praise and worship music is intertwined with traditional songs can be found in a growing number of contemporary urban churches. The reasons offered by the praise and worship leaders at Greater Christ Temple, Perfecting Church, and St. James Baptist Church—a pastor's insistence that the traditional songs not be discarded, another pastor's penchant for mixing a variety of genres, and a praise and worship leader's sensitivity to the requests of the older members—provide insights into why the inclusive model is used in many congregations.

Randy Short offers another explanation: "The Bible speaks of not destroying the old landmarks. I don't believe you can just remove traditional music from worship service. Modernize it, update it, whatever, but don't get rid of it. . . . Revelation of praise and worship gives a better understanding of traditional music. I know why my mother and grandmother sang [those songs]. It gave them hope!"[87]

There are, of course, other models for the use of praise and worship music. Some churches, such as Detroit's Dunamis Outreach Ministries, use praise and worship music almost exclusively. Dunamis's pastor, Reginold Lane, writes many of the songs that are a part of their services. In fact, it is reportedly the central music form used by that congregation. In contrast, other churches, such as Unity Baptist Church, have no plans to incorporate praise and worship music, at least not in the foreseeable future. Unity's minister of music, Dorgan Needom, shares why he and Pastor Valmon Stotts have been reluctant to follow other churches, including their peers at St. James Baptist Church, into the trend. First, there are what he refers to as "too many gymnastics . . . the 'stand up, sit down, touch your neighbor,' which seems to be the standard thing I've seen. I think there is a difference between coercion and sincerely motivating people to come into the presence of the Lord."[88]

Needom also raises questions about the ramifications of designating a solitary part of the service as "praise and worship": "The whole 11:00 service was [once] entitled 'worship service.' Then why do we have a period defined as praise and worship? Is the rest of the service something else? The word 'praise' was not included in that, but that was what it was supposed to be." He and Pastor Stotts have not ruled out praise and worship forever. Needom concludes, "There needs to be greater understanding regarding praise and worship. I have not had the opportunity to take advantage of any seminars. If we [at Unity Baptist] were going to do it, it would be where we would sing the hymns from the hymn book, sing some of the praise and worship . . . and leave out the gymnastics."[89] The pattern he describes sounds much like the inclusive one being used in many churches already.

As thousands of churches have incorporated praise and worship music into their services, challenges have arisen that some congregations have already handled and others are still trying to resolve. Among the more common problems I have heard named are arrogant praise team members, songs that are too complex for the congregation to sing, and praise and worship that is "practiced" rather than spontaneous. Judith Christie McAllister offers this cogent analysis of what has led to the first problem, arrogance: "that ['see me'] spirit has somehow crept into the church and has set up residence in many ministries, particularly the music and or the arts ministries. Hidden agendas, secret motives have been fed by the desire to be up front."[90]

Carolyn Cole, a nationally recognized organist, singer, and choir director employed by the Hope United Methodist and Hartford Memorial churches in Detroit, believes that arrogance can set in because the praise team members are usually handpicked and, therefore, not open to "whosoever will." For that reason, she states, "Pastors have to be careful not to allow the praise team to act as if they are a step above other singers, since that can lead to divisions and resentment."[91] EMI recording artist and praise and worship leader Darwin Hobbs offers these thoughts on the phenomenon: "To say that the worship team is such a focal point is a fact . . . but the TRUTH is that it shouldn't be! . . . This is serious business. We need to change the name from 'worship team' to 'team of worshippers.' . . . Maybe this will focus the attention more on the real reason for such a component in our corporate worship experiences."[92]

A second problem many have noted is the selection of songs that are not conducive to audience participation. Cole explains: "If the praise team brings music that has two verses, a chorus, a bridge, and a special chorus, that's a choir song and too difficult for the average church member to follow easily. That can be seen as just another segment of entertainment with the members in the pews serving as mere observers in their own church."[93] In effect, then, the praise team becomes just another choir, not the group that leads the congregation into corporate worship.[94]

Finally, Cole believes there is a problem of praise and worship music and behaviors becoming so rehearsed that the very thing the praise team is there to implement cannot be achieved. She recalls being "completely turned off" at a major local church as she witnessed what appeared to be rote participation in the praise and worship part of the service, including the entire congregation speaking in tongues as soon as the pastor started and stopping as soon as he stopped. "With that kind of predictability from the church, the choir, and the band," she explains, "there is no room for the Holy Spirit to come in."[95]

With a growing number of workshops, including the Gospel Heritage Foundation's praise and worship conference and the I Hear Music in the Air conference, addressing these and other related topics, there are various opportunities for churches to identify ways to have their praise and worship teams enhance rather than detract from the worship experience, which many of them may have to do in the near future for the sake of peace and harmony in the sanctuary.

Two decades after some black churches began incorporating praise and worship music into their services, it is safe to characterize this new element within the community as something more than a "fad," if, what is meant is something that comes in and leaves quickly. Gospel record stores have sections devoted to this music form, and in many, such as Detroit's God's World Records, it has been the best selling form since 2002, according to store owner Larry Robinson. But since "rhythm and praise," urban influenced gospel will usually do better at the cash register, there is clearly more to be considered in assessing the acceptance of praise and worship music.

Pastor William Murphy III, the native Detroiter who is both composer and lead singer of the hit recording "Praise Is What I Do," views the rise of praise and worship in the Black Church as a reflection of a specific need among and within worshippers:

> Everybody wants to go to the next level. Everybody wants the "better." Praise and worship is taking people to that next place in God. That's why it's become so popular because there's a release . . . for instance, on the song that God gave me "Praise Is What I Do," there's a release on that song. The song releases a glory that "I Don't Feel No Ways Tired" didn't release. So as people began to grow in God and as churches began to grow and as people became tired of religion, they discerned that worship—not just praise—but worship releases "the more."[96]

Those who would comprehend the success of the genre might want to turn their gaze to the church itself, which is where the phenomenon began and where it is practiced widely. There they will find praise teams and congregations engaged in worship using music from top-selling recordings such as *Throne Room*, by CeCe Winans, *Pages of Life Chapters I and II*, by Fred Hammond, and *The Next Level*, by Israel and New Breed. But they are also likely to hear refrains that have been part of the Black Church experience for generations, evidence that despite the presence of innovation, there remains a place for "the sound of old gospel," at least for now.[97] Where praise and worship music will be in a quarter century, to what extent it will be practiced and in what configurations, will certainly be worth tracking.

RIGHT UNDER OUR (UPTURNED) NOSES

THE PHENOMENON KNOWN AS THE GOSPEL
MUSICAL STAGE PLAY

Scene: Handsome Shemar Moore, as Joshua King, the spiritually centered voice of reason in *Fabric of a Man,* has just told his female friend Dominique Majors (R&B singer Cheryl "Pepsi" Riley) that he will pick her up for their date after he takes a shower. Moore (from television's *The Young and the Restless, Soul Train,* and *Criminal Minds*) has just come from the gym, working on his "six weeks to a six pack" program, he reports—which must be successful because when he lifts his shirt squeals of delight emanate from the largely female audience in the theater. After a brief "see you in a few minutes" and a musical interlude, Moore appears to be in the shower—water, soap, and all—and though he is only revealed from the waist up, there is pandemonium in the audience for several minutes. My niece RoseAna, who is attending her first gospel drama, comments, "If all of the gospel plays are like that, count me in, Aunt Deborah!"

Scene: Identical twin angels have just come to the rescue of a black male who is in peril in the play *Real Men Pray.* The audience is abuzz, in part because the character is being visited in biblical fashion by these ministering, celestial beings. But the audience is decidedly more entranced by the biceps and triceps of these massively cut figures. This time, it is a Jewish friend, Gail, another first-time visitor to a gospel musical play, who speaks to me: "If people thought angels really looked like that, there'd be a lot more bodies in church on Sunday morning."

She is probably right. But until the church decides to depict angels as incredibly buff or can spread the good news exclusively through the likes of Shemar Moore, there is the gospel musical stage play. As David E. Talbert, the playwright behind *Fabric of a Man* and eleven other dramas explains, "Gospel theater is a ministry in the form of entertainment."[1]

There are various kinds of productions, presented everywhere from church basements to the stages of Broadway, that have combined the good news of Jesus Christ with gospel music. Still, the form known as the gospel musical stage play is a distinct, controversial entity. As presented since 1989, these plays can be seen as a unique combination of religious and dramatic conventions and subtle and overt cultural symbols, including music, modes of advertising, and choices of performers, which convey meaning to black audiences. In an article published in 1991, theatrical historian Warren Burdine critiqued the gospel musical play as it had been staged to that point by writing that the form lacked innovation and was at the brink of extinction, in part because it had not produced a "crossover" audience during the 1980s.[2]

In the time since that assessment was made, not only has Burdine conceded that the productions have staying power, but scores of new productions operating under the heading "gospel musical stage play" or "urban inspirational play" have become a theatrical phenomenon, attracting large African American audiences and generating millions of dollars for their producers across the United States. While drama critics have reprimanded some of the playwrights for offering poorly developed plots and stereotypical characters, these same plays have also been routinely applauded for the celebratory nature of their musical performances and the reality of the social issues they address.[3]

Despite the enormous popularity of the gospel musical play, some reviewers have wondered whether the productions, with such evocative titles as *Momma Don't*, *Mr. Right Now*, and *If These Hips Could Talk*, are merely gospel concerts in disguise. The question remains unanswered, in part because only a few academic articles have focussed on the gospel musical at all.[4] A scant number of scholarly essays have centered on the gospel musical stage play as it has been shaped and presented in the last twenty years, a period during which it has become a dominant theatrical form in black America.

It would be easy to charge elitism and arrogance on the part of scholars and to assume that the plays have been dismissed as an ephemeral part of popular culture. However, the truth is that the contemporary gospel musical probably remains unexamined because it has been, by design, hidden in plain view from mainstream and academic communities. The gospel musical stage play as it has appeared since 1989 is a vibrant theatrical form for, by, and about black people. Rather than a lesser form of other kinds of theater, it represents a viable continuation of the dramas and rituals of the Black Church. For these reasons it, like the church play, also known as the sacred drama, is deserving of closer academic scrutiny.[5]

Defining the Genre

According to some scholars, the term "gospel musical stage play" refers to a production in which the action is similar to that found within a conventional drama, unlike gospel musicals such as *Mama I Want to Sing*, which some scholars have called musical revues or pageants.[6] More than a clever turn of phrase by academics, this specific label, gospel musical stage play (or urban inspirational play or gospel drama), is often incorporated within the advertising for the plays because it denotes a unique combination of elements for its target audiences:

Plots based on the challenges of contemporary life: adultery, prodigal children, drugs, child and spousal abuse, AIDS, the difficult search for a loving partner.

A cast of characters representative of the tug of war between good and evil.

A denouement that offers one remedy for the aforementioned ills: acceptance of Jesus Christ as Lord and Savior and a daily walk with the God of the Bible.

A score consisting largely of either existing gospel songs and/or of inspirational music written specifically for the play; these songs are often augmented by R&B songs familiar to the audience.

A combination of both dramatic and humorous passages.

Actors and/or singers who have marquee value within black America.

Charles Stewart and the Reach Ensemble of *Mama, I Want to Sing.* Producer, writer, and director Vy Higginsen proved with her production *Mama I Want to Sing* that a targeted marketing plan and gospel music sung enthusiastically and well could draw thousands of African Americans to the theater. Courtesy of the Mama Foundation for the Arts.

Rather than suggesting that there is a formulaic sameness to these productions, this list indicates that, as with other theatrical genres, there are specific conventions that define a gospel musical stage play, conventions that compel the target audience to return often.

The Plays and the Playwrights

Langston Hughes has been cited for demonstrating with *Black Nativity* that black music in general and gospel music in particular have a place on Broadway. Similarly, Vy Higgensen has been recognized for proving with *Mama I Want to Sing* that gospel music and smart marketing strategies could draw thousands of African Americans to the theater.[7] But thousands of black theatergoers view Michael Matthews as the grandfather of the gospel musical stage play since he is credited with giving the genre its current shape: that of an urban morality drama.[8] David E. Talbert, Angela Barrow-Dunlap, and Tyler Perry have followed his lead and achieved noteworthy success with their target audience.

A former theatrical booking agent and singer originally from Saginaw, Michigan, Matthews began writing gospel musicals in the late 1980s after his brother became a cocaine addict. The devastating effect on the family and Matthews's own faith in God compelled him to write to warn others of the evils of drugs and God's ability to change lives. *Wicked Ways, Momma Don't, Come Out of the Rain, I Need a Man, Mama I'm Sorry,* and *Love the One You With* [sic] are among his best-known works.[9] Matthews, along with most of his colleagues, has been accused of presenting the worst sins of the genre—stereotypical characters, poorly developed plots, and awkward combinations of comedy and humor.[10] However, his ability to punctuate the most emotionally involving plots with black stars his audiences want to see has assisted in lifting the gospel musical play to the point where its popularity outpaces that of most Broadway dramas and musicals.[11]

Momma Don't, which opened at Detroit's Music Hall on May 19, 1989, after sold-out performances in Flint and Saginaw, can be considered a classic Matthews drama. The protagonist, Linda, is a young woman who is introduced to crack cocaine by her best friend and cousin, Kim. Linda begins to abuse her children and prostitute herself to support her habit. After Kim and her daughter are killed on the mean streets, Linda's children turn against her, and the entire family is evicted. Linda finally faces the chaos crack has produced, "returns to her life as a good mother and Christian, vows to give up crack, and starts on her long path to rehabilitation."[12]

Matthews has proof, beyond the usually sold-out theaters, of having connected with his audiences with plots such as this. When his first play, *Wicked Ways,* opened for one night only, he remembers seeing a line of people wrapped around the corner waiting to get a seat. After the play was over, he recalls, "People came out and they were crying and talking about how it changed their lives. So I said, 'Okay, this is my ministry.'"[13]

One of Matthews's most successful peers is four-time NAACP Image Award winner David E. Talbert. The great-grandson of a Pentacostal preacher, Talbert, who holds a degree in marketing from Morgan State, began writing gospel plays in 1991. Among the genre's most prolific writers and producers, he has written and produced twelve plays: *Tellin' It Like It 'Tiz* (1991), *Lawd Ha' Mercy* (1993), *What Goes Around Comes Around* (1994), *He Say . . . She Say . . . But What Does God Say* (1996), *A Fool and His Money* (1997), *Talk Show Live* (1998), *Mr. Right Now!* (1998–99), *His Woman, His Wife* (2000), *Fabric of a Man* (2001), *Love Makes Things Happen* (2002), *Love on Layaway* (2003), and *Love in the Nick of Tyme* (2007). Talbert, who has also completed several books, was tapped by Oscar winner Jamie Foxx to write, coproduce, and stage his 2006 NBC television special, *Unpredictable: A Musical Journey.*[14]

Through Talbert's website (http://www.davidetalbert.com), potential theatergoers can click on the list of his complete works (which include books, music videos, and an upcoming theatrical film) and his biography, join his VIP mailing list, and read about his AIM (Arts in Motion) program that introduces inner city youth to the theater. They can purchase soundtracks from and videos of his plays, including what Talbert reports to have been the first gospel musical stage play available on video, *Mr. Right Now!*

In *Mr. Right Now!* Angel, a single mother, is looking for Mr. Right, but according to her son and her mother, she has been out with twenty losers who have broken her heart. After Darnell, the attractive entrepreneur she notices during a church gathering, "finds" and returns Angel's wallet, the two become a couple. She does not know he is a womanizer who is with her only because she is a senior bank loan officer. Waiting nearby is a man who truly cares for her, Walter, a plumber, who eventually avenges her honor and shows himself to be her Mr. Right, a revelation that comes only after she falls on her knees and asks God's forgiveness, redemption, and direction.

Perhaps the most successful woman in the genre is Angela Barrow-Dunlap. A native Detroiter, Barrow-Dunlap was enrolled in theater and communication at Wayne State University when she joined a Mike Matthews tour. During an audition, she met Lizzie Berry. Singly and together, they eventually "doctored" ten plays written by others, work that can entail, according to Berry, changing titles, rewriting scripts, turning a play into an actual musical, and recasting the actors. Eventually, the pair created their own work, including one of the highest-grossing gospel musical plays to date, *Why Good Girls Like Bad Boyz.*[15]

When Barrow-Dunlap began this work in 1989, she was unaware of some of the challenges she and Berry would encounter; the most surprising hurdle was gender, with several of their male collaborators "wanting us to remain the assistants with no credit and no compensation."[16] Now, with her extensive proven track record, Barrow-Dunlap no longer encounters such overt sexism and receives many scripts from those wanting her to co-produce or serve as a retooling expert on their work. Among the other plays she herself has written, directed, or produced are such titles as *Real Men Pray*, *If These Hips Could Talk*, and *My Sweet Potato Pie*. The president of Faith Entertainment in Detroit, Michigan, she believes her success rests in her combination of titles, casting, content, and purpose, with the latter always being her primary concern. "I've had lots of opportunities to do things that did not minister, but I've chosen not to," she explains.[17]

If These Hips Could Talk has been so successful that it has played twice in some cities, including Detroit, Philadelphia, New York City, and Chicago. Using an interactive television show within a play scenario, she presents four women whose program offers "healing, inspirational programming for sisters," hence the acronym "HIPS." Both the on-stage television show guests and the ticket-buying audience in the theater have the opportunity to share, testify, and connect with others whose experiences are similar to their own. Of course, the most riveting aspect of the show involves the drama in each host's life—marital infidelity, weight issues, cancer—which is second only to the moment when she realizes that only through remaining true to God and their sisterhood can she find peace in a turbulent world. Just as Talbert's website provides space for feedback, *Hips* audiences can offer reviews and a variety of thoughts on the play's official website (http://www.ifthesehipscouldtalk.com). The confirmation of the healing nature of *If These Hips Could Talk* has come through e-mails, telephone calls, and letters.

While Talbert has been the most prolific among the top tier gospel musical dramatists, arguably the most successful playwright now working in the genre is Tyler Perry, whose personal backstory of being physically abused as a child and living in his car during part of his adult life is as compelling as what he writes for the stage. With several plays to his credit, including *I Know I've Been Changed* and two stage collaborations with Bishop T. D. Jakes, *Woman, Thou Art Loosed* and *Behind Closed Doors*,

A scene from *Real Men Pray*, by Angela Barrow-Dunlap. Pictured are Deonne and Deronne Dotson (angels), Ernest Pugh (ministering angel), and Samson Logan (street person). Courtesy of Faith Entertainment.

Perry was already filling his share of theater seats when he created his most unforgettable character, Mabel a.k.a. "Medea" Simmons.[18] The 6'4" tall Perry decided to don a wig and a fat suit and cast himself as Madea, a term of endearment many African Americans give their grandmother (a shortened form of the words "Mother Dear"). In creating Madea he brought into black popular culture—to the delight of some and the consternation of others—a well-meaning matriarch with an edge, a Hennessey drinking, pistol-toting, straight-talking firebrand. Madea has become so popular that Perry had to create sequels (including *Madea's Class Reunion, Madea's Family Reunion,* and *Madea Goes to Jail*) on stage, video, and theatrical film to satisfy the demand from regular fans as well as such superstar devotees as Aretha Franklin and Oprah Winfrey. A marketing genius, Perry further enhanced the gravitas of his movies and increased the probability of attracting audiences from across generational and racial lines by casting such icons as Cicely Tyson and Maya Angelou.[19]

Some of the work by the August Wilson–inspired Perry has earned acclaim and been described as Broadway-quality. However, it is Madea who has allowed him to purchase a million-dollar home, land covers on *Jet* magazine, sit next to Oprah, and be included in articles in *Newsweek,* the *New York Times, Essence, Entertainment Weekly,* and other publications. Each of Perry's plays has a plot with intersecting storylines, as is the case with *Madea's Class Reunion:* a young wife fights to hold onto her marriage after being unfaithful to her spouse, a middle-aged wife discovers on her anniversary that her husband has a mistress, and a hotel maid is fired after decades of faithful service. Though each of these stories hinges on the characters relying on or realigning themselves with God, it is the joke-cracking, cantankerous earth mother Madea who has emerged as the reigning serial marquee-value character in today's gospel musical plays. While she does not often practice Christian values herself, she is the one who pulls the audiences in, thus serving as the magnet that allows them to witness the transforming power of God in the lives of the other characters while getting a good laugh.

Second only to Madea in popularity in Perry's plays is her next door neighbor, the tight polyester suit–wearing Mr. Brown, who is also the father of Madea's daughter, Cora. Played hilariously by David Mann, whom gospel music fans came to know as a member of the Family, the group with which Kirk Franklin originally recorded in the 1990s, Mr. Brown has been featured in several of Perry's plays, including *Meet the Browns,* one of the few in which Madea does not appear. He has also released his own CD, *Good Ol' Time Church,* with a mix of traditional songs and humorous reflections on such topics as caller ID and Madea outside the gates of heaven.

Perry has taped and sold several of his plays on VHS and DVD. But the theatrical film adaptations of his work have catapulted him to another level of fame and success. The film version of *Diary of a Mad Black Woman* was produced for $5.5 million, grossed more than $22 million its opening weekend, and had reached the $50 million mark by March 24, 2005, weeks before the highly anticipated DVD sales had begun.[20] His subsequent films *Madea's Family Reunion, Daddy's Little Girls,* and *Why Did I Get Married?* have been equally successful. Perry has emerged as the king of the gospel musical genre.

The Forerunner: The Church-Based or Sacred Drama

One key to comprehending the popularity, significance, and influence of the work Perry and his colleagues create lies not in comparing it with the

Mr. Brown, portrayed by David Mann, has emerged from Tyler Perry's stage plays as a character who is second only to Perry's Madea in popularity. This flyer is from the play *Meet the Browns*, in which Brown and his brightly colored polyester outfits and humorous take on life were featured. Courtesy of Tilly Mann Records.

works of August Wilson and Lorraine Hansberry but in perceiving it as part of a different tradition: the church-based drama. The roots of these African American sacred folk dramas can be traced to the slave plantations. There, the spirituals were not only sung but were frequently dramatized by bands of shouters, who often "became" triumphant biblical characters as they sang their part-African, part-American religious music and received a sense of transcendence, change, and worth.[21]

The first known religious plays, described as "crudely presented," seem to have emerged during the first and second waves of black amateur theater, 1865–1920 and 1920–50.[22] Folklorist Debbie Bowman characterizes these folk dramas as "episodic performances" that "(a) employ a variety of techniques to focus attention; (b) exist as public action of a small, community level group, sharing a system of understood motives and symbols; (c) have a foreknown resolution; and (d) are related to game, play and ritual."[23]

These early black folk productions, called "dramas of self-celebration," were based on the experiences and style of black Americans, and their formula for success was a combination of music, dance, and a thread of a plot.[24] While most of these early musicals, such as *Slabtown Convention* and *Heaven Bound,* were written to coincide with existing sacred songs, that changed when William Herbert Brewster, one of the prolific early gospel music composers, wrote new music specifically for his sacred dramas.[25]

By the end of the nineteenth century, the sacred drama had become an important feature in many black churches. Playwrights often served as social commentators and believed their combination of sacred music and drama could transform lives and society as well as assist in spreading the gospel.[26] Gospel superstar Mahalia Jackson, who acted in several plays during her youth, recalled them as bringing enjoyment to both audience and actor.[27] Sarah Haygood, a popular Sunday school teacher and leader in Detroit's religious community, also remembers the church plays as being a vehicle for bringing everyone together, from common folks to the "muckety mucks," her term for doctors, lawyers, and educators. "The muckety mucks would not be invited to our parties; nor would they have gone if they had been," she states. "But, they would come to see a play and laugh like everybody *else* because we all knew somebody like the characters. For us, it was entertainment."[28]

Black Theater for Black Audiences

The success of the gospel musical stage play is quantifiable and impressive. A single play can reportedly attract twenty thousand people in a week, three-quarters of whom are black females twenty-five to fifty-four years of age.[29] Larry Robinson, the owner of the Detroit gospel music store God's World Records, where thousands of these tickets are sold each year, agrees that black women predominate in the audiences and says that the average ticket buyer has a good income and prefers her entertainment to be easily accessible. He continues: "She likes to have a good time with her friends, go see wholesome entertainment where nobody is trying to hit on her and where there's something on stage she can relate to."[30]

The ability to comprehend the significance of the gospel musical play is related to a great extent to whether one takes an insider's assessment of structure or an outsider's panoramic view of the art form. Theatrical historian Warren Burdine charges that at best the gospel musical has settled for preaching to the converted; at worst, it has shown "a marked lack of respect for the audience's intelligence, broad-mindedness, and ability to consider new concepts and ideas."[31] However, the enormous popularity of the gospel musical stage play, and the fact that thousands of black patrons are repeat ticket buyers, suggests that, rather than being insulted by producers and playwrights, they are enjoying the experience of having many of their entertainment needs met in the theater.

Rhett S. Jones offers an intriguing assessment of why, as of 1991, black theater had not consistently attracted and held black consumers. Among the reasons, he argues, is that too much of it, like European American theater, is experimental and chaotic and too little of it draws upon black American traditions. The core problem is the lack of "a set of familiar figures, rituals, environments and plots," such as the ones found in sports and the Black Church, where everything and everyone has rules, roles, and parameters. Consequently, the theater has been for many black people a "disorderly structure," presenting chaos and disorganization for individuals who, Jones says, have enough surprises already from powerful, rich institutions they do not control, from white culture, as well as from their own community. For these reasons, many of them prefer order and predictability in their entertainment.[32] Or, as playwright Bill Harris puts it in a similar analysis, "The more complex the real world gets, the simpler you want your entertainment to be; you don't want to be challenged by your entertainment. That line of thinking transcends racial lines—that's why television is as popular as it is."[33]

While Jones's theory may appear simplistic to some (and Jones does offer exceptions and qualifiers), the fact remains that the success of the gospel musical stage play seems to prove his point. It offers familiar figures—Jesus and Satan as shaped by black culture, as well as characters reminiscent of those audience members may have seen in their own communities.[34] The plots contain well-known elements of the Black Church ritual (gospel music, calls to Christian discipleship, and ecstasy), and the audiences, which are almost exclusively black, watch these elements presented in the company of other patrons with whom they share similar frames of reference. There is no experimentation in the auditorium seating, and while some playwrights have surprised audiences with innovative touches, such as the shower scene featuring soap opera heartthrob Shemar Moore mentioned earlier, generally, the gospel musicals offer very little that could prove unsettling for someone seeking escapist entertainment. And, of course, the plot's direction is crystal clear: everyone knows that Jesus and his followers will win in the end.

Like its predecessor, the church drama and sacred pageant, the gospel musical stage play contains various elements that reflect the cultural values and religious interests of black audiences. Since the end of slavery, there have been repeated calls for a theatrical tradition that would continue to provide performances by and for black audiences, one of the most controversial ones emanating from the late Pulitzer prize–winning playwright August Wilson in 1997.[35] Perhaps the best known, or at least the most frequently quoted, list of criteria for black theater was issued by W. E. B. DuBois in 1926:

> The plays of a real Negro theater must be:
> 1 About us. That is, they must have plots which reveal Negro life as it is.
> 2 By us. That is, they must be written by Negro authors who understand from birth and continual association just what it means to be a Negro today.
> 3 For us. That is, the theater must cater primarily to Negro audiences and be supported by their entertainment and approval.
> 4 Near us. The theater must be in a Negro neighborhood near the mass of ordinary Negro people.[36]

As the following will demonstrate, the choices made by the producers and playwrights of music, advertising channels, storylines, and performers, have enabled them to turn the theater, which some may have perceived as unfamiliar and uninviting, into something that is viewed as welcoming and comfortable for thousands of black theatergoers.

The Music

Gospel music has significance within African American culture that reaches far beyond its religious text and the church context in which it was created, which is one of the reasons the attendance is so high at many gospel musical plays.[37] Emerging first in its transitional stage before the turn of the twentieth century in the storefront black churches of the north, gospel entered its full traditional form toward the end of the 1920s. It was then that a blues piano player and Baptist minister's son named Thomas A. Dorsey combined the sound of the folk church with new secular music forms, jazz and blues.[38] Since gospel music's earliest days, it has attracted both saint and sinner. The evidence is its so-called crossover record sales, placement on playlists of nonreligious radio stations, and inclusion on mainstream television programs.[39] The fan base for gospel music, then, is not the church community alone, for the same people who embrace other black art forms can and do embrace gospel music since it is a synthesis of various patterns of black speech, music, and dance.[40] This, of course, means that the potential audience for the gospel plays is deep and broad.

For that reason, the ads are not relegated to Christian or gospel outlets. James Chapmyn, whom Henry Louis Gates Jr. interviewed for his study of the "chitlin circuit," explains that the active black theater-going audience gets its information from the church bulletin, from a flyer placed on their cars while they are in night clubs, or on the black radio stations to which they listen. In fact, the producers, Chapmyn reports, bypass cities that don't have at least one such station.[41] Al "the Bishop" Hobbs, chair of the Gospel Announcers Guild of the GMWA, is among those who use the apt description "the churched and the unchurched" to characterize this audience that listens to black radio for most of its entertainment, spiritual, and informational needs.[42] By utilizing black radio, the producers are communicating volumes about their desire to have those from both categories in the audience. Equally important in attracting potential audiences is the language employed in the advertising ("electrifying," "soul stirring," and "inspirational"), which can summon images of church services or revival meetings, places where the potential audience would have undoubtedly witnessed dynamic musical performances in the past.

One of gospel music's most powerful roles within the African American community, according to Mellonee Burnim, is that of communicating the historical past while at the same time addressing contemporary issues and looking toward future remedies.[43] This holds true even when the context of the music is changed from the church to the theater. That is one reason an older classic gospel song can instantly create connections and rekindle memories for audience members. "Jesus Can Work It Out," a part of which is included in Talbert's *Mr. Right Now!* is a perfect example of how historical links can be made in the midst of a gospel musical stage play. The two friends, Angel and Lola, sing just a little of the special chorus from the perennially popular version recorded by Dr. Charles Hayes and the Cosmopolitan Church of Prayer almost two decades ago.[44]

On that recording, lead singer Dianne Williams creates some of the most familiar lines in gospel while the choir chants "work it out" behind her—lines about rent being due and the baby needing new shoes even though you're out of money. The words—along with the rest of the lyrics of the special chorus—have taken on a life of their own within the gospel community. Besides being sung for years by local church choirs and community ensembles, other national recording artists have "borrowed" or recontextualized Diane's words within their own songs.[45]

But it is in the service of thematic continuity that the song is used in *Mr. Right Now!* Talbert has structured parts of the drama in a manner reminiscent of a traditional performed sermon. Early in the delivery of a sermon, the preacher must announce his or her theme. Then, that message is reinforced; each time the minister shares an example, there is a bridge that connects that individual story to the original theme.[46] In *Mr. Right Now!* the opening narration states in part: "If only she knew that God has prepared her destiny. And like her, he [Mr. Right] waits. But to see him, she must look through God's eyes and not her own." These words function the way the pastor's thematic announcement does in that it alleviates any ambiguity about the direction of the play and establishes that Angel's perspective is flawed.

"Jesus Can Work It Out" functions as a bridge back to the main theme. A few lines from this classic allow the audience to reflect on the personal challenges God has brought them through and perhaps the number of times they have sung along with the song in their cars and at church. However, it can also rekindle memories of how God has brought the black community through as a people ("Didn't He, didn't He work it out?"). The evidence of this kind of connection is the call and response a song like this can evoke from the audience, along with head bobbing, hand clapping, dancing in the aisles, and other visible signs of affirmation.

During the musicals, a more contemporary-sounding gospel composition can also be used to connect the audience with the theme, personal and communal memories, victories and needs, and one solution, Jesus Christ. "God Has a Plan for Your Life," which is part of the musical score written specifically for *Mr. Right Now!* serves as such a connector for its audience members. Angel and Walter perform the song as a duet, though neither is aware that the other is singing. While the song is new to the audience, the concept of God having a blueprint for his children's lives is based on Scripture ("The steps of a good man are ordered by the Lord," Psalm 37:23). At the end of the song, both singers adlib specific Bible verses, such as "Weeping may endure for a night, but joy comes in the morning"—which helps give this contemporary song a traditional connection for the church-going part of the crowd. The singers also add in the words "God will work it out," another thematic bridge to the main message. The duet is made even more heart-rending, however, because many in attendance are interpreting the lyrics based on their own (and their loved ones') challenges to finding Mr. Right.

Robinson, the gospel record store owner in Detroit, has observed that "the women who attend the plays tend to identify with the problems, and they are able to see what they or their female relatives went through."[47] The comments from playgoers who sent e-mail to Talbert's website corroborate Robinson's observations. Diane B. from Newark wrote, "I can identify with the main character Angel. A lot of the things she was going through I have went through. This play brought tears to my eyes. . . . But, I know now who I belong to and I know that God does not want his daughter to go through this stuff."[48]

Interestingly, many of today's gospel plays can also include R&B selections, some with the original words, some with the words altered. In one of Matthews's plays, the Temptations' hit song "Treat Her Like a Lady" was performed verbatim by its original lead singer, Ollie Ali Woodson, as he played the part of a church deacon. The deacon uses the song to explain to a younger man how to conduct himself around his girl-friend. As Woodson sang, one lady hollered, "Sing it, baby," as if she were back at the old Motown Revue, clearly enjoying herself and seemingly oblivious to the Christian/gospel context in which the song was being reinterpreted. Though others did not call out to him in the same manner, they did clap, sing along, and smile as they enjoyed the performance and perhaps were transported back in time to their favorite performances by the Temptations.

While some might balk at the inclusion of secular songs within this gospel context, their incorporation actually helps the producers to under-score their intention to reach black audiences. And, because there is a black aesthetic that encompasses both the sacred and secular art forms, R&B, when framed properly, can be a dynamic element in a production. Ultimately, then, the words "electrifying," "soul stirring," and "inspira-tional" have as much to do with what the audience brings to the perfor-mances and how they interpret them as it does with how the singers and actors perform.

Familiar Adversaries

Religion is the underpinning of the traditional cultures of black people throughout the African diaspora, specifically in the United States, the West Indies, South America, and West Africa.[49] Consequently, the pro-ducers, by emphasizing this aspect of the plays in their advertising, are again demonstrating their understanding of what is important to many black audiences. It is usually made clear from the radio, television, and print materials that the forces of good and evil will fight over the protag-onist(s) and that by the play's resolution, through the power of God, good will indeed triumph over evil. The precedent for vividly depicting these warring spiritual factions runs through the church-based gospel plays of the first half of the twentieth century, as such titles as *The Devil Play* [sic] and *Hellbound* indicate. Of course, it can also be traced back further to the spirituals in which Satan was referred to as a cunning force around which the believer should be wary.[50]

The tradition continues, both in today's church-based plays and in the big-budget touring spectacles as well. The devil and Jesus are some-times presented in full traditional attire or in a modified version of said

In 1976 gospel singer Alex Bradford and writer/director Vinnette Carroll created *Your Arms Too Short to Box with God.* Audiences packed auditoriums to see exuberant performances, first on Broadway and then in auditoriums around the country, featuring choirs, dancers and soloists like Jennifer Holliday, and in a later version, Patti LaBelle and Al Green. *Arms* helped to pave the way for the contemporary gospel musical. Courtesy of the E. Azalia Hackley Collection, Detroit Public Library.

clothing, or their presence and effect may be suggested in characters that embody their philosophies. William Wiggins explains that in Margarine Hatcher's *In the Rapture,* a church-based drama that has been seen by thousands in Indianapolis, Indiana, over the last three decades, the more graphic route is taken. The narrator, in between twelve carefully selected songs, spins a tale about the tug of war between the devil and Jesus over the souls of men and women. The devilish character in the play, besides carrying a pitchfork, is presented as a dandy. He wears complete black formal attire as well as top hat, sunglasses, and a black cape with red lining. He entices his prey with various glittering temptations, from a fake diamond ring to stacks of counterfeit money. In contrast, Jesus, without saying a word, offers salvation, comfort, and hope to those whom the devil has spiritually duped and broken. Unlike the devil, Jesus is arrayed as he is in many Western artistic renderings with a crown of thorns atop his long hair, a beard, robe, and bare feet.[51] Usually depicted as white in much of Western art, Jesus and his representatives are always black in the gospel musicals.

While the devil and Jesus Christ physically appear in this and many other church dramas, they are usually represented in surrogate form or by suggestion in the gospel musical stage plays. The illustration used to promote *Momma Don't* includes three images: a woman's face with a tear running down her right cheek, a woman in silhouette with her hand at her forehead, and a large vial of crack cocaine. While there is no straightforward depiction of the devil and Jesus in this production, the audience, familiar with grim headlines and with friends and loved ones that have succumbed to similar temptations, recognize the enemy and cheer and even cry when "Jesus"—a return to righteous living based on the teachings of Christ—wins in the end.

The enmity between the devil and Jesus is, of course, at the center of basic Christian doctrine (see Genesis 3:15). However, Wiggins writes that *In the Rapture* is reflective of several cultural attitudes found throughout the African diaspora. The devil is presented as a trickster hero, as seen in the Brer Rabbit tales of black America, the Anansi tales of the West Indies, and the exploits of Legba in the Yoruba religion.[52] That same trickster surfaces as the con artist and duplicitous lover in *Mr. Right Now!* as well as the friend who gets Linda hooked on crack in *Momma Don't* (the devil can be depicted as female). "The enemy," as churchgoers often call him, manifests in various other guises, including a wide range of attractions and addictions, such as those presented in *Why Good Girls Like Bad Boyz,* a play in which the protagonists struggle with the devil in his most tempting, sexual incarnation.

Satan's nemesis, Jesus, is characterized throughout the African diaspora as one who hides his emotions and "never says a mumbling word," as one Negro spiritual describes it, during the time leading up to the crucifixion.[53] In Hatcher's play *In the Rapture,* he affects the cool pose found throughout urban black America, the inscrutability of the John Canoe dancers of Jamaica, the Geleda mask wearers of Nigeria, and the devil mask tradition bearers of Liberia.[54] Jesus is depicted similarly in the gospel musical *Perilous Times,* in which he counters the compelling temptations of the devil with a quiet strength and demonstrations of love for humankind, including going to the cross without murmuring. Often, however, Jesus is not portrayed, but his values and truths are personified in a God-fearing preacher (*Momma Don't*), a good-hearted fellow (Walter in *Mr. Right Now!*), or other characters who are longsuffering, faithful, and forgiving of the sins of the protagonist, such as Faye in *If These Hips Could Talk,* who is the first of three friends to pray for a fourth who tries to add tabloid television drama to what has been "healing, inspirational programming for sisters."

Combining Tragedy and Comedy

The protagonists in the gospel musical stage plays are often ensnared in some of life's biggest challenges, issues that are of imminent concern to many in the audience—AIDS, substance abuse, incest, and so on.[55] Tyler Perry, who addressed spousal abuse in *I Know I've Been Changed,* agrees with comedian Steve Harvey, who once told him, "You can tell Black people anything if you make them laugh."[56] The feedback about which Matthews and Talbert speak is quite typical of what the playwrights hear when they focus on an issue that is close to a patron's own situation or frame of reference.

Herein lies the basis for some of the most biting critiques aimed at the gospel plays, that is, that they deal with such topics awkwardly by juxtaposing social maladies with comically portrayed characters—the pimp, the finger-popping homosexual, the loudly dressed, shouting church saint, just to name a few. Gates sums up the enigma of this aspect: "All the very worst stereotypes of the race are on display, larger than life. Here, in this racially sequestered space, a black audience laughs uninhibitedly, whereas the presence of white folks would have engendered a familiar anxiety: *Will they think that's what we're really like?*"[57] In fact, the comedic moments within the genre, like the plays themselves, can run the gamut from the clever and sophisticated to the obvious and offensive. They include puns ("Your problem is that you're a nun. You ain't never had none, and you don't ever want none!"), sight gags (a would-be ladies' man trails toilet paper from the back of his pants), and references to contemporary culture (a gunshot victim says from a prone position, "I've fallen and I can't get up," a line from an infamous medical alert television ad).

The question of what is tasteful, acceptable, or even truly funny within black America is not new and has been addressed by individuals from various disciplines. In the early 1920s, DuBois offered his perspective on how black people should be portrayed, noting that many wanted stories about the black community to amount to "justifiable propaganda," depicting "the best and highest and noblest" aspects. But, he said, "We have criminals and prostitutes, ignorant and debased elements just as all folk have." As for why some black people could not find humor in certain portrayals, he added: "The more highly trained we become the less can we laugh at Negro comedy—we will have it all tragedy and the triumph of dark Right over pale Villainy."[58]

Another who has assessed black comedy and comedic portrayals, Mel Watkins, observes that the humor of nearly all minorities reveals a tendency toward self-deprecation. He concludes that a survey of many jokes seems to confirm a "self-debasing tendency" in black humor; yet, he also identifies an extensive use of irony and a "creative resourcefulness in reversing an accepted joke and turning it to one's advantage." Ultimately, Watkins reminds us, that of course whether something is seen as humorous depends on the perspective of the one hearing the joke.[59]

Simply stated, the reasons for the laughter and high attendance at the gospel musical plays may be as unique as are the people who buy the tickets. In some instances, the laughter is a reflection of the extent to which audience members recognize and can relate to what unfolds on stage. In other instances, it serves as a mechanism by which they can diffuse some of the discomfort and pain of being confronted in the theater by the difficult issues with which they or a loved one may be grappling. The irony and truth of the gospel musical plays is that while audiences purport to buy tickets so that they can receive a spiritually uplifting message, there are those who at least talk more about the humorous aspects of the productions. This is what Tony Mayberry, the former manager of God's World Records in Detroit, saw with his customers over the years. "Almost without fail," he said, "they return to the store, reporting about and laughing at the funniest scenes and actors in the production, except when it is a biblically based play like *Perilous Times*."[60]

That these gospel playwrights seem to tread onto this difficult territory where humor and pathos meet could be attributed to their backgrounds as well as their missions in undertaking this work. Many of those currently writing gospel plays are not trained in that discipline, though at least one acclaimed playwright, the late Ron Milner, wrote two gospel plays—*Don't Get God Started,* which ran on Broadway, and *Inner City Miracle.* He also directed another for a short period, *If These Hips Could Talk.* Most of these writers come from the community and were initially compelled to write because of their faith, a fact that connects them to early sacred pageant writers like Brewster and is a further demonstration that these plays spring from a different heritage than that of the Broadway play, a heritage that is viable in its own right.

Performers with Marquee Value

One of the most telling signs that the gospel musical play is designed for black audiences is its presentation of performers who have marquee value and history within that community. "They are," as my friend and fellow playgoer Rosemary Reed remarked, "like a 'welcome' sign, telling black audiences that their patronage is wanted." The producers obviously know who can create good box office traffic. But they may also be aware that for many black audiences, certain performers—singers, musicians, and comedians among them—create something that is beyond entertainment. That is, they are seen as producing performances that have the feel of ritual and that allow for individual and communal catharsis.[61] Thus, the experience of the gospel musical is heightened and enhanced for audiences who are able to witness on stage those who in another setting have moved them spiritually or energized them through acting, singing, dancing, or even joke-telling.

Some of the performers have starred in or been featured in various television shows or made-for-television movies. That long and ever-growing roster includes Tichina Arnold, Pam on the Fox sitcom *Martin* and the wife on *Everybody Hates Chris;* Malik Yoba, J. C. Williams of *New York Undercover* fame; and Lawrence-Hilton Jacobs from *Roots, Cooley High,* and *The Jacksons.* Feature film actors, like Billy Dee Williams (*Lady Sings the Blues* and *Star Wars*) and Margaret Avery and Akosua Busia (both from *The Color Purple*), as well as top-selling R&B artists, including An-

Playwright Ron Milner. Courtesy of the Milner Family.

gela Bofill, Cuba Gooding Sr., and Sean and Gerald Levert, have helped draw audiences to the plays. Even nonactors with high visibility, such as attorney Johnnie Cochran and real-life judge turned television adjudicator Greg Mathis, have made appearances on these stages. Gospel performers, the upcoming stars and superstars alike, among them Kirk Franklin, members of the Winans family, and the Clark Sisters, have all lent their talents to gospel musical stage plays and have, in turn, seen their record sales increased. In fact, artists in all these categories have benefited from the exposure that comes with being a part of the gospel musical stage plays.[62]

The star-studded cast may be one of the most nonnegotiable factors in building a successful play. One play launched in 2004 with all the other elements in place and plans for a several month run returned early for retooling, one insider reports, because there was only one known star in the cast. The playwright/star probably would have been more successful by returning to the formula that has made several peers prosperous in this arena.

Recent Changes

Since the publication of the first version of this article in 2000, a significant change has occurred in the staging of gospel musical stage plays. Poverty and its attendant ills are no longer the leading challenges for the protagonists. Just as the black-oriented feature films have generally moved from the boyz in the 'hood to the upscale sisters and brothers in suburbia, the central characters in the gospel musicals have done the same. Now their dilemmas include working too many hours, mishandling the abundance, and placing jobs before family and God.

Conclusions

Linking the gospel musical stage plays to the religious dramas that are part of the black church experience is not an attempt to have them perceived as inferior to those dramas that are considered part of "legitimate" theater. Rather, it is a call to have them assessed as an outgrowth of a tradition of cultural and religious elements that resonates with meaning and entertainment value for black audiences. It is an acknowledgment that these playwrights and producers have learned how to transform disorderly structures into inviting spaces, spaces where thousands of black folk, including "muckety mucks," can and often do find entertainment, validation, and inspiration.

MUSCLE T-SHIRTS, TIGHT JEANS, AND CLEAVAGE

(W)RAPPING THE GOSPEL FOR A NEW GENERATION

If the Son therefore shall make you free, ye shall be free indeed.
    JOHN 8:36

If Vickie and CeCe [Winans] had really been set free, they would not have performed in pants.
    Gospel announcer and missionary BERTHA HARRIS

I've been shown a freer way, and I am walking therein.
    Gospel artist VICKIE WINANS

For centuries, black men and women have dressed up to go to church.[1] Over time, "dressing up" came to mean shirts, ties, and suits for men, and dresses or skirts and blouses for women, including what I call "divine divawear," dresses and suits that range from conservative yet chic to show-stopping and even flashy attire, including garments accented or covered in rhinestones and beading. And, of course, there were hats for both sexes, glorious, colorful crowns of every shape and size. Many still dress in this manner when attending church or gospel music events. But just as artists have expanded the sounds and styles that can be considered gospel, a growing number of them have also chosen to dress less conventionally.

Their decisions have been met with applause, ambivalence, and even flat-out disapproval by some of their peers and audiences.

Virtually every person who meets another individual for any reason "reads" the garments of the other as if they were actual texts or books, determining, based on personal criteria or sociocultural conventions, the appropriateness of the clothing. The same is true for those witnessing a gospel music performance; they too judge whether the clothing is attractive or distracting, secular or sacred, traditional or contemporary, decisions that can be as subjective as the judgments made about the music itself. Alison Laurie has theorized that clothing is itself a language, that there is a vocabulary of dress that includes hair styles, accessories, jewelry, make-up, and body decoration, as well as actual garments.[2] Whether we view the clothing of gospel artists as text or as vocabulary words, the consequences are the same: performers must have a solid understanding of the varied and sometimes intense responses their outfits and their movements in them could receive from fans. They could find their music embraced, but their CD covers could be viewed skeptically. Or they could receive cat calls and boos because of the assessments made by the audience. Though the rallying cry is always that the message of gospel music is paramount, a number of artists have discovered that a misstep made in their sartorial choices can severely disrupt the communication of their message.

When artists make garment selections that go beyond the traditional boundaries of the Black Church or gospel music world, they generally do so for several reasons. What may appear to be a flagrant disregard for the rules of dress and decorum can be more appropriately understood as the existence and assertion of multiple identities within "the body of Christ," the name Christians often use to refer to fellow believers and their institutions. Whereas earlier generations seem to have prioritized projecting a certain image through attire—"I am Christian and, therefore, not worldly"—a growing number of turn-of-the-century gospel artists are selecting ensembles and accessories that underscore the various identities they embrace and that allow them to declare through their selections, "I am young *and* Christian *and* 'fashionably correct.'"[3] Such perceived proclamations are controversial in some circles because they highlight the existence of differing values and aesthetics, divergent interpretations of relevant Scriptures regarding adornment and the body, and challenges to denominational mores in the Black Church and gospel music worlds, where, for years, many have viewed conformity as a sign of membership. In fact, this celebrated virtue has never been as uniformly practiced as many believe.

Clothing remains one of the most visible signifiers of identity within cultures, including religious communities. For example, men who are about to be ordained as Buddhist monks and novices wear white robes during the ordination ceremony and then change into the saffron robes that signify their new status.[4] The Amish wear plain clothing to encourage humility, to underscore that they are separate from the world, and to express their faith.[5] And black couples may intertwine materials from West Africa, including fabrics, designs, or accessories, with their Western finery in order to emphasize their cultural and ancestral heritage during their wedding ceremonies.[6] It is no less so within the Black Church and gospel music communities.

In fact, this penchant for not merely dressing but for asserting identity through dress can be found throughout African American history. Southern slaves often created specific clothing for social occasions, including weddings, birthday and holiday celebrations, and, of course, church.[7] Oral histories, diary entries, and illustrations from the nineteenth century document the fact that the slaves, even those who received only one garment per year from their master, often created "dress-up" attire for themselves. Their "wardrobe" could include everything from the master's and mistress's castoffs, which were often given to slaves who worked within the home, to corn stalks and other plant leaves, which were sometimes innovatively woven into hats and other accessories by those with more meager resources. Through attire, the enslaved were able to communicate several messages: their desire to distance themselves from the clothing provided by the master, their sense of individual style and taste, and their connection to the aesthetics of the community.[8]

Since gospel music was created within the Black Church, one way to understand the "rules of attire" that operate within the realm of gospel music is to evaluate the principles that apply to dressing up for worship. Most of the regulations concerning proper attire in the sanctuary of the Black Church have roots that can be traced to the very beginning of Christian Church history (100–500 A.D.). The Bible is not as specific as many imagine regarding clothing; it says virtually nothing about what men should wear and nothing about the length of women's garments. In the Old Testament, there are warnings against wearing clothing of mixed fibers and against cross dressing, that is, men are told not to wear women's clothes, and women are instructed not to wear men's attire (Deuteronomy 22:1, 5).

In the New Testament, the general directive from Paul is that women should be "modest" in their clothing and adornment: "I also want women to dress *modestly,* with *decency* and *propriety,* not with braided hair or gold or pearls or expensive clothes, but with good deeds, appropriate for women who profess to worship God" (I Timothy 2:9–10, emphasis added). The apostle also decrees that women should have their heads covered, whatever their role within the church.[9]

Beginning a mere three decades after Paul wrote these words to Timothy, the early Church fathers, with their knowledge of biblical sanctions and of "the specific evil evoked by lust," codified what would be viewed as unacceptable attire for women.[10] For example, they were to avoid wearing "soft, clinging" fabrics as well as hemlines that were above the ankles, since the mere sight of any flesh, even an ankle, could be provocative. Clement of Alexandria insisted that women wear veils with the exception of purple ones, since that color "inflamed lust." Red was also on the list of colors to be avoided. As Enoch, another early Church patriarch, wrote, "If God wanted dresses made of purple and scarlet wool, he would have created purple and scarlet sheep." Enoch is also credited with observing that "women learned about cosmetics from the fallen angels."[11]

As the Church attempted to make the female body less sexually desirable, there were at least three unintended results: (1) women learned to signal or suppress their sexual intentions by revealing or hiding parts of the body; (2) all parts of the body came to be considered sexual, since "body parts that have been covered can be uncovered"; (3) men knew which women to approach for sexual encounters and which to avoid based on what these women wore.[12] Two thousand years later, there are varying levels of uncertainty, discomfort, and tension within local churches and across denominations, as some individuals adhere to the time-honored standards about what constitutes sacred attire while others communicate their own definitions of "modesty," "decency," and "propriety." The varying interpretations of these words keep some Christians focused on their fellow parishioners—and gospel artists—as they try to determine who has crossed the narrow line that separates the sacred from the secular.[13]

Since the 1800s, the African American Church, the most important religious and social center within the community, has understandably developed a variety of mores regarding dress. For almost two centuries, one standard was virtually ubiquitous. "Sunday best," that is, dressing up as described earlier, was generally deemed appropriate for men, women, and children. Despite our collective memory that the rules were standardized and adhered to without deviation, dressing up was as varied as the people who attended the churches; however, it was widely assumed that each person would demonstrate that serious effort was put into looking appropriately dressed and well groomed when attending church and that there would be a discernible difference made between what was worn for worship and what was worn for work. This was especially important since church was one of the few venues where the black community could assert individuality and status while demonstrating their flair for adornment that was often hidden by the service uniforms many had to endure during the work week. Beyond looking suitably attired, individuals could or were instructed to select or delete certain colors, fabrics, hats, gloves, jewelry, shoes, and other elements of adornment as dictated by their denominations or local pastors.[14]

If there is one item of clothing that demonstrates how differently individuals and organizations have and continue to interpret Scripture, it is women's pants, just as the quotes that open this chapter suggest. Until the last quarter century, there were few if any women who openly wore pants to a Black Church service other than prayer meeting or auxiliary meeting. Traditions about dressing up as well as prohibitions in certain denominations about wearing pants were in full effect then. But today the female parishioners and gospel singers who wear pants are being challenged or looked at askance by some because of differing interpretations of the biblical statement about women wearing "that which pertaineth to a man." For a variety of reasons, including the growing acceptance of casual dress within American culture, an ever-increasing number of black churches have become less rigid in this area of dress.[15]

One of the churches I visited in the mid-1990s that had embraced more casual dress was Greater St. Stephen Full Gospel Baptist Church in New Orleans. Bishop Paul Morton, who was already known for his dynamic singing and preaching, was also drawing attention because he often delivered his sermons while wearing jogging suits and casual wear. He had also instituted three "Come as You Are" months during Louisiana's hot summers. Even during the other nine months, there was no pressure to dress up, according to his chief administrator and sister, Gwen Morton. As long as worshippers were decently attired, they could enter wearing whatever they found comfortable: "We wouldn't encourage women to wear halter tops, but we would never stop them from entering the service. We'd just give them a sweater."[16]

In a 2006 interview, less than a year after Katrina devastated the largest of the Greater St. Stephen church buildings and its surrounding neighborhood, Morton explained that the dress code remains in place in the two remaining sites in New Orleans: "Katrina robbed many of the parishioners of their homes and so much more, so we allow people to dress as they choose. We just ask them to be modest." Post-Katrina, Greater St. Stephen is now described by Bishop Morton as "one church in two cities." He and his wife, Elder Debra Morton, divide their time shuttling between New Orleans and Atlanta, where they are nurturing a new congregation that includes many former New Orleanians who were displaced. As for attire, "We brought the same flavor to Atlanta," according to Gwen Morton, a flavor that she has found to be counter to the way a number of other churches dress. "In many of Atlanta's black churches, people still dress up, while we often come to service in jeans."[17]

Across the country, thousands of other African American churches have become more relaxed regarding dress. At Detroit's Second Ebenezer Church, pastored by Edgar L. Vann Jr., members can be seen wearing jeans, shorts, leggings, T-shirts, and other casual attire during services, though a number of others still arrive for worship in traditional Sunday best. Hartford Memorial Church, also in Detroit, is sometimes referred to as a "silk stocking" church, meaning that a sizeable percentage of its members are middle to upper middle class, well educated, and well dressed.[18] In fact, despite this perception of the church, there is no restrictive dress code. Hartford has a Saturday night service that was created initially for the baby boomers' children but that is now attended by members of all ages; relaxed attire is the standard for that service. The congregants, praise and worship team, and even the minister for the evening are usually dressed in jeans, cut offs, leggings, and other casual items.

Another aspect of dress in the Black Church that can be read as a step away from the old rules of dressing up is the inclusion of African attire.

In some churches during Black History Month, both the congregation and the choir may be asked to wear clothes from the Motherland. At Hartford, African attire is requested for the last day of the fall revival. At a number of African-centered churches, the pastor and the members wear African attire to indicate their ties to and reverence for the African continent. For example, at Fellowship Chapel in Detroit and Trinity United Church of Christ in Chicago, the pastors, the Rev. Wendell Anthony and Dr. Jeremiah Wright, respectively, and a sizeable number of congregants frequently wear African attire. At the Shrine of the Black Madonna of the Pan-African Orthodox Christian Church in Detroit, members adorn themselves in red and black, two of the colors of the flag of the African diaspora introduced by Marcus Garvey. Nkenge Abi, a bishop in the church and manager of its cultural center, explains that the colors, which were decided upon by the founder and first bishop, Jaramogi Abebe Agyeman (Albert B. Cleage), serve to both help identify and foster unity among the members of the church.[19]

A more recent phenomenon entails congregants "dressing down" for Easter Sunday, traditionally one of the days those attending church could be depended upon to be resplendently attired. However, during the last few years, a number of churches have sent announcements to various gospel and church radio programs, including mine, inviting nonmembers to attend and to dress casually. Easter 2006 was no exception; when I asked listeners to let me know whether they were dressing up or dressing down for church, several called in to report that their pastors had "mandated" or "requested" casual attire, reflecting the desire to "put the emphasis on the resurrection of Christ, not on our clothing." One listener, with sentiments representative of another way of thinking in my decidedly unscientific poll, explained why she was dressing up: "We are children of the King. God gave us His best, and we should act like, look like and dress our best."[20]

Many churches, some with youthful pastors and others with more seasoned leadership, adhere to the traditional dress code for the exact reasons articulated by the listener just mentioned: they view dressing up as a sign of respect. Within this category are churches that have even displayed signs in the vestibule that state that women wearing pants will not be permitted to enter the sanctuary at any time. Detroit, for instance, has several Baptist, Pentecostal, Deliverance, and Holiness churches with specific prohibitions regarding women and pants in the sanctuary, and some ban them during outdoor events and church maintenance projects as well.[21]

Besides women's pants, other aspects of dress, including skirt hems, have also come under scrutiny. Many church women, including those who attend some of the major church and music conventions, such as Pentecostal Assemblies of the World and the GMWA, can and do buy oversized, decorative handkerchiefs, often from on-site vendors. These hankies are used to dab tears, accent their outfits, and most important, cover their laps, particularly when they are facing the pulpit and could possibly reveal too much of themselves to the minister.[22] Full-sized sheets are even implemented in some churches. If a woman becomes filled with the Holy Spirit and her movements threaten to uncover her legs or more, nurses, ushers, or members of the mothers' board may rush to her and either cover or wrap her with a bed sheet.

Women's hair can also be a site of controversy. In some denominations, it is to remain uncut. Other local churches and denominations stipulate that women must wear a head covering, which can include a hat or a doily-like piece of fabric. Both of these regulations are based on a literal interpretation of the Apostle Paul's instructions about women's hair and heads (I Corinthians 11:5–6).

Da'Dra Crawford Greathouse of the urban contemporary gospel duo Anointed recalls her feelings upon learning that the church in which she grew up had not been welcoming to those who had on what was considered inappropriate attire, including women wearing pants: "I was hurt. . . . I don't want anybody to feel that they can't come into the House of God because of what they have on. We need to win as many people to [Jesus Christ] as possible, so when they come in, I don't want to feel that we place such an overwhelming burden on what they have on."[23]

But it is not only within individual churches or denominations that such regulations have been enforced. It has just been since the turn of the twenty-first century that the interdenominational GMWA, which was founded in 1968, has permitted women to wear slacks during mass choir rehearsal. And there are still very specific rules regarding the other times during the convention when women can wear pants (not during communion and nightly services) and when either gender can wear shorts (never).[24] Greater Christ Temple Church in Ferndale, Michigan, a suburb of Detroit, is representative of those congregations that have seemingly found a middle ground. No visitor is turned away because he or she has on inappropriate garments. But according to the church's minister of music, Carl B. Phillips, "Once they choose to join, Bishop Holland [the pastor] shares with them 'the rules of the house'—shirts, ties, and sports coats for men and dresses or skirts for women."[25]

The initial problem for many churchgoers who are gospel artists involves staying within the confines of the dress code outlined by their local church. However, once they choose to move into the larger worship and performance arenas where multiple denominations are represented, the decision regarding dress can become more complex since, despite the use of the collective term "the Black Church," as Gwendolyn S. O'Neal has noted, "there is no essential African American church dress."[26] The test, then, is to negotiate the various interpretations their audience members have of what is appropriate, since it is important not to offend by violating the rules of propriety, if the artist intends to be heard that is.

Within gospel music, clothing choices reflect denominational teachings, to be sure, but other elements are at play, including personal style. But the garments selected by the artists can also be read as markers of important shifts and innovations taking place within the general culture and within gospel music. For that reason, many clothing pioneers within gospel have often created controversy by mirroring contemporary dress modes, only to be widely imitated a few years later. Among those unfamiliar with the dynamic nature of gospel music and its performance styles, there is a tendency to think of the image of the "gospel singer" that appeared on hundreds of thousands of church fans for decades. In it, the female singer—sometimes Mahalia Jackson but often an unknown soloist—was adorned in a simple, dark-colored robe with a plain, white collar, the kind often worn for high school graduations and by Jackson in the emotional funeral scene in the 1950s version of the movie *Imitation of Life*. Despite the prevalence of this conservative style, there were those who did not conform to it.

When *Ebony* magazine referred to Clara Ward as the "glamour girl of gospel singers" in a 1957 article, it did so because of the elaborate wigs, rhinestones, and vibrantly colored robes and gowns that she and her singers favored—attire that placed them in stark contrast to most of their contemporaries.[27] It is this type of adornment, the "divine divawear," that

Clara Ward and the Clara Ward Singers. Courtesy of the *Michigan Chronicle.*

a majority of women in gospel music eventually adapted and wore on stage while attending gospel conferences, musicals, or various other events. In 1991, for example, during the funeral for the late King of Gospel, the Reverend James Cleveland, there were female performers, including some of the former members of the Caravans, whose garments were highlighted with sequins at 10:00 AM. Those artists and audience members who still view glitter as a necessary part of their church and gospel wear do so, to some extent, because of the Ward Singers and Rosetta Tharpe, who initially took some of their dress cues from the secular music arena in which the female secular performers wore show-stopping gowns.

The Mighty Clouds of Joy of Los Angeles, California, one of the most acclaimed gospel quartets of the last fifty years, caused a stir within the field when they first sought out a tailor who worked for Motown's Temptations. The Clouds emerged wearing red, lime green, and even orange suits that made them first the talk of and later the pace-setters within the quartet circle for decades.[28] Alex Bradford and the Bradford Specials, the first all-male gospel group that did not sing in the quartet tradition, further set themselves apart from that tradition by replacing the standard suits and ties with billowing robes, often accented with pastel or other brightly colored stoles.[29]

These innovators of the past were often those who were also making other significant changes in the gospel arena. The Ward Singers along with Rosetta Tharpe, who is considered a forerunner of today's pop gospel performers, were among the first to take gospel into nightclubs.[30] And while appearances in such venues were cause for negative comments from some, others applauded them for proclaiming the gospel outside of the traditional church walls. The Mighty Clouds of Joy are called the first gospel quartet to be self-contained, that is, to travel with a full band at all times. And Bradford was one of the early architects of the gospel musical, having played a central production and performance role in such major Broadway and road hits as *Your Arms Too Short to Box with God* and *Black Nativity*.

Today's gospel artists who have introduced cutting-edge attire, including CeCe Winans, Kirk Franklin, Mary Mary, Tonex, and Yolanda Adams, clothe themselves—or are dressed by image consultants—in a way that assists them in one of their greatest desires: reaching new, generally younger, multicultural audiences. In the process, their style choices often help to reshape, or at least challenge, widespread ideas about what constitutes appropriate gospel performance attire. A multiple Grammy Award winner, CeCe Winans was among the first in the current generation of gospel singers to wear pants regularly during her performances.

In fact, Winans adopted a number of personal changes, including wearing makeup, jewelry, and pants, all of which were particularly noteworthy since she was raised in a denomination (Church of God in Christ) in which these items were frowned upon and since the transformation first occurred while she was a regular performer on the *PTL Club*. While the cohost, Tammy Faye Bakker, was known for her elaborate use of

Tonex. Courtesy of Sweet Finesse Entertainment.

makeup, Winans reveals in her autobiography, *On a Positive Note,* that it was not Tammy Faye but a friend who told her she needed to face the daily cameras with more than lip gloss and a dusting of powder. When Winans protested that such actions violated biblical instructions, the friend challenged her to check for herself. After doing so and finding no specific warnings against cosmetics, Winans was convinced that she could in fact venture into this previously forbidden territory (121–24).

The talented and attractive singer, composer, and record label owner has created platinum selling recordings, both alone and with her brother BeBe and has earned countless awards from gospel and mainstream entities. As a result, she has performed many times on television (including acting roles and a series she hosted on cable), made several appearances at the White House, and has served as spokesperson for such national sponsors as Crest toothpaste and Kmart. Still, her nontraditional image and music provoked some disapproving responses. Winans writes in her autobiography that, regardless of these negative assessments she and her brother BeBe sometimes attracted, they achieved their most cherished goal:

> Despite years of criticism about the untraditional sound of our music, our message not being Christian enough, and even our *look* being too slick and sophisticated, after nine years our music had won the respect and admiration of both those in the industry and those beyond the industry.
>
> Although we were grateful for all the acclaim and were excited by all the doors and opportunities that became available to us as BeBe & CeCe, we were especially proud of the fact that our songs were doing what God wanted them to do, that both core gospel fans as well as mainstream audiences found hope and inspiration in our music. (207–8)

Kirk Franklin is another who was criticized because of his look and approach to the music. When his first recording for Gospo Centric Records was released in 1993, that year became, according to Horace Boyer, a "watershed in gospel," just as 1969 was when Edwin Hawkins's "Oh, Happy Day" was released: "Gospel and pop music lovers alike turned to Franklin for the new sound in gospel. Franklin obliged by introducing many hip hop elements into gospel and, like the Winans and the Clark Sisters, blurred the lines between sacred and secular music. While the text of Franklin's songs are religious in nature, he is particularly interested in reaching the 'unsaved' youth, and places his lyrics in the music 'of the world' to reach those in the world."[31]

Franklin's music and attire, like that of his urban contemporary colleagues, underscore who he is and the audience he hopes to draw to the gospel. His clothing can vary from urban casual wear, as in his "Looking for You" video, in which he wears designer jeans and a T-shirt, to urban chic, the look he projects in the "Hosanna" video, in which his attire consists of a black designer suit with elongated jacket.[32] His clothing can also highlight other aspects of his personality—his background as a break dancer and his calling as a minister of the gospel.[33] It also speaks to a large segment of the audience he has energized, those teenagers, younger men and women, and even a sizeable number of older adults who were dissatisfied with the more traditional music of the church, those who had left the church, or those who had never attended in the first place.

The popularity Franklin and his peers have attained underscores a significant difference between them and their predecessors. According to Boyer, during gospel's beginnings and its golden age, younger artists received attention just because they were youths who sang the music of their elders. But, he writes, "When 'O, Happy Day' became a major hit, it was the beginning of young people taking over gospel. And they have never given it back."[34] Boyer is being somewhat humorous and hyperbolic in his statement, for there are many seasoned artists who are still making a living and earning major awards in gospel for singing traditional gospel music.[35]

However, Boyer is correct about one aspect of his statement: many of the artists already mentioned as well as several of today's emerging gospel performers, such as Tye Tribbett and Stellar Award winner Kierra "KiKi" Sheard, are young, and while their lyrical content is scripturally sound, they are performing music that is aimed at younger ears. The whole image they display, then, is one that speaks to their personal identity—young and Christian—and to the fashion consciousness they share with their core audience members. But from a ministerial standpoint, it reflects what many of them see as another important drawing card: attire that does not make a visible distinction between "us," those who are in the church, and "them," those who are either unchurched or nonbelievers. Kirk Franklin offered *Vibe* magazine his assessment of the possible influence of gospel singers who dress in contemporary styles: "Now you're going to have some little girls watching the videos," he says, "and saying, 'You mean, I can wear pants and still love Jesus? Because I go to a church that don't allow girls to wear pants.' Come on man, that's setting them free."[36]

Mary Mary, Yolanda Adams, and Trin-i-tee 5:7 were described by *Entertainment Weekly* as "a style-conscious set of almighty altos [who] are helping to make gospel look very chic." Tina Campbell, one half of Mary Mary, explained succinctly the mission she and her sister Erica have when selecting their performance attire: "We want people to know that people who love God are not old, fat, and boring."[37] The term "boring" could hardly be applied to the Stellar and Grammy Award–winning siblings

Trin-i-tee 5:7. Photograph by Robert Ascroft. Courtesy of Spirit Rising Music/Music World Entertainment.

who sing and produce, as well as compose songs for themselves and others. Their first CD, *Thankful* (2000), went platinum (one million units sold); the second, *Incredible* (2002), has surpassed gold status (five hundred thousand units sold); and the third (2005), which is self-titled, sustained the national and international acclaim they have received since their debut. Known for their urban flair that surfaces in designer attire, in funky, sometimes edgy hair styles (including braids and Nubian knots), and in vibrant hair colors (fire-engine red has been a favorite for Tina), Mary Mary has been featured in fashion layouts in *Essence* (October 2000) and other lifestyle, hair, and beauty publications.

In an interview with Gospelflava.com, Tina Campbell reveals how clear she and her sister are about the purpose of their music ministry:

We want the platinum sales and all, but we want people to see that they can live saved. You can be young. You can be cool. But you can still praise God. We can still pray and give God the glory and honor for all of His blessings. We can still try and clean some of the things in our lives that aren't right. This is what we want. You don't have to have a turtleneck on, a long dress, clear nail polish and no makeup on with a bob, carrying your bible around to be saved. You may not be able to go to church every Sunday, Thursday, Friday and Saturday night, but that does not mean you can't have a relationship with God.[38]

Erica sees the image she and her sister project as assisting them in drawing those outside of the church to the message of the gospel: "We're trying to give them God in a way that they'll listen. They still have preconceived ideas of what it should be, what it should sound like, what you should look like. What we're ultimately doing is bringing more people to Christ. That's the point. If we're not doing that we might as well sit down. I might as well go on, put me on a little bitty skinny little dress and sing R&B."[39]

Yolanda Adams, one of today's most popular female gospel artists, is also clear about what compels her in making decisions about her music and ministry: "You always have to be aware that you are helping somebody make it through. I have to make sure I understand that this is not about me. This is about souls." Adams, whose statuesque figure caused comedian Jonathan Slocumb to teasingly refer to her as "Barbie," prepares to meet that diverse audience of souls, consisting of churchgoers and non-churchgoers alike, by practicing advice she was once given by a preacher who told her, "You have to look like something before anyone will ever pay attention to you."[40] Her designer boots, dresses, pants, including bejeweled jeans, along with her contemporary hair styles have drawn the applause of her fans, but undoubtedly others have not been as pleased with her bold, sometimes body-conscious fashion statements. Still, knowing what is at stake, Adams called for support, rather than judgment from the church and gospel communities, during her acceptance of a Stellar Award in 2003:

To everyone in this building, trust and know that every time you see a gospel artist on mainstream TV, we are there to make sure Jesus is represented. Please, please don't look down on us. Please pray for us because you never know what goes on backstage. All you see is what the camera shows you. You never know what goes on backstage. We are asked to pray for people. We're asked to lay hands on people. But you . . . we need y'all. We need you. We need the church. We need the bishops. We need the evangelists. We need the elders. We need y'all behind us one hundred percent. *Even if you can't agree with what we have on, just agree with the message of Jesus.* (emphasis added)

This phenomenon of holy women *and* men wearing clothing that generates amazement, befuddlement, and even disdain is not found solely within the Black Church and gospel music communities. One Jewish friend and colleague explained that he left the temple to which he belonged, not because he objected to women cantors, but because the young women who served in that capacity wore their skirts so short, he found their attire distracted from the worship experience.[41] In an article titled "Put on Some Clothes," Valerie G. Lowe discusses "the storm over immodesty . . . in the body of Christ" and the "alarm" caused by the "sensual, skimpy, low-cut, too-short, revealing clothes worn by believers." Among the guilty is an unnamed female evangelist who apparently wore an outfit that was so tight, the organizers of a Pentecostal conference for which she was the main speaker went to the attendees and promised never to invite her again. The article also quotes a young woman who left a church near Atlanta that she was visiting when, to her surprise, "the pastor and many of the church's male leaders [were] dressed in sexy-looking, tight muscle shirts. 'I left because I struggled with lust in the past, and I didn't want to take myself through that again.'"[42]

While accusatory fingers are often pointed at such visible cultural icons as Destiny's Child, Christina Aguilera, and Britney Spears for creating the trend of short, tight, revealing garments, Lowe contends that the record companies are equally culpable and that Christian performing artists are not exempt from the pressure to wear provocative attire. According to Lowe's article, the members of Out of Eden, three sisters with six recordings and sales of more than half a million copies, reported that some record labels would not even talk to them because they insisted on dressing to reflect the sexual purity they sing about in their songs.[43] Gospel music fans as well as colleagues in the industry have commented on one of the latest topics of conversation: the rising incidence of cleavage being shown by some of the most visible women in gospel on award shows, in their videos, and elsewhere. Even "toe cleavage," evident through sexy, high-heeled sandals worn by both traditional and contemporary gospel singers, has made some observe, "It's gotten where I can't tell the saved folks from the unsaved folks until they open their mouths."

For many of the artists in question, that is the whole point, their reason for dressing as they do. Wearing clothing that makes Christian performers look contemporary rather than "boring," some artists believe, draws the attention of the audience for a positive, spiritual end. The concept that audiences, rightly or wrongly, give artists instant assessments before they have heard them sing a note,[44] or before they discover the behind-the-scenes ministering about which Adams spoke during the Stellar Awards speech, is one that singer, composer, producer Fred Hammond has also referenced. During a pre–Motor City PraiseFest interview in 2003, he told my radio audience to "go home and change clothes after church" so that the non-churchgoers would see church/gospel folks as approachable and welcoming.

Since Hammond's former Zomba Gospel label mate Tonex emerged on the national gospel music scene, he has challenged the strict dress code that he believes those inside and outside of the church have tried to impose upon gospel performers and one another. Tonex's music is often described as urban contemporary, but those words do not allude to the fact that he also produces choir music, soulful ballads, and rap with equal dexterity. Nor does it cover the yodeling he includes in some of his songs to create a special effect.[45] During the taping of the thirty-sixth annual Gospel Music Association Awards, Tonex performed "Alive 2," a song from *Out the Box,* the double CD that earned him six Stellar Awards in 2005. He described the song as "what would happen if Led Zepplin, George Clinton, and Prince [had] all just found Jesus."[46]

In keeping with the "vibe" of the song, Tonex chose an outfit that was straight from the rock/funk/fusion stage: "a red & black, long fur coat with a light brown razor cut wig topped with a three tier diamond choker. Underneath, he wore an ordinary sleeveless t-shirt, black jeans and black boots."[47] Tonex, who often changes during the course of an evening from rocker to hip hopper to fiery Pentecostal preacher, explained later to the press that his goal that night was to convince audiences who are often caught off guard by his chameleonlike transformations to judge him and his colleagues, not by what they wear, but by the message they present.[48]

Though Tonex has preached this sermon continuously, many gospel artists apparently are not leaving to chance their reception by often judgmental consumers. Their strategy for gaining acceptance among those who are not regular church goers includes presenting themselves with a level of sophistication, professionalism, and glamour that the gospel arena has not uniformly required in the past. For those whose ministry is solely within the local church, the need for glitz and glamour varies from sanctuary to sanctuary, but generally, parishioners come to be ministered to and inspired and are not usually expecting the razzle-dazzle of the concert stage.

But anyone stepping into the music industry encounters audiences who have paid to hear them and therefore demand both inspiration and entertainment for their dollar. Once in that arena, new artists soon discover an important fact: the three key components of the gospel music *industry* are not God the Father, Son, and Holy Spirit but "the music, the technology, and the business."[49] Those who would succeed in this twenty-first-century world of the gospel music industry need to both sound and *look* as if they are ready for prime time while being spiritually prepared for all that is required of those asked to be sacred in a secular space.

That list of those who regularly move within that secular world and face its demands includes Adams, BeBe and CeCe Winans, Donnie McClurkin, Franklin, Hammond, Mary Mary, Trin-i-tee 5:7, and Smokie Norful. All of these and others have had gold- and, in most cases, platinum-selling releases because their recordings are compatible with a variety of radio formats, including urban and urban adult contemporary, Christian hit radio, and urban gospel. Their successful recordings and presentational styles have opened venues that were previously closed to such artists because of their race or simply because gospel itself was not welcomed. But noteworthy changes, including Adams and Mary Mary becoming the first gospel artists in the almost thirty year history of the American Music Awards to receive the Favorite Contemporary Inspirational Artist designation (in 2002 and 2005, respectively), have scores of other artists scrambling, sometimes ambivalently, to get ready for their television, cable, or movie screen close-ups as well.

Most of their ambivalence is rooted in the contradictions that today's gospel music industry presents as it always has. Don Cusic, in *The Sound of Light: A History of Gospel and Christian Music,* describes the essential problem when he writes that there is "a certain schizophrenia within the gospel world—trying to live in the world but not be of the world" (362). How can one appeal to the world without becoming transformed by it? In fact, many gospel artists, including those from gospel's earliest years, have managed to create a balance that works for them, one that, at least in their opinion, does not equate to compromising the message of the gospel but results in using the best aspects of secularization to promote it. One such example is Professor Thomas A. Dorsey, the man universally called "the father of gospel music." Jerma A. Jackson, author of *Singing in My Soul: Black Gospel Music in a Secular Age,* explains:

> For many African American singers and musicians, religious conversion prompted a wholesale renunciation of secular music. Dorsey, however, did not take that path. Rather, he sought to put the skills he had learned as a bluesman to sacred ends. Some years earlier, he had been deeply moved by a musical performance in which a Baptist minister riveted his audience by embellishing a hymn with the twists and turns that bore a striking resemblance to the enhancements Dorsey used to give his blues songs emotional force. As Dorsey began to compose religious songs, he sought to create the same effects. (54–55)

Dorsey initially thought the correct route for him was to play both gospel and secular music. But after several illnesses, he came to understand that his call was to mingle his gospel with blues, as Jackson has described. With his fellow pioneers, he took this blues-infused music into any church that would allow them in; together, they revolutionized black sacred music. His "gospel blues" electrified the worship experience in a way that satisfied millions both within and outside of the church in the early and mid-twentieth century. Beginning in the late 1960s, Edwin Hawkins and his contemporaries, including Andrae Crouch and the Rance Allen Group, followed Dorsey's lead as they sought to apply their R&B skills in the creation of their gospel compositions. And the pattern continues with today's urban contemporary performers who express their desire to use their talents to win the hearts of the youth for God.

Jeff Grant, vice president of promotions for Zomba Gospel, and others contend that there are many positive aspects of secularization. However, one of the biggest problems, Grant believes, is the tendency to overdo it, particularly in the area that is the central issue of this chapter, clothing: "We try too hard to be secular, for example, with our dress. We try so hard to be hip that we end up appearing wack [silly, out of our element] and have no street credibility from the people that we are trying to impress. . . . The world, when it needs help . . . they don't necessarily need help from someone who looks and acts just the way they do."[50]

Tracey Artis, a vice president with GospoCentric, the label behind the success of Franklin, Dorinda Clark Cole, Kurt Carr, and others, is also concerned about what artists wear for performance: "There is a general trend to be 'free style' rather than dressed for church. But if a Yolanda Adams is singing a ballad, I prefer to see her in a gown. When you begin to talk about the church, there is a standard wardrobe that is not offensive. I don't want to see [female] artists in pantsuits. If you are before God's people in church, remember I'm from the church; that's my experience, so come before me with a dress or skirt on."[51]

An examination of the responses generated by the female trio Trin-i-tee 5:7 is particularly germane to this discussion since they have been both applauded and vilified because of the visual image they project. Known for their distinctive singing voices, the individual members were hand-picked by their original manager, Kenneth Grant, to become part of a trio that would "appeal to the masses" by offering young people the female urban flavor of groups like TLC and En Vogue.[52] Their self-titled debut CD, released in 1998, featuring the hit "God's Grace," was produced by R. Kelly and reportedly was the first by a female gospel group to sell five hundred thousand copies and thus be certified "gold."[53] While their subsequent CDs *Spiritual Love* (1999) and *The Kiss* (2002) also offered the group's signature sound and earned them five Stellar Award nominations, it is their image, described by Saul Eady Jr. as encompassing "immaculate make-up, stylish, form-fitting attire, and a sexy mystique," that has had some traditionalists shaking their heads.[54]

"Sexy" is a word that generally is not applied, at least not aloud, to gospel singers, probably because of the discomfort it gives some to think of the messenger of God and sexiness simultaneously. "I don't need sex to sell Jesus," one popular male vocalist told me. "You can't turn Jesus on." Though he and his contemporaries have performed or posed for photographs in leather, a fabric generally thought of as sexy rather than utilitarian, it is doubtful that their purpose was to "turn Jesus on" but rather to get the attention of the contemporary consumer.[55]

While this is probably the largest crop of gospel singers, male and female alike, to which the "sexy" label might be applied, they are by no means the first for whom the term would be fitting. According to Anthony Heilbut, author of *The Gospel Sound*, "Gospel is, in some ways, a sexual music. Its performers sing with their bodies and move with a thrilling grace and physical abandonment. This sexuality is taken for granted and is, I think, largely innocent" (76). Still, in the film *Say Amen, Somebody*, Willie Mae Ford Smith talks about a not so innocent preacher who said he wanted to pat her hips while she was ministering in song.[56]

Jules Schwerin writes in his biography of Mahalia Jackson, *Got to Tell It*, that the singer was warned by certain ministers and elders that unless she agreed to wear appropriate robes, "she would risk forfeiting church engagements, maybe even jeopardize a career if it came to singing in their churches." After Jackson acquiesced, Schwerin concludes that "she ascended to the performing pinnacle of the gospel circuit like lightning" (61). Heilbut reports, "Some churches exiled her for her rocking beat, others for her 'snake hips,' and at least one admirer called her 'the sexiest thing out there' because of the way she would raise her robe as she danced and swayed while singing her praises to God."[57] Apparently wearing a robe does not shield a gospel performer from being labeled as sexy.

Sam Cooke, who became a star within gospel as a lead vocalist with the Soul Stirrers in the 1950s, has frequently been called its first sex symbol. He was so appealing vocally and physically that when he crossed over to soul music later in the decade, his female audience, who frequently swooned when he performed, followed him.[58] Though Kirk Franklin has only written and performed songs with gospel texts, he like Cooke, has been called "a gospel-pop sex symbol [who] has on occasion been pulled off stage, kissed and had his clothes ripped by adoring fans anxious to meet the man behind the sacred music."[59] The runway-beautiful Tramaine Hawkins also created a regular buzz, both as one of the Hawkins Singers and as a solo artist, because of the songs she performed—from the church staple "Changed" to the disco favorite "Fall Down." But her wardrobe and her ever-evolving glamorous image during the 1970s and 1980s were also a definite part of her appeal.[60]

Tramaine Hawkins's talent and style so inspired Trin-i-tee 5:7's Haynes when she was growing up that she once wrote to her idol, a fact recounted on the group's CD *Spiritual Love* on which they chat briefly about and sing one song with Hawkins. Like the award-winning Hawkins, the members of Trin-i-tee have their own specific ideas about style. Contralto Haynes summed it up this way when speaking to *Entertainment Weekly* in 2000: "I'm 21 and I want to look like a 21-year-old."[61] That same year, the group served as spokespersons for Revlon, which was a good fit for Trin-i-tee 5:7 since they confess to enjoying color and to having fun experimenting with makeup on themselves and on one another.[62] Angel Taylor explained the rationale behind their look: "We want people to listen to the message that we are disseminating rather than paying so much attention to what we are wearing. The glamour is just the eye-catcher. The message is the meat that makes the difference and is good for the soul."[63]

While the group's fans would agree, their detractors assert that the message sent by their image undercuts the potency of the gospel lyrics of their songs. The video for their recording of "Put Your Hand in the Hand" typifies Trin-i-tee 5:7's approach of using popular sounds and visuals in their attempt to bring audiences to the good news. First, the song itself includes lyrics from several songs from the past: two are gospel, one is inspirational, and one is R&B.[64] The resulting song and Trin-i-tee's choreographed video performance mirror what Melanie Clark and Stan North have written, that is, the group "never shies away from either component of the words that make up their musical category—contemporary and gospel."[65]

The video opens with a wide shot of an empty blue room with a number of geometric cuts in the walls through which light shines; the most prominent shape is an oversized cross cut into the back wall. The ladies, Adrian, Angel, and Chanelle, respectively brunette, blond, and auburn-haired in the video, wear three outfits. One features casual pants and brightly colored shirts; a second is an attention-getter: blue leather two-piece ensembles executed differently for each singer with a combination of capri pants, skirts, and fringed edging. The third outfit is a two-piece dress with floor-length skirt that appears to be made of tie-dyed material in various shades of blue. Both the eye shadow and lipstick worn by the group are in bold colors that seem to vibrate with the music.

Worth noting are the points in the video at which they wear each outfit: the pants and shirts are chosen when each member is shown singing alone in a corner of the blue room. The blue leather outfits are the ones worn when they execute choreographed moves before an audience and in front of a high stepping group of male dancers in muscle T-shirts; they are also the last outfits we see as they end the video. Whenever the ladies sing in front of the cross, they are in the floor-length skirts.

I asked seven church-going gospel music lovers, virtually all of them in their twenties or thirties, to serve as my feedback interview crew for several videos, including "Put Your Hand in the Hand" and "The Nu Nation Tour," which features Kirk Franklin, CeCe Winans, and Trin-i-tee 5:7 in concert.[66] They were as divided as the rest of the gospel community appears to be in assessing what is acceptable and what is outside the boundaries in terms of appropriate dress for gospel artists. Four of the seven found the group's makeup, attire, and moves in both videos "too sexual" and concluded, in the words of one, "It's all too much; I can't hear what they're saying for looking at what they have on." One respondent commented that "even the way they move their hair" was seductive. But the other respondents saw Trin-i-tee's look as being a way of getting young men and women to pay attention to the gospel message within the song and video.[67]

It is that very contemporary look that some have castigated that makes another video performance of a song from that same CD extremely powerful and relevant. "My Body," the video for which again features the young women in multiple outfits, including beautiful dresses and white pantsuits, extols their determination to abstain from sex until marriage. In fact, they actually use the word "celibacy" within one of the verses. "What part of 'no' don't you understand?" each member of the trio sings to an attractive man, the kind that many young girls would, unfortunately, not refuse sexual favors. Haynes, for example, moves her date's hand off her knee, slides out of the car, and closes the gull-wing door of his two-seater Mercedes Benz without looking back. Before the end of the video, the men that have been turned down by the young women are chanting the words of the chorus: "Don't mess with me—God's property." The song was in the top 100 for 1999 at urban stations such as FM 98 WJLB in Detroit, because of the sound, of course. But the lyrics were also a welcome change from the "anything goes" variety that is more often part of urban radio. Those who saw the video did not witness singers who were "old, fat, and boring," to use Erica Campbell's words, and less likely to be propositioned but attractive young ladies in trendy clothes encouraging other young people to live by what they believe are God's rules for singles.

Unfortunately, the kind of negative assessment mentioned earlier was very probably behind what happened when Trin-i-tee 5:7 performed by invitation during the Holy Convocation of the Church of God in Christ held at the denomination's headquarters in 2002. When I told industry colleagues that I was researching contemporary gospel attire, at least three of them within a twenty-four-hour period began talking about this incident without my ever mentioning or alluding to the female trio or the performance site. According to their reports, Trin-i-tee 5:7 performed "Put Your Hand in the Hand" while wearing trousers. While theirs was a performance during a musical event and not a worship service per se, it appeared to these informants that it was the combination of the song and the attire that prompted the audience to boo the group "as if they were at the Apollo. I was expecting the Sandman to come out," said one witness.

Equally compelling, however, are the group members' recollections about the evening. According to Haynes, "We were actually on stage one night at a gospel concert, and we were booed by Christian people. . . . It wasn't a stage; no, it was a church. And they invited us, and I'm scratching my head thinking, 'Well, you asked us to come, you know, and you knew we were going to be ourselves.' . . . So that kind of threw us for awhile, and every time we would perform that particular song, we would tense up [she grabs the other members' hands] and say, 'OK. Here it goes again.'"[68]

While some would clearly argue that it was the group's "secularized" (often meant as "sexy") look and sound that brought about the poor treatment, other informants have described the response of the audience as the epitome of what happens when secular overtakes the sacred in other areas as well. One lifelong member of the denomination remarked:

The crowd that would have booed them would have been that new, "freed" generation—free to be boorish, free not to have good manners, unchurched, and just believing that anything goes. They bring that secular behavior into that sacred environment. And become many of these mega churches cater to them, they just respond in the moment instead of with love. In the old days, the mothers of the church would have "sat on them" [looked at them in silence]. Afterward, they would have taken them aside and instructed them on what to do and wear next time.... In Jeremiah 31:3, the Lord says, "With loving kindness have I drawn thee." Where is the love when we boo one another?[69]

Anointed's Da'Dra Crawford Greathouse, while not specifically address-ing the Trin-i-tee 5:7 incident, raises another point, that is, whether the negative response could have been envy driven by size-ism: "I have no-ticed that there are women in the two-hundred-, three-hundred-, four-hundred-pound range—and it is challenging to find clothes that fit prop-erly—who wear clothes that are too tight here or there. And yet I've never seen anyone rebuke them. . . . If you are a size 6, 8, or 2 and very shapely, if your clothes are a little form fitting, there will be an industry buzz about it. Is it that we feel their clothing is inappropriate, or are we just jealous or envious of their size?"[70]

In fact, the number of overweight artists in gospel, particularly those with widespread name recognition, appears to be dwindling despite the reported obesity epidemic in America. What makes it noteworthy is that it is occurring in a music form whose artists have often been known for their big voices and equally substantial physical size. Today's trimmer artists reportedly achieve their body size through a variety of methods, some worth emulating and all reflective of what the larger culture pro-motes for those interested in achieving good health and youthful attrac-tiveness.[71] While there are certainly exceptions to the rule, their contem-porary silhouette is more likely to be slimmer, such as the case with Yolanda Adams, Vickie Winans, and Dorinda Clark Cole, rather than full figured as was the case with Mahalia Jackson and Willie Mae Ford Smith.[72] This is not to suggest that they are all reed thin; however, the most popular female gospel artists in particular appear sizes smaller than the image on the church fans of a generation ago. That silhouette is per-haps as responsible as the attire and the beats for further blurring the lines between sacred and secular, thus providing many of the gospel artists with one more element, their own physiques, that can be used to draw the at-tention of their target audience.

Cosmetics aside, however, there are important health and spiritual im-plications of the healthier and generally trimmer gospel artist that can-not be underestimated. Vickie Winans, for example, used to be a 230-pound serial dieter and even created a "diet medley" as part of her comedic banter between songs on her album *Share the Laughter.* However, not only

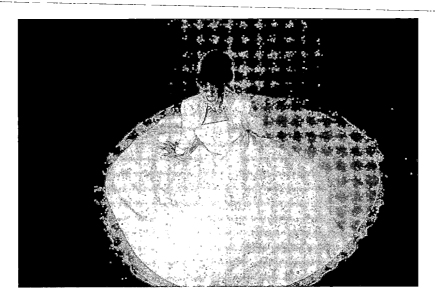

Vickie Winans demonstrates the range of wardrobe options she feels are hers as a gospel artist—from glamorous gowns to casual pants—now that she has been, in her words, "shown a freer way." Photographs by David M. Deutsch Photography. Courtesy of Vickie Winans.

has she taken and kept off seventy-five pounds through a regimen rich with fruits and vegetables, but she joined forces with the National Cancer Institute to promote Body and Soul: A Celebration of Healthy Eating and Living, a program for African American churches. Marvin Winans explains that the fitter physique of today's gospel artists can also be viewed as a reflection of "a godly lifestyle, which is a temperate lifestyle in everything. So you can't eat that entire bucket of chicken." In his estimation, the new silhouette is not important because it is sexy but because, by example, the artists can encourage audiences to join them in practicing godly discipline regarding eating and exercise.[73]

So, if the new silhouette speaks to discipline and a healthier way of life, why, then, are so many uncomfortable with the clothing that often accompanies it? The reasons are probably as many and as unique as the individuals who look askance at muscle T-shirts, tight jeans, and cleavage being displayed by gospel artists. They include those with their brows furrowed as they critique Trin-i-tee 5:7 in pants at Holy Convocation as well as those who look disapprovingly at the contemporary female group Ramiyah without knowing why they were in form-fitting outfits during their first Stellar Awards performance.[74] They might also include the ones who wondered what to make of the cover of Bingo Kenoly's CD titled *H.O.G. Life* on which he wears an athletic T-shirt and displays tatooed, ripped biceps rather than a traditional suit and tie.

But another list of questions needing straight answers comes from younger gospel artists. The Ambassador, a member of the Christian rap group the Cross Movement, has written a compelling song, "My Clothes, My Hair," found on his second solo CD, *The Thesis*. In it, he laments the focus many have on "right attire" rather than on reaching out to everyone with the message of the gospel:

I could weep
So many people never heard of the name
Yeah they heard the word "Jesus" but never heard of His fame
They feel cut off from Him
Not just 'cause of their sin
But because of their clothes, hair, or their color of skin
And they've been afloat—drowning in sin, we're in a boat

Bingo Kenoly. Photograph by Michael Cairns. Courtesy of Wet Orange Studios, Orlando, Florida.

> Yet they've never been approached
> 'Cause we see them as different folks
> God's offer's universal—yeah
> He wants you in His circle—yeah
> He wants you in the do-rag
> And He wants you in the purple hair.

While Jeff Grant would agree with the Ambassador that God looks at the heart, he knows that human beings often get sidetracked by clothes. For that reason, he offers these words of caution to those preparing to minister in song: "Be aware of where you are and for whom you are singing. If I am coming into the pulpit of the Church, I need to ask myself: Do I look like everybody else in here?"[75] Evangelist and recording artist Esther Smith conveyed the story of a newly saved woman who, after attending her first gospel concert, was "traumatized" because the performers wore the same outfits she had seen in the clubs. With that in mind, Smith said that while she never plans to "point a finger or criticize any artist for their choice of dress during performance," she prefers to sing in "elegant, classy" dresses and gowns because she "doesn't want to put the audience through the type of trauma" the new Christian apparently experienced.[76]

Teresa Hairston, founder and publisher of *Gospel Today*, believes that what some have called egregious errors in judgment are what can logically be expected when something is so new: "There are bound to be some awkward steps. . . . So we have someone wearing leather pants and someone else in a low-cut outfit. [The artists] are not in the traditional sequined suit because that's not who they are. They want to be who they are and still be respectable. They are getting the big gigs, but they don't all have stylists who know what to do. And since we don't have a Sean John making gospel attire, these artists are still trying to figure it out, and it's a job."[77]

In just two decades, the gospel industry has seen dramatic changes in the choices some artists make regarding their attire. In the past some audience members might have whispered to their neighbors simply because a female artist wore pants; today, those same audiences might witness entire concerts during which every performer, male and female, has on jeans. Dr. Bobby Jones, host of BET's most popular regular program, once remarked in the mid-1990s that given the nontraditional clothing some artists have worn on his program, criticism about their attire did not surface nearly as often as he expected. After sharing that one woman had written, "I can't get any more joy [from your show] because of the way the women dress," he concluded, "Women should have a choice, and it doesn't have anything to do with their spirituality."[78] In that same article, Vickie Winans agreed with Jones: "There is nothing wrong with dressing in the traditional way, which I do whenever I am in a sanctuary, but not even the strictest pastors have been able to show me that wearing pants is a sin. Your anointing is not dictated by pants."[79]

And so, regardless of the controversy they create, today's innovators push the boundaries with their clothing, just as Tharpe and Ward and others did in earlier times. Simultaneously, today's traditionalists try to hold the line just as their historic counterparts did decades, even centuries, ago. And the debate about what gospel singers should wear if they have really been set free continues.

FROM PRINCESS PREMIUM STUFF
AND MISS MANDY TO HOLY BOLDNESS

THE INFLUENCE OF WOMEN GOSPEL ANNOUNCERS

Gospel music and radio have been inextricably linked since each was in its infancy in the 1920s. Consequently, there has always been a need for gospel announcers, who, regardless of gender, generally perform two very different tasks as they work. They provide a music ministry for those who accept the spiritual premise of the lyrics of the songs they play while they enhance the popularity and viability of the music within the commercial marketplace.

A closer look at the work of women gospel announcers, however, reveals that by using gospel music as the vehicle and radio as the medium, these broadcasters often empower their listeners and communities by modeling spiritual, maternal, entrepreneurial, and womanist characteristics. Their dynamism on the radio coupled with their various endeavors within and for the cities in which they work qualify them to be seen as othermothers and community leaders whose value to their listeners extends far beyond the music they present.

This chapter looks at women gospel announcers with special attention given to Irene Johnson Ware of Mobile, Alabama, and Martha Jean "the Queen" Steinberg of Detroit, Michigan, both of whom attained near legendary status locally and nationally. Through on-air language that sounds "deceptively chatty" and singularly spiritual at times, women gospel announcers frequently become guides, goads, and nurturers because of their ability to use radio for multiple sacred and secular purposes, often simultaneously.[1] The two central figures in this chapter further enhanced their lofty reputations because of the social and political activism they practiced in their communities with activities ranging from getting out the vote for the Reverend Jesse Jackson to building low-cost housing and providing college scholarships for inner-city residents. Prominently featured are performance-centered analyses of their broadcasts during which they demonstrate their phenomenal ability to multitask—praise God while spiritually inspiring listeners and moving them to some needed action in the community or in their personal lives.[2]

Since at least the 1940s, African American women have served as gospel announcers, introducing gospel music and artists, inspiring listeners with a skillful combination of music and words, recreating aspects of the Black Church experience, and linking listeners and advertisers.[3] Unfortunately, the histories that have focused on black radio or gospel music often fail to explore the presence and importance of these women. To understand the context in which women gospel announcers entered the gospel music tradition, it is important to review briefly how and why gospel music and radio initially intersected.

First, gospel music emerged in its early transitional form at the end of the nineteenth century, as African Americans were beginning the Great Migration. During this period that continued into the 1920s, the rhythmic congregational songs of the Pentecostal and primitive Baptist churches coexisted with early gospel hymns by the Philadelphia-based minister Charles Albert Tindley.[4] Beginning in the late 1920s, blues pianist, composer, and arranger Thomas A. Dorsey provided gospel music with what is universally recognized as its "traditional" sound when he created a fusion of blues, the music of the Black Folk Church, and the various other new rhythms of the urban black populace.[5]

During the 1930s and 1940s, Dorsey, along with such contemporaries as Sallie Martin and Roberta Martin, composed gospel songs, established choirs, and identified performance venues across the country that would be welcoming to the music and its upstart performers. In so doing, they provided new audiences for the music and paved the way for its eventual acceptance within the more conservative "mainline" churches, many of which rejected gospel music initially.[6] Concurrent with all of this was the rising popularity of gospel music and its placement on the increasingly important medium of radio.

Gospel music has been broadcast on the air almost since radio's beginnings. In the 1920s, multiracial audiences made the church and music broadcasts that featured gospel music among the most popular on radio.[7] An equally significant occurrence that decade was the emergence of the first black announcer, Jack L. Cooper, in 1926; his initial program, *The All-Negro Hour*, highlighted various aspects of black life, including the newest forms of music, jazz, blues, and gospel. By the end of the 1940s, gospel and its sister, the blues, had become the "backbone" of black radio, according to the August 24, 1953 *Sponsor* magazine (69). Eventually, gospel music fans wanted more than the occasional song sandwiched between other forms of music on variety shows like Cooper's or on all-music programs hosted by disc jockeys that specialized in other musical genres. That demand led to the creation of the gospel music program and, in turn, to the emergence of the gospel announcer, the on-air personality whose sole purpose would be to entertain and inspire using this sacred music.

Besides being the first black announcer in the United States, Jack L. Cooper was also in the vanguard of placing black women on the air as announcers.[8] He employed several women in his various enterprises; they wrote show segments, sold airtime, and performed on-air. Among those who were associated with Cooper was Rosalie Latimer Wood. In 1932 the pair cohosted a Sunday afternoon broadcast featuring religious music and poetry, making Wood, a CPA with the Metropolitan Funeral System, among the first black women to present black religious music in this type of format.[9] Gertrude Roberts, the daughter of a Chicago minister, became Cooper's third wife in 1939 and helped him as a radio announcer, musician, and program director, according to the obituary that ran in the *Chicago Sun Times* in May 1992. Hosting shows on four different local stations, she became the leading black female broadcaster of her day.[10]

While it is fairly easy to document that these women who worked with Cooper played gospel recordings along with other musical forms popular with their black listeners, trying to discover the first women to host programs completely centered on gospel music is more challenging. Though a number of histories have been written on black radio and on gospel music, rarely, if ever, are women gospel announcers included. If they are, it is only a nominal mention in a sentence or paragraph with several other names.[11] Rarely is any biographical information or analytical perspective provided. However, using oral histories and interviews and extracting information from various popular magazines reveals interesting details about when and where these women entered radio.

After Cooper's historic entrance into radio in the 1920s, other pioneers followed in the 1930s, including Eddie Honesty in Hammond, Indiana; Ed Baker and Van Douglas in Detroit; Bass Harris in Seattle; and Hal Jackson in New York. These were black men whose performances mirrored those of the successful white men who were popular on radio at that time. Their speech patterns enabled them to challenge racial stereotypes and to make room for a black presence on radio beyond the caricatures offered on what historian William Barlow calls "blackface radio."[12]

The emergence of all-black radio in the late 1940s and early 1950s provided many commercial opportunities for sponsors and performers attempting to reach black audiences.[13] Black DJs also reached new heights in number and popularity during this time. The ones who became most successful presided over programs whose content and style "gave legitimacy to the black lower-class experience."[14]

Interestingly, but not surprisingly, women gospel announcers were part of this new wave. Though no women are listed in the December 1947 edition of *Ebony*, for example, in which sixteen "sepia spielers," that is, black radio announcers, are discussed (44), oral histories suggest that women gospel announcers were indeed becoming active in this aspect of radio. An excellent example of this is Mother Mattie Davis of Muskegon, Michigan. In 1947, the same year that the *Ebony* article was published, Mother Davis launched the first of her two broadcasts, which made her, according to her recollections, the first black woman on radio in that city. *The Heavenly Echoes,* heard on WMUS 1090 AM, featured live music provided by local groups. Her second program, *Quartets on Parade,* which went on the air in 1955, introduced the recordings of both African American and European American quartets among other features.[15]

In its October 10, 1949, issue, *Sponsor* noted that the number of black disc jockeys had risen to over one hundred (55). Women gospel announcers were also becoming more numerous by this point, though their visibility may have been obscured by the fact that they were in smaller cities, such as Muskegon, Michigan, or by the fact that they often handled multiple duties on air. In a display ad dated September 20, 1954, in which ten on-air personalities are pictured, Mama Lou of WBOK, New Orleans, is described as hosting a "homemaker and spiritual program." So, along with dispensing household tips, as several of the pioneering black women on radio did, it is highly probably that Mama Lou also presented some forms of black sacred music.[16] Another publication also places a growing number of women on radio during this period. In the August 1951 issue of *Our World,* a feature with the headline "Negro Women Become Disc Jockeys" explores the range of radio formats handled by black women. Next to the photos of the women DJs who presented fashion and entertainment, there is Frances White of WOOK-AM, Washington, DC, whom the magazine calls "a different disc jockey using only religious records" (11).

Later in that decade, according to her own oral history, Vermya Phillips, a teacher, choir director, and soprano soloist, began cohosting gospel radio programs with her husband, John. Commencing March 1, 1957, they broadcast on KTYM, Inglewood, California, on a program they called *Moments of Decision.* Following that, they were on KFOX, Long Beach, for five years (1965–70) and then were heard for the next fifteen years (1970–85) on KKGO-AM, Los Angeles. Finally, they returned to their original station, KTYM, where they remained together until Vermya passed away in 2004. Besides spending more than forty-five years as an on-air team, the two were national officers with the Gospel Announcers Guild (GAG) of the Gospel Music Workshop of America, Inc.[17]

Pauline Wells Lewis was also serving as a gospel announcer in the 1950s. Known as Aunt Pauline throughout Baltimore, Maryland, and the gospel music industry, she was a founding member of the GAG and was known as its dean because of her seniority in the field. She was actually introduced to radio in the 1940s when she and her sister, Sylvia, sang duets on a local weekly church broadcast on WITH-AM. As an adult, she became a noted emcee, traveling around the country to introduce such luminaries as Mahalia Jackson. Her work as a gospel announcer began at WANN, Annapolis, Maryland, in the late 1950s and continued at WSID-AM in 1959, where she remained for twenty-three years, and at WAYE-AM, which later became WBGR-AM. Aunt Pauline retired in 1992 from WEBB-AM after ten years of service; while there, she became one of the first in her area to play gospel music on FM on WEBB's affiliated station.

In retirement, Aunt Pauline remained a sought-after emcee because of her creative introductions for artists. A choir director at the same church for more than fifty years, she was involved in various public service activities, such as the pantry she maintained for the needy, which accounted for her being known throughout Baltimore and among other gospel announcers as "the People's Friend."[18] Testaments to the effect the late announcer had on her city include the Aunt Pauline Wells Legacy Choir and a full-size wax figure of her that has been on display since 2002 in the National Great Blacks in Wax Museum in Baltimore.

Wells not only helps to establish the emergence of women gospel announcers during this era, but she also points to a long-standing tradition of gospel announcers working within the community as well as on air, as at least one other scholar has noted.[19] She is also one of a long line of women gospel singers who later became announcers, a custom that includes those with local followings as well as those who have achieved international success. In 1950 the great Sallie Martin, one of gospel's pioneering performers and publishers, moved from Chicago to Los Angeles and became one of the first female announcers in that city. When she went on the air in March of that year, the *California Eagle* called her "California's first religious disc jockette." Later, Martin's daughter, Cora Martin Moore, a choral director and composer in her own right, spent two years as a gospel announcer in Los Angeles.[20] Years later, other prominent gospel singers followed their lead.[21]

Clearly, the period between the late 1940s to the late 1950s is a critical point at which women gospel announcers became important participants in radio and paved the way for those who would enter the field behind them, such as Irene Johnson Ware and Martha Jean "The Queen" Steinberg. Steinberg, who did not focus on sacred music in her programming until the 1970s, was one of the most successful personalities, male or female, to have emerged from the post–World War "second wave" of black disc jockeys. Born Martha Jean Jones September 9, 1930, in Memphis, Tennessee, and educated in a Catholic mission school, Steinberg practiced nursing for a year and then for two years went into business, which included producing and commentating weekly fashion shows for churches in Memphis. Her training for these events came from a Mrs. Lansky who had attended modeling school and whose brother outfitted Elvis Presley. Lansky taught Steinberg, a statuesque, attractive young woman, what she had learned about modeling; Steinberg, in turn, taught the black women who participated in the fashion shows what she had been shown. Through these productions, Steinberg came to the attention of A. C. "Moohah" Williams, an on-air personality at WDIA, the nation's first station to offer a complete "Negro appeal" format. Williams suggested that she become a public relations person for the historic station.[22]

Steinberg came in a close second in a contest to replace the host of the homemaker show, and after being deemed "a natural for radio" by the program director, David James, she was assigned to several programs, beginning in 1954, one of which was aimed at a male audience. The show was called *Premium Stuff,* and Steinberg was named "Princess Premium Stuff," an appellation she described as "kind of sexist" during a 1993 interview.[23] After existing with that title for a while, the day came when Steinberg told a board operator, "Your behind is mine if you call me Princess Premium Stuff today." Believing her threat to be real, he opened the mic and said, "Ladies and gentlemen, Martha Jean . . . Martha Jean . . . 'the Queen.'"[24]

Steinberg's move from Memphis to Detroit transformed her life, the direction of three Motor City radio stations, and the listening patterns of thousands of Detroiters for almost three decades. After Dr. Wendell Cox and his wife, who were co-owners of WCHB, a black-owned-and-operated radio property, heard Steinberg while driving through Memphis in 1963, they invited her to visit the station where she met their co-owner, Dr. Haley Bell. Recently divorced and intrigued by the opportunity to move to a new city, she accepted their offer to join WCHB in Detroit and became a huge hit.[25] Because the talented, personable, straight-talking announcer was a southern transplant speaking to southern emigrants, she was an immediate and enormous hit with listeners. Steinberg proved to be another of the black disc jockeys Gilbert Williams aptly describes as "cultural heroes."[26] When personality radio was phased out, Steinberg rose to the occasion and conformed to the demands of Top 40 radio, a response indicative of the decisive stances she would take throughout the rest of her broadcasting career.[27]

In 1966, just a little more than two years after coming to Detroit, Steinberg was recruited by WJLB, where she was hailed as "the only female radio personality in the city and the nation to so steadily command the air waves."[28] But on February 2, 1972, her direction changed. Steinberg

Martha Jean "the Queen" Steinberg and B. B. King, two of WDIA's early radio stars. Photograph by Ernest Withers. Courtesy of Diane Steinberg-Lewis.

"broke format," and, in her words, "received the power of the Holy Spirit."[29] The change in her programming was marked. As one writer explained, "After 25 years of selling people on products, 'The Queen' started selling people on GOD!"[30]

Three years later, she founded the Order of the Fishermen Ministry, a nondenominational organization with a focus on obedience to God and compassion for others. Upon that foundation, she opened the Home of Love in 1975, a community center and church on the west side of Detroit.[31] She remained WJLB's midday announcer until 1982. By that time,

Martha Jean "the Queen" Steinberg at WDIA, Memphis, 1954. Photograph by
Ernest Withers. Courtesy of Diane Steinberg-Lewis.

the station had left its old AM frequency and had become an FM urban
contemporary powerhouse looking to attract younger audiences, demo-
graphics its research said were vastly different from those listening to
Steinberg's program.[32] Booth Broadcasting moved her to 5:00 AM, and
for a year, she did not go into the station; rather, she recorded her program
in her home studio and sent the tapes. During that time, she and associated investors bought the old WJLB-AM 1400 and named the new property WQBH, acronym for "Welcome the Queen Back Home" or "the
Queen Broadcasts Here." On May 12, 1997, Martha Jean "the Queen"

Steinberg became not only the president and general manager but the owner of WQBH, the Queen's Broadcasting Corporation, and thus one of the first black female radio owners in the country, thereby capping a most remarkable career in radio.[33]

Steinberg's friend and colleague Irene Johnson Ware can also lay claim to becoming one of radio's most successful and visible women gospel announcers ever. Ware, who was born April 24, 1935, in Blacksher, Alabama, entered the world already deeply connected to the gospel tradition. She is the granddaughter of the late Reverend J. B. Weaver, who, for forty years, was the pastor of the church she still attends, Greater Mt. Olive Baptist Church in Mobile. Her grandmother, Savannah Georgia Jones, was a missionary and church mother. Her father, Dr. James Edison Weaver, was a deacon in that church for more than sixty years and, though he was not a minister, earned a doctor of theology degree because of his desire to know more about the Bible. Ware's mother, Everlean Williams Weaver, was a professional cook who worked for the school system and local hospitals and served in various capacities in the church, including the usher board and the gospel chorus.

Ware's endeavors on radio and within the community reflect her Christian upbringing and exposure to church activities. She has sung gospel music most of her life; she began with the Sunday school choir and then moved on to an all-female group she helped to form called the Spirit of Heaven Singers. Performing in the traditional gospel style of the Ward Singers and Davis Sisters, who were stars of gospel's golden age, the Spirit of Heaven Singers were popular enough to open for all the major groups that came through Mobile. Today, Ware still sings alto and leads many songs as a member of Greater Mt. Olive's Hubert Baker Choraleers. The first female trustee at her church and the only woman to have served as the chairman of that board, she remains an active part of that auxiliary as well.[34]

From the very beginning of her broadcasting career, Ware displayed an ability to handle successfully several tasks at once. After graduation from high school, she attended Besteda's School of Cosmetology from which she earned her license in 1961. That same year she accepted two positions at WGOK-AM, Mobile: gospel announcer and receptionist. Unlike many aspiring broadcasters who have played gospel music on radio as a way of getting into the industry, Ware never desired to present anything

Irene Johnson Ware (*far right*) with participants in WGOK's Good Neighbor Contest, Mobile, Alabama, 1970. Courtesy of Irene Johnson Ware.

but gospel music. For almost forty-two years, she continued to do so gladly because of who she professes to be and what her programming entailed: "I am a Christian . . . the program is a ministry."[35] That is undoubtedly why she initially accepted the position of host of WGOK's *Miss Mandy Show*, during which she was to dispense household tips between gospel songs, a format followed by the two other women who had previously been in that slot. "OK" Radio Group owners Jules Paglin and Stanley Ray, who had stations in Louisiana, Texas, Alabama, and Tennessee, routinely gave names like "Miss Mandy" and "Topsy Turvy" to their black on-air personalities. Ware remembers that she, like her predecessors, was required to wear a white robe during promotional engagements, though she refused to do so after the first time.[36]

Assigned and assumed names have always been an important part of black radio. While such radio titles as "Honeyboy" and "Golden Girl" had been seen as simply that by most disc jockeys and listeners, many within Mobile's black community, including a local civil rights group called

Irene Johnson Ware receives the Living Legend Award during the Urban Network Convention from Dr. Jerry Boulding (*left*) and Ray Harris, 1992. Courtesy of Irene Johnson Ware.

NOW (Neighborhood Organized Workers), characterized the names "Miss Mandy" and "Topsy Turvy" as "Uncle Tom." Ware believes the names were used to conjure up images of the good old days of slavery while simultaneously enabling the owners to replace the on-air personalities at will without loss of continuity for the audience.[37] But just as NOW, with which Ware was affiliated, demanded fairness and respect in other arenas of Alabama life in the mid-1960s, they called for the announcers to be able to use their own names on air. Once that goal was achieved, Ware ran a contest to have her listeners name the show. It was called *The Brighter Day* from that point (around 1965 or 1966) until her tenure at WGOK ended in 1999. In taking back the use of her own name, deciding how a new title would be selected for her radio program, and refusing to wear the station's "costume," Ware established a pattern of holy boldness that she has continued to follow throughout her career. She explains that she is guided by the Holy Spirit, who tells her "when to roll it and when to fold it" regarding matters both inside and outside of broadcasting.[38]

Both Steinberg and Ware displayed their spiritual directedness, not only in the genre of music they played, but also in the selection and pacing of that music. Ware's understanding of music and recording eventually led to her being named a vice president at Jewel Records, where, among others, she signed the Reverend C. L. Franklin to a historic contract.[39] On a more personal level, her expertise was displayed daily during her radio broadcasts. In November 1996, Ware explained to *Billboard* how the musical continuity for her show evolved:

> "I mix my music," Johnson-Ware explains of her balance of contemporary and traditional, upbeat and stately, tunes. "When I come on in the morning at 10, I play an inspirational tune, something that says, 'Thank you, Lord, for another day.' As I get into 11 AM, I have a funeral home that sponsors the hour, so I play something uplifting with a beat to it, so if the family is listening, it gets them through the day. I try to be kicking—I'm up against *The Young and the Restless* and all that! I encourage people to call and tell a friend. At noon, when everybody's going to lunch, I try to play . . . the hits, music that is really hitting: Kirk Franklin, John P. Kee, Dorothy Norwood, new group the Williams Sisters— they are very strong—and Beverly Crawford. Music that's good and up-tempo."[40]

In her own programming, Steinberg, rather than haphazardly presenting whatever came to mind, centered her music on particular themes based on the day of the week. For example, Tuesday could be "bank of faith" day; Thursday, "salute to all men" day; and Friday, "contemporary gospel day on the Q." Within the show itself, which ran from 11 AM until 2:00 PM, Steinberg did not speak until noon, other than on audio recording. This meant that all the music that preceded her live presentation functioned much like the presermonic music within a traditional black church service, that is, it paved the way for the high point of the "service," or, in this case, the broadcast: the delivery of the spoken word. In fact, besides the music, what has given both Ware's and Steinberg's programs durability is their skill in recontextualizing aspects of the black worship experience. Ware incorporated a look at the Sunday school lesson for the week, the discussion of which might involve a roundtable with local ministers and Christian education teachers.

And there was, of course, the meditation period, the hallmark of each of their programs. The "praise and progress reports" from Steinberg's listeners simulated the testimonial service that many churches still hold, and she was often known to use Gregorian-like chants, the most popular of which incorporated words from the Psalms. So those who appreciate gospel music as a reflection of black culture—or as just good music—could simply enjoy the flow and the artistry. And those who accept the spiritual premise of the lyrics could find within these programs replications of the elements Arthur Paris identifies as "major subsegments" of the black worship experience.[41] When told that her program did seem to recreate aspects of a church service, Steinberg remarked that it was not her conscious decision. Rather, in keeping with her deference to the Holy Spirit, she said it was just what she felt led to do.[42]

Spiritual courage underpinned the careers Steinberg and Ware forged, and it manifested itself both on and off the air. On their radio programs, this spiritual audacity was demonstrated as they addressed national and local issues that others often avoided. However, they always believed they were divinely inspired to broach the hot topics of the day, a conviction that set them apart from many of their peers in gospel radio whose commentary focused on the music, the artists, and spiritual matters, not on civil issues. There was no set time on Ware's program for her commentaries: "Whenever the Spirit leads me to deal with it, I do that," she explained during a telephone interview. In the 1970s with the passage of legalized abortion, she denounced the practice and declared, "If we allow it, the spirit of death will be rampant in this country," a prediction she believes has come to pass. Following the report of the dragging death of black pedestrian James Byrd in Texas in 1998 by avowed white supremacists, Ware issued a warning to her audience. She recalls declaring, "If we sit back as black American citizens and ignore what is happening, we're going to go back and be worse off than we were in the fifties." And when Reynard Johnson, a seventeen-year-old honor student was found hanged after dating a white girl in Mississippi, Ware called a local television station to ask why they had not commented on the incident. About her willingness to address more than scriptural passages, Ware states: "My whole thing has always been this: either you stand for something or you'll fall for anything."[43]

Steinberg was equally intrepid in the topics she raised, but she reserved a specific period for these meditations. *Inspiration Time* began each day at noon—ironically the same time her sexy *Premium Stuff* program had aired on WDIA. *Inspiration Time* grew out of the leadership role she took during the 1967 disturbance in Detroit that many called "the riot" but that she always referred to as "a rebellion." For forty-eight hours, she served as a voice of reason, pleading with people to get off the streets and return to their homes. As gospel choir director Minister Donald Vails recalled, "[Steinberg] was not a religious announcer at the time. She was R&B. But something happened in that whole experience with the riot and so forth, and she became the voice of black Detroit."[44] After the disturbance abated, she continued to use a period in every program to nurture, advise, and comfort people and to encourage them "to change their lives through her strong belief in God."[45]

Steinberg explained the marked transformation to the *Detroit News* in 1996 when she was named one of the newspaper's "Michiganians of the Year":

> "It changed my whole life," she recalls. "After the '67 rebellion, and after I realized that people had problems that civil means and legislation just could not solve, I realized that people had to have a new kind of thought process about themselves. I did not have the answer. In desperation, I prayed. All of a sudden, something happened that I can't explain. It was like an empowerment, a boldness. I talked a different way. I felt different about myself. I had to get rid of anger and teach people to get rid of anger. We had to project love."[46]

Whether discussing politics or alerting women that the various auto makers were issuing cost of living or bonus checks (an alert sounded to the chagrin and anger of some men), Steinberg remained resolute in her belief that her statements were God-inspired. That included explaining to Detroiters, "God told me he would bless the city through casino gaming," a concept she not only embraced on air but supported as one of the minority investors in the MGM Grand Casino in Detroit.[47]

But these were more than spiritual women when they got behind their microphones; these were gifted communicators who proved over several decades their ability to sell for advertisers, attract loyal listeners, and move audiences in any number of ways. Verna Green, former general manager of WJLB (1982–99), paints this picture of Steinberg's verbal dexterity:

If you listened with a casual ear, it sounded just kind of chatty. But if you listened with a focused ear, you could tell that she was strategic in her comments.
. . . She came along when announcers really had an art of conversation with or
to listeners, so there was a feeling that you really knew this person on air and
that they could take liberties in saying things and instructing you and direct-
ing you. If there was a breadwinner who was male—and mostly women were
listening to her—then she saw that as a platform for helping them know what's
going on in terms of family finances and literally encouraging them to take action.[48]

Both women, equipped with impressive verbal skills, sales and marketing acuity, personal charisma, and popularity in their markets, were
able to attract high numbers of local and national accounts for their programs and stations. Steinberg, for example, while employed at WDIA,
was the first to present a Crest commercial on black radio.[49] In Detroit,
Steinberg's affiliation with the Black McDonald's Association lasted for
more than twenty years and included not only on-air buys but paid appearances at individual restaurants, where her presence always drew a
crowd and allowed her to receive four figures per hour. Several local sponsors were willing to pay a higher talent fee to have the Queen voice their
commercial announcements, and some even paid a premium beyond that
to have her talk to them "live" about their business ventures at the conclusion of her popular *Inspiration Time*.

Steinberg, a consummate salesperson, once described her friend Ware
as being able to sell anything to just about anybody.[50] Ware's track record
attests to that fact. Once, after a representative for Coca Cola declined to
buy her program, she challenged the wisdom of his decision with facts and
her persuasive powers. By the time she was finished, not only had he
bought an extensive schedule on the station, but he allocated dollars for
marketing and promotion as well. Politicians frequently sought Ware's
valuable endorsements, though 2000 was the first time in almost twenty
years that she had agreed to appear in television ads for a candidate. In
1984 she lent her support to the presidential candidacy of the Reverend
Jesse Jackson, perhaps helping to make the Deep South the site of Jackson's strongest showing that primary season.

Ware's ability to sell herself, her products, and her show is most evident, however, in her rise from a gospel announcer to station manager and

finally general manager of two stations. Before that, Ware's show was the top-rated gospel program in the market. She was the most successful at sales within WGOK, and she had shown her creativity in adapting great contests for their audience. "Everybody listens to various stations now," she explained, but back then, there was basically black radio and white radio." Ware knew how to create contests for black radio, including a soul food contest in which callers had to identify the name of the soul food that would be announced next on an audio list of foods. Another contest was a money game that allowed listeners to win from nine cents to nine hundred dollars.[51]

Ware was rewarded for her creativity and sales abilities with a promotion to station manager when Roberds Broadcasting bought WGOK-AM. Three years later, she was promoted again, this time to general manager. And when the owner found an FM property, Ware was tapped to be general manager of both; as far as she knows, she was the only gospel announcer in the country at that time running two stations, a twenty-four-hour AM gospel, which she also programmed, and an FM station. While the FM was finding its way in the marketplace after being aimed at mainstream (white) audiences for years, Ware's gospel station, which was ranked number 1 among all stations in Mobile, was able to support itself and the new property, to a great extent because of Ware's marketing and sales savvy. "Selling is just a gift God gave me," she declares in a matter of fact manner.[52] Because of her accomplishments in radio, Ware was named announcer or manager of the week, month, or year by such organizations as the Gospel Music Workshop of America and publications that include *Billboard, Record World,* and *Black Radio Exclusive.*[53] It is apparent that neither Ware nor Steinberg squandered the favor they built with their listeners through their gifts. Ultimately, their sales skills not only helped to enrich the stations and finance their programs but also brought them the kind of financial revenues, stability, and status within the industry relatively few announcers earn.

Any review of the careers of these two announcers reveals that they were always activists involved with causes that affected their listeners, coworkers and industry colleagues. After Ware ended her broadcast day, her ministry continued in the greater Mobile, Alabama, area. She reached out to and thus endeared herself to her community through blood drives and positive activities for young people, mothers, and the city at large.[54]

Ware's assistance and mentoring extended far beyond her coverage area, however. To date, she is highly regarded within the radio industry as the longest-serving and the most successful president to have headed the National Black Programmers' Coalition. The organization, originally called the Young Black Programmers' Coalition, represents radio program executives from around the country but primarily from the South. Ware proved to be a stabilizing influence and agent for growth, for under her watch the organization grew in visibility, became financially solvent, provided wider opportunities for networking and education among its members, and raised scholarship money for college students.[55]

Steinberg also demonstrated her commitment to improving the lives of others. While still at WCHB, whose studios were located in Inkster, approximately a half hour drive from downtown Detroit, she would note the road crews hard at work on the highways connecting the cities of southeastern Michigan. One day in the late 1960s, she decided to give a verbal tip of her hat to those crews, only to have other workers call and ask to be included the next time. Those verbal toasts evolved into her "Blue Collar Salute" during which she regularly celebrated "the forgotten man," those who "made their living by the sweat of their brow." That salute and Steinberg's affection for the community became the springboard for various enterprises, first under the name of the Blue Collar Workers of America and later under the title the Queen's Community Workers. These included but were not limited to refurbishing housing and selling them at low prices, owning and running rent-controlled apartment buildings, and setting up a delegate agency for Head Start that serviced over 450 children and parents in Detroit.[56]

Steinberg and Ware also combined their formidable confrontational and verbal skills when they decided they would no longer allow the male majority of NARA, the National Association of Radio Announcers, to exclude women from the business meetings. In 1965, less than two years after the two had connected by phone, they planned, with the other female members, to take their demands to the convention floor. Unfortunately, most of the other women backed out, but Steinbeg and Ware persisted although the crowd was drinking and smoking and initially turned their backs on the women. Steinberg took the microphone first and proclaimed that, while producing fashion shows was fine, the women in that organization were capable and ready to be included in the business sessions.

When it was Ware's turn, she explained that she had never been part of an organization that did not begin with prayer. As she recalls, Tommy Smalls, owner of Small's Paradise in Harlem, invited her to go ahead and pray; she apparently took the entire room by surprise when she did just that. When the prayer was over, both she and Steinberg were voted in as members of the executive board. The anecdote is one that Ware, other people within the industry, and even those who were not there delight in sharing as an example of Steinberg and Ware's willingness to fight for women and to display holy boldness in a most unlikely place.[57]

Steinberg's finest hour as an activist in Detroit, besides her forty-eight-hour radio stint during the 1967 rebellion, is undoubtedly the time she led the strike against her own employer, Booth Broadcasting, around 1969 because WJLB was a black-oriented station without black management of any kind. Having become "the voice of black Detroit," she was able to rally churches, pastors, and community people by going on the air and requesting their support. There were men within the station who assisted, but Steinberg was clearly the leader; under her direction, they were able to hold the station hostage for more than a week. She even contacted sponsors and asked that they withhold their dollars from the station until there was a positive resolution. The outcome was that Norman Miller, then the station's news director, was promoted to station manager. According to Jay Butler, there were several similar boycotts staged around the country near that time for the same grievances, but only the strike of WJLB was successful for these reasons: "Queen wanted black management. . . . And she had the power to rally people."[58]

H. LeBaron Taylor, who became senior vice president of corporate affairs for Sony Music Entertainment after serving as a radio personality, explained that one of the elements that made announcers like Ware and Steinberg stand out is the fact that once they were situated in the industry, "they believed it was their obligation to help others."[59]

The Queen's penchant for bringing people together for positive ends was tapped again in 1971. In the aftermath of the Detroit rebellion, the Police Committee of the Greater Detroit Chamber of Commerce decided to launch a radio program titled *Buzz the Fuzz,* a weekly half-hour featuring police commissioner John F. Nichols. They invited Martha Jean the Queen to serve as cohost, and she accepted. According to the assessment made on the Chamber of Commerce's historical website, "Initial response [was] so great that the station's phone lines [were] jammed."[60]

This picture of Ware and Steinberg would be incomplete without some assessment of their personal style and flair for the dramatic. Both women were fully aware of and relished their ability to create a stir when they entered a room. George Stewart, founder of the American Quartet Convention, summarizes this aspect of their appeal: "When they walked in you had to go, 'Who is that?' . . . Part of their radio legacy is the presentation standard that they set for women. They had style and knew how to carry themselves. They presented the 'ahh' or the 'wow' factor when they walked in. People want to know that the radio personalities are a little bit different—at least they used to."[61]

When asked to respond to being described as possessing the "ahh" or the "wow" factor, Ware shared one telling story. She and "Queen," as she called her friend, were invited in 1996 or 1997 to Aretha Franklin's annual Christmas benefit to be held at New Bethel Baptist Church, where her father, the late C. L. Franklin, had been the pastor for many years. Steinberg wore hot pink and silver, and Ware had on black-and-gold brocade and beads. Each had on coordinating, custom-made hats. When they entered, the gospel quartet called the Jackson Southernaires was performing, but the crowd stopped to "ooh" and "aah" at the announcers' outfits. Later, one member of the singing group laughingly shared the group's mock irritation with having been upstaged.[62]

Though silver and gold attire may seem extraneous to a discussion of these radio pioneers—and Ware and Steinberg did have a good laugh about creating such scenes—in fact, these women were as careful with their clothing as they were with their speech, sales, and activities. Their choices of garments were not for the timid and retiring. As Stewart noted, "They had the personae to go along with the presentation."[63] When Steinberg was inducted into the Rock and Roll Hall of Fame, she wore a bright lime green hat, but her comment about it—"I wore this hat because I wanted to stand out among all these good-looking men"—spoke to the occasion as well as to her entire career. Steinberg and Ware stated through their choices in clothing as well as in their demeanor that "they would not be denied," as Bishop Sam Williams has expressed it: "And to this day,

Irene Johnson Ware refuses to compromise in a man's world or conform, which is why she is no longer with those two radio properties."[64] Here, Williams refers to Ware walking away without regrets from WGOK after thirty-nine years and from her last station, WDLT-AM (1999–2002), after just three. In one case, she was asked to keep silent about community affairs and just "stick to the log." In the other, her commissions from her sales efforts were to be eliminated. Reflecting on both situations and her decision to walk away from a career that was four decades in the making, Ware commented, "If I have to buy time and have my own show as a nonsalaried person, that's what I'll do. . . . These new station owners, the conglomerates, don't want people who are strong in the community any more; I'm not the one to stay and be silent."[65]

Through most of Steinberg and Ware's tenure on radio, the medium remained male dominated. Industry professionals offer several opinions as to why it has been more challenging for women to enter and succeed within radio. Veteran DJ Eddie Ojay remembers a time when women's voices were not considered good enough and that some even called them "irritating," while Jerry Boulding of American Urban Radio cites a study in the mid-twentieth century that found that men and women preferred male voices on radio.[66] Teresa Hairston, publisher of *Gospel Today*, talks about the time-consuming aspects of the job, particularly for those who were offered brokerage agreements with radio stations; they had to go door to door and sell their programs, perform on those programs, and keep their homes running.[67] Still others, such as Lisa Collins, publisher of *The Gospel Music Industry Roundup*, believe that the challenges for women in radio are posed by the same individuals who do not embrace women in ministry and see gospel announcing as an extension of the pulpit.[68]

Despite these historic challenges, gospel radio is populated by hundreds of women, some of whom are already making major contributions to their stations and the community. Examples from the national arena include contemporary trailblazer Willie Mae McIver. From 1999 until July of 2006, she served as program director and midday host for the ABC Radio Network's twenty-four-hour music format *Rejoice! Musical Soul Food*, which was heard in forty-nine markets. Now, she is vice president of programming for the Urban Choice Media Group, which acquired *Rejoice! Musical Soul Food* from ABC in July 2006. Her affiliation with the ABC network began in 1989, when she was hired to create, produce, and

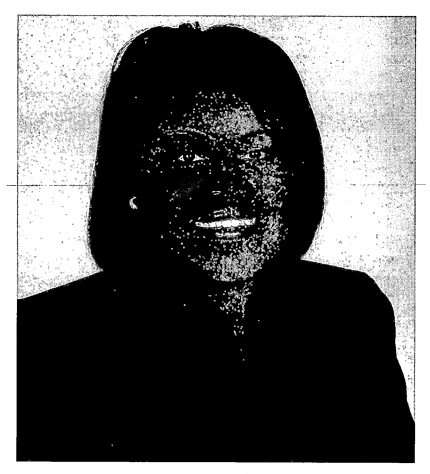

Willie Mae McIver. Courtesy of Willie Mae McIver.

host *Gospel Inspirations*, the first live satellite gospel program in the nation. A 2004 inductee into the Broadcasters' Hall of Fame, she has been
in radio since the early 1980s, initially as a programmer for gospel and urban stations in Las Vegas and later as on-air talent in Dallas. She meets
the challenge of serving the cities in which *Rejoice* is heard through a
range of initiatives. There are weekly and monthly drawings for everything from CDs to trips, and each month a church is awarded one thousand dollars through a random drawing. Health is an important part of
the network's agenda as well. Diabetes, HIV/AIDS, sickle cell anemia,

hypertension, and abstinence awareness are each the focus of a month-long campaign. On the website, visitors can find scriptures for challenging times (Overcomers Bulletin), post their prayer requests ("I was laid off and my bills are piling up; please pray for me!"), and much more.[69]

Pastor Juandolyn Stokes, like Steinberg and Ware, is a nationally recognized radio personality. She can be heard weekdays 8 PM–midnight and Sundays 6–11 AM in over fifty radio markets through the gospel radio format the Light, a division of the Sheridan Broadcast Network. Previously, she was on Atlanta's WCLK-FM as host of *Joy in the Morning*. Stokes, who was named one of "America's Ten Most Powerful Female Pastors" by *Gospel Today Magazine*, is the founder, senior pastor, and prelate of Deeper Life in Christ Ministries, with locations in Decatur and Conyers, Georgia. The chaplain for the Gospel Announcer's Guild of the Gospel Music Workshop of America, Stokes is equally comfortable as a program emcee. Her prowess in this setting has been showcased in the series *Gospel Today Presents: Praise and Worship* on Verity Records, where her ability to flow within the moment is called "peerless" by many of her colleagues. An author and teacher, Stokes serves as a board member for the E. C. Reems Women's International Ministries and the Gospel Heritage Foundation.[70]

Several other women have achieved national prominence through hosting nationally syndicated programs, including McIver's and Stokes's colleagues on their respective networks and individuals like Vanessa Vaugn, who presides over *Inspirations Across America*, a two-hour weekly gospel show that is carried on more than one hundred stations.[71]

Syndicated programs such as these provide tightly packaged programming for scores of markets and serve as an important source of inspirational music, which is especially critical for those cities that are without their own locally produced gospel programs. However, the local announcer is still the one listeners most frequently turn to for music, inspiration, community support, and events, as ten pages of gospel radio listings demonstrate in *Gospel Industry Today 2007*.[72] Stellar Award–winning Gospel Announcer of the Year Tracey Bethea, for instance, on WHAL 95.7 FM Memphis travels to various churches and works out with her listeners through her Healthy Lifestyle Ministry. Another Stellar Award winner, Tracy Morgan in Washington, DC, has officially launched her back-to-school shoes program for children in the Heaven

1580 AM coverage area, a major feat after two years of lining up sponsorship dollars for the project.

Sister Louversey Green, who for thirty years could be heard early Sunday mornings on Detroit's WMUZ, the Light, now broadcasts on 1340 WEXL AM. She is the founder of the Meditation Outreach for the Blind and Radio Ministry, Inc., which since 1977 has provided music lessons and performance opportunities for visually impaired persons. Initially, she was also the driver for the ministry, making certain that the participants were picked up and brought to her home, the original site for the meetings. Unlike Bethea and Morgan, who are employed by their respective stations to do their on-air work, Green is a broker, which means that she has the extra task of raising money to pay for her weekly broadcasts and sustain the outreach ministry. This she does through writing grants and creating partnerships with advertisers to defray the expenses.[73]

An example of a local personality who embodies the othermother spirit that many women gospel announcers often display is another Detroiter, the Reverend Norma Jean Pender. Given her demeanor, she could not have chosen a more appropriate radio name than the one she uses: Reverend Mother. The host of a daily 5–8 PM program on 1340 WEXL-AM, she admonishes ("You need to get to somebody's church this Sunday!"), explains ("In times like these, I'm telling you, you need to keep your Bible turned to Reverend Mother's favorite scripture, Psalm 27. Keep that right there near the front door, so you can see it as you come and go"), and encourages ("Jones family, you know Reverend Mother and the entire WEXL family are holding you up in prayer as you prepare to bury your father tomorrow").[74] The associate pastor at New Jerusalem Temple Baptist Church for more than twenty years and the public relations director for the GMWA since its inception, Pender has become one of the Motor City's most popular women in the gospel music and church worlds because of her delivery style and her involvement with several community organizations.

Women gospel announcers, too many to discuss here, continue to model for their radio audiences broadcast excellence, spirituality, commitment to community, and style. Whether they are iconoclasts who challenge the status quo, savvy communicators who subtly create the othermother persona while broadcasting, or ministers who see radio as the

most effective way to reach thousands, their listeners will continue to benefit from their radio programs and community service, particularly if they
are executed with the spiritual audacity that took Ware and Steinberg
from their early labels of Miss Mandy and Princess Premium Stuff to
their legendary status in black radio and gospel radio history.

PREACHERS IN DISGUISE

Holy hip hop (HHH) artists, particularly those solely devoted to communicating the gospel message through rap, are among the most controversial of today's ministers of music.[1] They are often shut out or looked upon suspiciously by gospel audiences who see them as mirror images of the hyper-sexual, hyper-materialistic performers featured in scores of secular music videos.[2] Conversely, those within so-called secular hip hop often dismiss HHH because the artists perform without the commercialized signifiers of street credibility (profanity and barely clad video dancers, e.g.) and are therefore perceived by some to be the less edgy, not-really-hip hop younger sibling.

Despite the questions some raise about what they see as the oxymoronic nature of holy hip hop—how could it possibly be holy and hip hop?—a closer examination of the testimonies and lyrics of these artists reveals that their approach to the ministry is generation-specific in its packaging but age-old in purpose, including the articulation of a plan of salvation, revelation of the changes God has made in their lives, and adoration for their Savior and Creator. For these reasons, holy hip hop can be viewed as an authentic part of a continuum that includes all other black sacred music and speech traditions. Holy hip hoppers are in fact preachers in disguise, to borrow the name of an earlier holy hip hop group (Preachas in Disguise—PID), as serious about their ministry and calling as any of the traditional gospel artists of today or of the early twentieth century.[3]

Anthropologist and ethnomusicologist Charles Keil has declared that the oral tradition is one of the "defining features" of black culture, one that easily separates it from mainstream culture. In his seminal work *Urban Blues*, he explains this essential difference: "In White America, the printed-literacy tradition—and its attendant values—are revered. In the Negro community, more power resides in the spoken word and oral tradition—good talkers abound and the best gain prestige" (16–17). African American history provides copious support for Keil's contention. Many individuals celebrated by African Americans have achieved prominence, at least in part because of their facility with language. Geneva Smitherman calls this veneration of "those who can perform stunning feats of oral gymnastics" a "residue of the African world view," which has survived both the Middle Passage and four centuries of contact with European Americans. Because this "residue" runs throughout African American history and culture, individuals who are as seemingly disparate as Muhammad Ali, the Reverend Martin Luther King Jr., and Oprah Winfrey—"preachers and poets, bluesmen and Gospel-ettes, testifiers and toast-tellers, reverends and revolutionaries"—are unified in their ability to "rap" and by the community's appreciation of their gift.[4]

Certainly, even a superficial glance at the history of the traditional Black Church reveals a deep reverence for the speaker and the spoken word. The apex of the worship event is, of course, the preaching of the sermon or the delivery of "the message," usually by the pastor or spiritual leader of the congregation. Everything that comes before the sermon—the devotional service, with its uttered prayers and testimonies, as well as the music from the congregation and choirs—paves the way for this pivotal juncture of the worship.[5] As a Baptist pastor's daughter, I have attended countless church services and made note of the fact that there is often a special stance taken by the members of the usher board as the sermonic Bible passage is read and the pastor "takes his text," that is, announces the title and direction of his or her message. The ushers prevent departures and entrances of any kind during that period, and they often stand in a linear formation, cross right hand over left, and then place both over their hearts in indication of the sacredness of the moment.

As for the preachers themselves, special designations are given to those who are particularly adept at delivering the sermon according to cultural guidelines. A particularly competent preacher may be described as "a whooper," a term that refers to a particular style of preaching and a unique sound made during the process; a "bench walker"; or "somebody's preacher," that is, a competent minister whom people gladly claim as their own. Grace Sims Holt, in the article "Stylin' outta the Black Pulpit," offers the terms "soul jerkers" and "spellbinders" as descriptive titles given to black preachers who use a range of rhetorical devices to captivate their audiences (196, 200).

The reverence for competent speakers within the Black Church tradition connects the contemporary African American with those who worshipped in the praise houses and "invisible churches" of two centuries ago. Within the slave community, there was an ample supply of impressive speech, much of it generated by the black preacher who was held in high esteem because of his rhetorical prowess.[6] In *God's Trombones*, poet James Weldon Johnson pays tribute to these traditional black "sons of thunder," as they were often called: "The old-time preacher of parts was above all an orator, and in good measure an actor. He knew the secret of oratory, that at bottom it is a progression of rhythmic words more than it is anything else. Indeed, I have witnessed congregations moved to ecstasy by the rhythmic intoning of sheer incoherencies. He was a master of all the modes of eloquence. He often possessed a voice that was a marvelous instrument, a voice he could modulate from a sepulchral whisper to a crashing thunder clap" (5).

Black America's historical appreciation for good talk has its roots on the African continent, where respect for the well-turned phrase and the phrase-turner is pervasive. The oral tradition, then, as Smitherman describes it in *Talkin' and Testifyin'*, is one of the essential cultural elements the African brought to America: "The pre-slavery background was one in which the concept of Nommo, the magic power of the Word, was believed necessary to actualize life and give man mastery over things. . . . In traditional African culture, a newborn child is a mere thing until his father gives and speaks his name. No medicine, potion, or magic of any sort is considered effective without accompanying words" (77–78).

Because speech is such a vital aspect of black culture, it was virtually inevitable that the gospel music community would create its own speech traditions. They include, but are not confined to, song introductions, testimonies, narratives (such as those told by extraordinary storytellers and gospel singers Shirley Caesar and Dorothy Norwood) and call and response used to involve congregations in musical program or services.[7] The oral customs also include the use of prayers and Scriptures for a variety of reasons, among them the transformation of otherwise secular spaces into "churches." They may consist in part of words and phrases from black sacred repertoire as well as idiomatic expressions from black secular culture, which Smitherman refers to as "black semantics."[8]

The Convergence of Hip Hop and Gospel

Given the importance of speech throughout the African diaspora in general and within African American culture in particular, gospel and rap were bound to converge. Holy hip hop, then, can be seen as a logical continuation of Black Church speech patterns. "Indeed," writes Horace C. Boyer, "many gospel music lovers insist that African American preachers were the first rappers and that gospel rappers have been long overdue."[9] Simultaneously, it is a sacred adaptation of what the Sugar Hill Gang first commercialized in 1979 with the release of "Rapper's Delight." By the mid-1980s the "long overdue" experiments with holy hip hop began. The late Tim Smith, acknowledged as a pioneer in playing holy hip hop on radio, recalled that before the actual emergence of the genre, Scott Blackwell, a prominent club DJ in New York, took a sermon and put beats behind it: "It was so cool. And it's like, 'This is what I hear on Sunday morning. Same thing.'"[10]

Both Allmusic.com and Cross Rhythms magazine concur with Smith that Stephen Wiley and Michael Peace, along with D-Boy Rodriquez, were the pioneers of Christian rap with their respective *Bible Break* and *Rock It Right* albums.[11] Music writer and historian Bil Carpenter categorizes Wiley's work as "too tame to be taken seriously by rap aficionados" while naming him "the godfather of gospel rap."[12] Smith, who recalled that Wiley rapped while wearing a suit, described his rhymes as having a "homogenized" sound: "It didn't have the heavy beats that you hear from Gospel Gangstaz [a popular HHH group that for a time was known as Camp 8], people like that. It sounded like 'Mary Had a Little Lamb' with uh, you know, I'm being real! It sounded like 'Mary Had a Little Lamb' with a bit of an edge to it. And that was our introduction to Christian rap."[13]

Whatever it may have lacked, there was apparently a market for it. Wiley's music often placed in the top five on the CCM charts since it was the white community to which he was catering, as Smith remembered. Carpenter, however, places Wiley within one of the early black megachurches; he was a youth minister at the fifteen-thousand-member Crenshaw Christian Center led by Frederick Price, which brought him in contact with other youth ministries. After selling a number of custom rap albums, Wiley was signed by Star Song Records, where label vice president Jeff Moseley is quoted as commenting about the artist: "His talents are large, but his heart for kids is even bigger."[14]

Michael Peace, just a bit later in the 1980s, introduced the "hard-edge" rap sound for that time, marked by "beats, his delivery . . . his street look," as Smith remembered. Not readily received by many churches in his prime, Peace reached out to those on the streets and worked with urban ministers and rapped to youth in schools, gyms, and anywhere else they would have him.[15]

In their willingness to stand on street corners and evangelize if necessary, Peace, his peers, and his successors are a throwback to gospel music's origins. From its emergence at the end of the nineteenth century through much of the first half of the twentieth century, gospel music was used primarily as an evangelistic tool within the context of church services, of course, but also during outdoor revivals, tent meetings, and other less structured settings.[16] Many contemporary Christian rappers, whose mantra is often "takin' it to the streets," continue that tradition and do so for at least two reasons: it allows them access to youth who would not ordinarily walk into churches and it provides alternative performance and ministry sites for their alternative ministry. Since Peace's emergence, the climate for HHH performers has been much more welcoming. In fact, increasing numbers of churches have been involved in encouraging HHH performers to minister on their premises and in assisting their own youth in developing their verbal skills. For example, Detroit's Rosedale Park Baptist Church, under the pastorate of Haman Cross Jr. and Pastor of Student Ministries Dennis Talbert, has hosted nationally recognized holy hip hop ministers for more than fifteen years, held regular HHH-centered services, and even seen the emergence of rappers within the congregation, including a group called the Mad Prophets. Both mainstream and Christian media report similar kinds of support in churches around the country.[17]

The alternative performance sites that have emerged include Christian "light" clubs, evening spots where Christian rappers as well as singers, instrumentalists, comedians, mimes, liturgical dancers, spoken word artists, and poets take the stage before audiences in an alcohol-free, smoke-free environment. In many of these sites, the audience also has the chance to line dance to prerecorded music, often played by DJs who are skilled in mixing thumping beats for a youthful, Christian audience. Dr. D, an HHH DJ in New York, ran the Gospel Light House, an early Christian night club, from 1995 to 2000; his target audience included those in their teens to those in their early forties.[18]

Detroit's Upper Room Entertainment Complex, which has been the site for a range of Christian performance arts and events, including the Autumn Blaze HHH Summit (2003), has been described as offering "a refreshing alternative to smoke-filled and booze-drenched nightspots." Other cities, including Dallas, Nashville, and Tamarac, Florida, are also part of a growth in the number of Christian nightclubs.[19] Then there are DJs like Esosa in the Motor City who mix and present urban contemporary artists biweekly in a variety of venues that they rent for these purposes. A growing list of conferences and festivals, those that solely focus on HHH as well as those that are enclaves within larger mainstream events, provide opportunities for HHH artists to display their skills, discuss their issues, and, of course, minister.[20]

Priming the Mainstream for Holy Hip Hop

The interest in HHH and its financial viability continues to build. Evidence of this can be found in the number of websites devoted solely to HHH, the local events and national gatherings that feature HHH/urban contemporary gospel summits and performances, and the fact that major gospel labels, including GospoCentric and EMI, and several of the independent ones, including Gotee, DoRohn, and Tyscot, have previously or are now distributing projects. These labels have aligned themselves with HHH, despite the fact that HHH's earlier artists, including Mike E, A-1 Swift, the Dynamic Twins, and SFC, and even most of today's HHH artists usually sell to a far more modest audience than their secular counterparts, as is the case with most nonsecular performers.

While a number of rappers have recorded songs with religious, inspirational, or spiritual themes, only a few have had major hits using specifically Christian references.[21] Ironically, high profile secular artists with only fleeting associations with the genre have recorded these hits, and their recordings, in turn, have brought HHH before a wider audience. Many rap and gospel music fans may recall Hammer, formerly MC Hammer, and his experiments in melding the two forms in his version of the hymn "Do Not Pass Me By," featuring gospel star Tramaine Hawkins and the original song "Pray"; still, in the minds of most, he will always be connected with less religious themes, such as his defining recording, "You Can't Touch This," and the controversial "Pumps and a Bump." In 2004 Kanye West's "Jesus Walks" proved to be one of the most popular songs from his *College Dropout* album. The song received airplay on gospel radio as well as on most urban contemporary stations and was prominently featured during a number of television specials, including the BET Gospel Celebration and the Grammy Awards.[22]

But the artist most responsible for exposing HHH to both the mainstream media and conservative churchgoers is Kirk Franklin. He and his "hip, 'singing'" peers, including Mary Mary and Tonex, "have been mistaken by the public as hip hop artists," in the words of publicist Kia Jones-Glenn.[23] Franklin has even been featured on the cover of the hip hop magazine Vibe.[24] Clearly, the use of hip hop elements, including rap, attire, and dance, has brought Franklin and these other artists the attention of fans and the media. Franklin's image as a hip hop performer is understandable since some of his biggest hit records ("Stomp" and "The Revolution") have rap elements and since he was both a self-described "church boy" and a break dancer known as Kid Fresh before becoming a record-setting international gospel artist.[25] His peer Tonex even has a different name—T. Bizzy—for the times when he displays his rap abilities.[26] But these artists' repertoires also include ballads, retro funk, and even Sunday morning– ready praise and worship songs. The good news for HHH is that these successful, high-profile gospel artists have been at least partially responsible for persuading radio programmers to broaden their play lists to include more of the urban contemporary music of emerging artists.[27]

One of today's most bankable gospel performers, Franklin has experienced crossover success few other gospel artists have achieved. He has reportedly sold 10–12 million recordings, making him the most successful gospel artist to date.[28] His music ranges from his first hit single, a ballad called "Why We Sing," to the song with the widest crossover appeal, "Stomp," from the 3.5 million– selling *God's Property from Kirk Franklin's Nu Nation*, which layers old George Clinton funk, rap, and a gospel message. Franklin's music has been nothing if not evolving, progressive, and controversial. In fact, the names of the groups with whom he has recorded speak to that range: the Family, God's Property, the Nu Nation, and the One Nation Crew, also known as INC. With each group, the music has been, as the names suggest, increasingly urban contemporary.

The Nu Nation Project, the first recording by a gospel artist to ship platinum, typifies the urban, in-your-face, not-your-mother's-gospel-music Franklin has produced. Rodney Batdorf, writing for *All Music Guide*, observes, "Kirk Franklin designed *The Nu Nation Project* as a revitalization of contemporary gospel, a way to bring it to an audience accustomed to the slick, funky innovations of hip-hop and rap. It's an ambitious project and one that's not too far removed from his earlier records … the end result is every bit as engaging as his previous records, thereby confirming his status as one of true visionaries in '90s contemporary gospel."[29] "The Revolution" from that project is a prime example of how Franklin has visually and textually layered the traditional gospel message with hip hop elements. The young people with whom I conducted feedback interviews reported that both the CD version and the video work to attract hip hop fans for several reasons: the incessant beats are there, it has the look of an R&B/hip hop video—quick cuts, multiple outfits on the main artist, various performance scenarios, along with stylized choreography—and the featured rapper is the esteemed hit-making producer Rodney "Darkchild" Jerkins, whose long list of credits includes Michael Jackson, Destiny's Child, and Mary Mary.[30]

The elements in Franklin's performances that attract hip hop lovers are also the attributes that repel his detractors. These components, in fact, allow Franklin to approach a new audience without looking, or sounding,

Kirk Franklin. Photograph by Mark Mann. Courtesy of Zomba Gospel, LLC.

radically different from them. In two of the three video scenes in "The Revolution," he and the singer/dancers perform in the casual and athletic wear popularized by hip hop culture. The choreography reflects Franklin's break dancing career in that it is far more street than sanctuary without being sexually provocative. The movements are energetic—at some points, the singer/dancers seem to bounce on and off the floor—yet it is never lurid, as both male and female participants are clothed in unisex athletic wear.

However, just beyond these exterior aspects, there are layers of other texts that allow this song to be viewed as an evangelistic tool. Franklin begins the song and video by reciting Revelation 7:16–17: "They shall hunger no more, neither shall they thirst anymore. . . . God shall wipe away all tears from their eyes." In between phrases, a young man talks back to him in church-styled call and response: "Preach, Preacher!" "Yes, suh!" At the end of the verses, Franklin puts everyone on notice that they should prepare themselves for the revolution.

The listener and viewer are told from the onset of the song that the focus is ministry through several elements: the church-appropriate call and response, Franklin's label as a preacher, and the directive from the young speaker to Franklin to do what he was called to do—"preach." Other texts help to place the song within the gospel music tradition, including a rap by Franklin that encompasses some widely held Protestant doctrine regarding the triune nature of God, including Jesus as the "true Son" who is the second member of the Trinity. Later in the video, DarkChild responds to those who negatively characterize him, Franklin, and their colleagues in HHH for their choreographed moves and allegedly worldly presentations. They are told that they move too much and too fast. But his rejoinder is that God is in the midst of their physical and spiritual movement. Block them, and you're blocking a move of God and those He's using to reach a generation. DarkChild warns the naysayers: dismiss me and my peers and you run the risk of missing out on something God has ordained.

The video version adds other texts that can be read as part of the gospel music continuum. Franklin, whenever he is within the "church" scenario, is in a white shirt, reminiscent of one a pastor might wear, and he completes his church ensemble with serious-looking black-rimmed eyeglasses. On either side of the church or chapel, there are pews, or at least benches that have the look of church pews. Finally, there are at least two prominent crosses within the video; Franklin preaches and the One Nation Crew sings in front of one, and a cross medallion apparently filled with diamonds swings across the screen at the very end.[31] These crosses replicate visually what Franklin indicates orally in the beginning by quoting biblical text, that is, that the focus of this video is the gospel of Jesus Christ.

While at least one of the seven feedback respondents found the dancing a distraction from the message, she did agree with the others that the gospel was definitely discernible within "The Revolution." The gospel message is also identifiable within the other hip hop– influenced songs Franklin has recorded, including "Stomp," which features Cheryl James Wray, formerly "Salt" of Salt-N-Pepa fame. It is also present in "He Reigns," a funky version of the popular praise and worship song "Awesome God," found on the CD *The Rebirth of Kirk Franklin.* In this case, it is introduced by former Jamaican dancehall king turned gospel rapper Papa San with additional choral lyrics from Franklin.

When added to the fact that the balance of Franklin's songs, such as "Hosanna," "Now, Behold the Lamb," and "My Life Is in Your Hands," are readily sung on Sunday morning by youth and senior choirs alike, Franklin can be rightly characterized as the perfect bridge between more mainstream gospel and those who perform straight holy hip hop, since he helped to make it possible for many who were unused to, fearful of, or dismissive of hip hop to view it as yet another viable performance mode for gospel artists.

The Cross Movement

The members of the HHH group the Cross Movement (CM), like their peers, such as Corey Red and Precise, Grits, Lecrae, and T-Bone, use rap as their primary evangelistic tool. The CM members, collectively and singly, are distinguished, however, by a remarkable level of success most of their colleagues have yet to experience. The group originally consisted of five young men who were solo Christian rappers until 1995, when they decided to combine their verbal skills and "reach out to persons who were a part of Hip Hop Culture like themselves but did not know God."[32]

The name the Cross Movement initially covered three entities that had similar missions but distinct personnel and officers: (1) the performing group now consisting of four—T.R.U.-L.I.F.E., the Ambassador, Phanatik, and the Tonic—and the rap songs they write and perform; (2) Cross Movement Records (CMR), the brainchild of the Tonic and former CM member Earthquake (an original member who now focuses on the label), who created the independent label so that "no one could ever ask an artist signed with the label to 'water down the Gospel'"; and (3) Cross Movement Ministries, headquartered in Philadelphia, Pennsylvania, which emphasized teaching and disseminating the gospel and was

The Cross Movement (*from left to right:* the Tonic, T.R.U.-L.I.F.E., Phanatik, the Ambassador). Courtesy of Cross Movement Records.

headed by the Ambassador and Phanatik.[33] The latter was recently re-placed by other initiatives, including ChristianHipHopper.com, a web-site that aims to articulate a philosophy for ministry and serve as a site that groups a number of effective Christian hip hop ministries.[34]

CMR, located in Deptford, New Jersey, is also home to Da' T.R.U.T.H. and Flame, rap protégés of CM who have each released three projects. Though both have been positively received by fans and critics, Da' T.R.U.T.H. has enjoyed heightened exposure due to his inclusion on the 2005–6 Hero Tour headed by Kirk Franklin, with whom he has also made several media appearances. Another CMR artist known simply as J. R.

is an R&B-styled vocalist, previously heard on such Cross Movement favorites as "Closer to You." His debut CD, *Metamorphosis,* was released in late 2005. The label has also introduced contemporary Christian/Latin vocalist Michelle Bonilla, whose debut project is titled *Phenomenal.* Recent additions to the roster include Ministri of Defense and Everyday Process.

In assessing the place the Cross Movement has held within the world of Christian rap, Kymo Dockett has said, "Whether you judge success based on the number of lives reached for Christ, the number of albums sold, or the amount of projects dropped, Cross Movement have quite remarkable stats on all three fronts."[35] The reasons for their three-pronged success are summarized by Jon Corbin, who writes that CM is "one of the groups that legitimized gospel rap to a mainstream audience. Their first record, *Heaven's Mentality,* took CCM listeners by storm: here was a group rapping entirely about Jesus Christ with no apologies. The difference between this group and previous artists who had made such an attempt was that these guys were actually good."[36]

CM, whose style generally reflects their East Coast roots, has a repertoire that includes songs with driving beats as well as those that are more midtempo. Gospel music producer, promoter, and artist Kim "Kiwi" Williams recalls the group vowing to steer away from singers on their recordings; yet they have been savvy enough to amend that statement and incorporate some R&B musical hooks, all of which can be attractive to the "curious" listener.[37] In fact, publicist and promoter Kia Jones-Glenn cites the Cross Movement and the Righteous Riders as being among the artists "clever enough to create gospel-friendly, sing-songy radio singles," such as "Cry No More" and "Sometimes I Wonder," respectively, that have helped to increase the acceptance of HHH on gospel stations and those mainstream stations that program gospel on Sunday mornings.[38]

The Testimonies

As is the case with other gospel artists, those whose performances are infused with hip hop universally declare that the gospel of Jesus Christ is the impetus for their music ministry. Throughout its twenty-plus-year history, however, the critics of HHH have viewed it as they would virtually any amalgamation of the sacred and the secular: as an aberration at

Kiwi. Photograph by TVisuals Photography. Courtesy of Kimberly Williams.

best and an abomination at worst, a form far removed from "pure gospel." HHH artists report being told that what they are doing is "of the devil."[39] One Detroit husband and wife team, the Quest, recalled being told that they were going to hell and taking others with them. Another pastor was so dismayed by their "worldly" performance style that he warned that they could neither worship with nor perform for his congregation again.[40]

Without question, the HHH performance style is markedly different from that of those who blazed the gospel trail in the 1930s and 1940s and stands in stark contrast to those who are now described as traditional artists. However, these performers display a passion for spreading the gospel of Jesus Christ that is identical to that expressed by other gospel artists. Like their forerunners and current counterparts, they have conveyed that their goal and calling is to communicate the full message of the gospel: God's love for humanity and the redemptive earthly journey of Jesus Christ.

For example, Madam Gertrude Ward, matriarch of the trailblazing Clara Ward Singers during gospel's golden age (1945–60), recalls that in 1931, a voice told her, "Go sing my gospel and help save dying and lost men and women."[41] That recollection dovetails with a testimony shared by the Ambassador (William Branch) of the Cross Movement, who told me during an interview, "When Christ snatched me up, it became logical for me to use [hip hop] to contribute to the Great Commission."[42] In his autobiography, *Church Boy,* Franklin writes that "regardless of the beat or the groove, the music has to draw us to the cross" (19). Similarly, CeCe Winans, whose repertoire runs from praise and worship to urban contemporary, declares in her autobiography, *On a Positive Note,* that she has a "lifelong commitment to sing God's glory" (xv), while contemporary gospel icon Vanessa Bell Armstrong tells Dr. Bobby Jones that after four decades of singing, she's "ready to go forth in this new generation and to help more people receive the gospel."[43]

Holy hip hoppers in Detroit are equally compelling as they discuss what prompts their ministerial zeal. Jason Wilson, who produces HHH under the name Maji, previously worked in secular hip hop. He recalls rededicating his life to Christ in 1996 and thinking he would need to leave hip hop behind. But after seeing the Ambassador of the Cross Movement perform a song called "Blood Spilla," Maji's direction changed. The Ambassador's "sincerity and skill level" and the fact that "the Holy Spirit was in him" inspired Maji, who says he knew he had to "keep pressing on with hip hop but yet this time do it all for the kingdom of God . . . I have a purpose now . . . to help change people's lives towards Christ. I have a compassion for the lost."[44]

Holy hip hop artists are also like their colleagues in other areas of gospel music in that their song lyrics detail the sins from which the Lord has delivered them. An oft-repeated floating lyric in the Black Church about having been changed by God is this: "He picked me up, turned me 'round, placed my feet on solid ground." In the Cross Movement's song "Rise Up," they offer a look back at their lives before they accepted Christ:

And though the world is godless
We thank God that God has called us
From bein' ballas, and playas, and pimps and alcoholics
Times are hard, but we must still run our hardest
"Run like Forest," wit a limp, but we run regardless

So no more weed in us, or Hennessey in us
We've been freed indeed, we've got His seed in us.

Just as the Apostle Paul could preach from experience about having a life-changing encounter with Jesus Christ, some members of the holy hip hop community, including the Cross Movement, can do the same. Tonic, for example, who told a *Washington Post* interviewer that he had been a heavy drinker in the past, said during that same interview: "Look at us. . . . We were violent, we were sexually immoral. We come from that, and look at how we changed. In our eyes, we're walking miracles."[45] The title of a song and CD from the Gospel Gangstaz, "Once Was Blind," echoes the story of Paul's Damascus Road experience, which found him blinded for a time until the scales fell from his eyes (Acts 9:1–19). These former Los Angeles gang bangers also pick up one of the most powerful phrases from Christian music: "I once was blind, but now I see." That set of words, of course, comes from the hymn "Amazing Grace" written by the eighteenth-century former slave trader John Newton, who recognized his shortcomings and turned his life over to God. But for those whose earlier lives were not laced with the drama of drive-by shootings, drugs, or sex, there is "My Story," the popular track from Da' T.R.U.T.H.'s debut CD, *Moment of Truth:*

I ain't got no horror story
God kept me in my youth; I give Him all the glory.
Thought my story wouldn't flow but now I know
The blood of the Lamb has saved my soul.
That's my testimony.

The Lyrics

The lyrics of the Cross Movement and their peers often reflect a dedication to the gospel that is completely congruent with the Great Commission of Christ (Matthew 28:19– 20); the difference is that the commitment comes packaged in cleverly worded lyrics and raps that not only reference the Bible but that may also link them to a variety of historical, cultural, and popular images. At the beginning of "Blood Spilla," the Ambassador describes the mission of the group: "We're the Cross Movement, which is an alliance of born again believers in Jesus Christ that are trusting God by His grace to become agents through whom He's gonna advertise salvation and also communicate His purpose for all of humanity." Though it is not the norm for HHH songs to have a spoken introduction before the fast-paced rap that is characteristic of the genre, these opening words from the Ambassador serve as both a description of their mission as well as a spiritual framing device for that which follows. The proof that they are on this specific mission comes from close textual reading of the actual lyrics of "Blood Spilla," which offer this quatrain featuring both cultural and spiritual allusions:

> (2X) It's the thrilla' in Manilla
> Jesus Christ versus every man's killa'
> Sin and death's got the whole world gettin' illa'
> But I praise God for the blood spilla'.

Here, the group alludes to the audacious young Muhammad Ali who, in 1975 as he prepared to fight Joe Frazier, coined the phrase "Thrilla' in Manilla" and then beat his opponent in a most humiliating fashion. The Cross Movement is using cultural shorthand, making reference to an occurrence that is three decades old, to convey their assessment of the contest between Jesus Christ and the twin adversaries, sin and death. It is a face-off that must occur for two reasons: it is a key biblical prophecy, and, the group says, the world is getting further away from doing what is right.[46] Since the face-off will result in the eradication of the two ills that destroy humankind, they thank God for the one who will be triumphant over sin and death: Jesus Christ, "the blood spilla." Kiwi uses that same phrase in the song "Tired":

As for me and mine's we on the for-real-a . . .
Always representing Jesus the blood spilla'
With or without the fat record deal-a
Me Kiwi be-be a demon killa.

Embedded here is a quick retort for those who report that HHH will
never be as big as its secular counterpart. It is not about the record deal,
Kiwi explains; it is about her commitment to bringing down the kingdom
of the one known as the adversary of Jesus Christ. The Gospel Gangstaz
recorded a song titled "Demon Killa" in which they describe themselves
as permanently seeking to wipe out Satan and any evidence of his work
within the culture. Papa San's song titled "Ste Pon Di Enemy" (Step on
the Enemy) puts that same message forward with his reggae/dance hall
flair. In all these cases, using language that is generation-specific, the
Cross Movement, Kiwi, the Gospel Gangstaz, and Papa San are express-
ing the intolerance all believers are supposed to display toward Satan, an
intolerance evidenced in old congregational songs, such as "Satan, We're
Gonna Tear Your Kingdom Down" and traditional gospel songs, such as
"Got the Devil under My Feet." It is the same message, just delivered in
a different style.

Eschatology, the study of the final prophetic events mentioned in the
Bible, is another topic to which Christian rappers have applied their skills.
Holy hip hop documentary filmmaker Shannon Gaston (Vessel) explains
why this theme is so prevalent: "As it relates to social issues, this generation sees 'the system' as irrevocably corrupt (and rightfully so), therefore
in their lyrics you'll hear more about eschatology and how things are un-
folding before our eyes or rhymes about their deliverance from the issues
they've faced as young African-Americans."[47] Though the very word "eschatology" conjures up dark, foreboding images for some, in "Cry No
More," the Cross Movement paints a picture, mirroring the book of Revelation, chapter 21, of an existence in which the most vexing aspects of this
world are absent:

One day I won't cry no more
Can't wait for the day when people won't die no more
Daddy's won't say, bye no more; lie no more
In the streets bullets won't fly no more.

Right after the singable chorus from which these lines are taken, CM goes into the spiritual reasons for wanting the prophecies to be fulfilled:

> One day we takin off baby and ever since the Lord saved me
> I've been waitin for the day we can say, it's all gravy
> It's all crazy tryin to see life when its all hazy
> How can I persist to do right when I'm all lazy?
> Feel me? Too much pain it all ails me
> Vexed, cause I can feel the effects of the Fall daily
> The pain in my chest is strong, let's get on
> Come Lord, quick, bring on the eschaton
> End the search, start the new earth, flex your true worth
> Honor your Son, let Him come, perfect the new birth.

In these lines lie references to several core Christian beliefs written in such a way that a listener can follow most of them without consulting a dictionary or biblical concordance. CM talks about the daily struggles of earthly life that can be traced to "the fall" of Adam and Eve. However, they explain their belief that there will come a time when this life ends and God's promised new earth will replace the current one, which is one of the central eschatological prophecies of the book of Revelation.[48] The group does not get embroiled in the pre-, post-, or midtribulation debates that center on whether believers will go through certain challenges during the end times or be spared from them altogether. Instead, they stick to the point on which all these groups agree: "one day we takin' off baby."

"Takin' off" ties into one of the most persistent images in black folktales and the traditional songs of the Black Church: flying away to escape the troubles of this world.[49] CM reminds their listeners that believers in the gospel look forward to the establishment of a new theocratically ruled world ("Honor your Son; let Him come"), where God will give the true believers the ultimate reward for their faith and faithfulness: eternal life with Him. CM's description of the afterlife also includes a hilarious reference to the fact that hair weaves will not be a part of this new world since believers will "feel your real hair."

Corey Red and Precise, who have been compared to secular artists Redman and Method Man because of their dynamic style, also examine the end times in several of their songs, including "The Answer" from the mix tape titled *Street Prophecy Volume II* in which they focus on what for some are the most baffling images in the Bible, those relating to the apocalypse. In fact, they admit that this aspect of the Bible is not for those who are new to confronting biblical text or those who are still caught up in worldly escapism:

> This verse beyond 4th grade level so catch the next rap
> You get high/I pray you drop your pipe on the next crack.
> Zion vs. Babylon, Christ vs. Abaddon
> Jehovah's Mighty-Men with javelins piercing Leviathan.[50]

The end-time prophecies of the Bible have challenged trained biblical scholars for years. So it is interesting that these artists, several of whom are themselves in theological seminaries or regular Bible studies, have decided to bring these challenging apocalyptic images to their audiences, especially since they do so by using a performance style that is more often used to encourage partying rather than pondering the end times.[51]

As in secular hip hop, holy hip hop is a male-dominated field. So it may come as a surprise to many that unabashed love for God is another subject expressed through its lyrics. Cross Movement member the Ambassador, in his solo project titled *Christology in Laymen's Terms,* offers these words in the piece titled "I Love You Jesus" in which he focuses not only on God's love but his own personal response and responsibilities because of it:

> Meet the God who died for me enduring all the verbal mockery
> Got to be cause He loves me like women love a shoppin' spree
> His agape be the love that got to me, He adopted me
> Now I'm in the family and I'm God's property
> And periodically some youth will want to copy me
> As I copy the Savior so no more living sloppily.

The love theme has also been picked up by B. B. Jay, one of a handful of gospel hip hop performers who have recorded for major labels. The artist, whose visibility was enhanced by CD and video appearances with gospel artists like Hezekiah Walker ("Let's Dance—Remix") and Mary Mary ("I Sings" [*sic*]), presents the ever-present nature of God's care and concern in the song "His Love." As a female vocalist sings the memorable R&B-styled chorus, which is an adaptation of the refrain of DeBarge's hit "All This Love," the rapper dedicates the song to mothers facing "mad drama" and anyone else dealing with challenges. Thus, he reminds them through both a sung and a rapped lyric that God's love is theirs for the asking.

The female Christian rappers are equally vocal about their love for Jesus Christ. Kiwi, who oversaw the production of the compilation *Pure Gospel, Pure Flava,* is also the writer and performer on the cut "Pure Flave." In verse three, she offers words that celebrate the love relationship she has with Jesus that began with his sacrificial death:

I'm in such a state of peace people can't understand
This kind of love flesh can't comprehend
Ain't no man in the land like my Man . . .
Jesus Christ, He's my First Husband
Like I said, Yeshua is His name
Worthy is the Lamb for my sins who was slain
I'm made white as snow due to His blood stains
That's why I owe my God my everything.

Here, Kiwi alludes to John 3:29, in which the relationship between Christ and the church is compared to that of a bride and a bridegroom ("my First Husband"). It is the same kind of personal love connection depicted in the Cross Movement's "Blood Spilla," which, while focusing on the sacrificial death of Jesus Christ, also articulates the profound reverence, love, and awe the group feels for their Savior because of the price He paid to bring humankind back to God:

I step back to take a chill pill
just to let the thrills build
back up and now I have to say that I still feel
goo-goo about the one the crew brings to you .
died to woo you and bring you back like part two—ooh!

As expressive as these words are concerning the love the group members feel for Christ, they are equally bold later in the song in drawing a line in the sand to challenge those who suggest their gods are on the same level as the God of the Bible:

If it's your god let him speak
I'll hide let him seek, I'll jump let him leap
Let him swim the deep. Did his blood leak?
Does your god love me?
Will he still propose even though I get ugly?
Can he turn trouble to ease?
Can his love make me "weak in the knees" like SWV?
If he can take the sins of the whole world—swallow 'em
Experience death then resurrect, then I'll follow him
But if he can't then I'm stayin' with my camp
We a pack of theocrats gettin' amped 'cause our God is champ!

Using the language of love affairs, including talk of proposals and "getting weak in the knees," CM delivers lines that are simultaneously clever, vernacular, and accessible.[52] They are clever here in that they take us back to the original allusion to Muhammad Ali and the inevitable fight between God and Satan, vernacular in their description of who they are ("we a pack of theocrats gettin' amped"), and, therefore, accessible, able to attract those who find HHH at times either too didactic or not as skillfully created as the work produced by secular artists.[53] As one reviewer explained, "with clever wordplay and quality production, the Cross Movement does not disappoint."[54] While this can be said of CM, these words can also be applied to many of their peers in today's holy hip hop: they are among those of their generation who have learned to balance both the message of the gospel and the skills required within hip hop.

Final Thoughts

Those who are not "children of rap" can sometimes look beyond the clothing and the beats, but they are often unable to grasp the spiritual depth of the lyrics because of the sheer speed at which those within the genre usually recite their words. While this insistence on ultra quickness is more related to rap's formative years, the fact is that those who were not raised on rap may still find it challenging to catch the lyrics no matter what the pace chosen by the lyricist at the microphone.

During a lecture on my campus in 2004, Pastor Marvin Winans, of the Winans, whose urban contemporary gospel hit "It's Time" featured rapped segments, raised the rhetorical question of why some gospel artists would choose a form that is attached to self-described thugs and "gangstaz." That statement was followed by the incomplete comment: "If they would just slow it down so I could understand what they are saying . . ."[55] Granted, rapping more slowly might make the lyrics more accessible to some, but if today's HHH slows down, it will be derided as it had been until recently for being inferior to its secular cousins. If the artists retard the pace at which they "spit" or "spurt" the gospel, they may well lose their appeal to their core audience, that is, unless their secular counterparts do the same thing.

Just as the music of Motown was the soundtrack for youth in the 1960s and 1970s, rap music is the lingua franca for many of a certain age. The core problem is this: these HHH ministers of the gospel have by choice ensconced their lyrics in vernacular language and beats that are a virtual signal of membership for those within their demographic category. Perhaps one solution is for those outside of hip hop culture to view HHH as they would any other style of gospel music that, while not their favorite, is a legitimate means of conveying the message. A great model for that would be Pastor Winans who, despite his statements in 2004, has since that time included the music of Da' T.R.U.T.H. and the Ambassador alongside the more sizeable repertoire of praise and worship and quartet music on his Sunday morning gospel music program on Detroit's 92.3 WMXD-FM. Another example would be traditional gospel music legend Pastor Shirley Caesar, who is joined by Tonex and actually raps herself on the title song from her 2005 CD *I Know the Truth.*

Those outside the hip hop generation could think of HHH as they would Japanese, Danish, or any language other than their own through which someone preaches the gospel, that is, as a means of acting upon the Great Commission and thus reaching "all the world." Finally, if they simply cannot embrace it to any extent, they could consider stepping out of the way of those who can carry the Word in that "unknown tongue" as others eventually made way for Thomas A. Dorsey and his gospel blues and, later, for Edwin Hawkins, Andrae Crouch, and Rance Allen and their R&B influenced gospel. For, like it or not, these preachers in disguise are here and could remain for some time to come.

EPILOGUE

Having worked in the gospel music industry professionally since the 1980s, I have witnessed more than a few shifts in sound, presentational styles, and aspirations among gospel music artists. During my tenure, I have interviewed a number of performers, several of whom I will never forget. One sticks out in my memory because of a solitary sentence. The interviewee, a member of a famous gospel group, was telling me about their new recording. When she got to one particular song, she said, "Now this song will be the crossover hit." "Whoa!" I said to myself. "She's smart enough to predict that?"

Of course, neither she nor anyone else can make such predictions with accuracy. At the beginning of the twenty-first century, thousands of gospel songs are recorded each year, and hundreds of CDs are marketed.[1] Only a percentage of them get significant airplay, a smaller number become hits, that is, become songs that the audience comes to know and embrace, and a mere fraction of that number captures the attention of both gospel and secular radio programmers and fans. Although today's gospel music is well-produced and sonically compatible with urban radio, almost always, crossover hits are a surprise; some say they are an act of God, while others see them as the right songs at the right time.

In the hyper-sexual music industry, gospel songs that are about faith, salvation, inspiration, and Jesus Christ are not the major focus of most secular programmers. However, there is another side to this reality: there is a large and loyal audience for gospel music, one bigger than those who buy jazz, and one that includes millions who hear that music first in churches and on gospel radio. And while most artists would love to be among today's gospel superstars, most of them will never be pursued by MTV, BET, or the Steve Harvey or Tom Joyner shows, all of which reach millions every day. There is no question that exposure through such television and radio powerhouses can often equal increased sales. But if the focus of the gospel artist is ministry, then the other good news is that there are more mediums and emerging performance modes than ever through which they can reach the masses, modes never even imagined by their forerunners.

Gospel plays, announcers, dress codes, rap and praise and worship music—the elements I have covered in this book—are just five parts of a gospel music ministry/industry matrix that becomes more fascinating and multilayered daily. They are also proof that innovation still begins in the local community and the local church. For just as certainly as the praise and worship movement brought a new subgenre into the Black Church, other popular forms and extensions of gospel music have their roots in the Church as well.

Near the top of that list is liturgical dance. While dancing for and before God is referenced throughout the Old Testament and is another element that defines cultures created by people of African descent, it has only been since the rise of the praise and worship movement that increasing numbers of black churches across denominational lines have added liturgical dance divisions. The popularity of liturgical dance has also been enhanced by the ubiquitous presence of choreography in the live and videotaped performances of gospel singers. Liturgical dancers range from the youngest of children to senior citizens, all of whom can now perform in attire specially tailored for sacred movement, that is, garments that keep the dancers' bodies covered so as not to titillate during the performance. While some parishioners are disconcerted by the presence of choreographed movement in the sanctuary ("There is no kind of dance that belongs in the church," they say), this is another application of gospel music with biblical and African roots that should be around for decades if not longer. And, as many grateful dancers have declared, liturgical dance proves that one need not be able to sing to make an important contribution to the worship experience.

One of the more unusual new forms is gospel mime. Twin brothers Keith and Karl Edmonds of Pennsylvania, who perform as K&K Mime, are called the "fathers of gospel mime," which involves silent, dramatic, choreographed interpretation of gospel songs. Dramatic gestures and facial expressions help the mimes to convey pathos, joy, and a variety of other emotions. Young people around the country, who have seen K&K perform on Bobby Jones Gospel and elsewhere, have started their own mime troops. Thus gospel mime has provided another way for youth to participate in gospel music ministry without having to be a vocalist or musician.

Gospel music can be experienced in thousands of places outside of the church setting, which may come as a pleasant surprise to those who still believe that they must wait until Sunday morning to hear the sound of gospel. While nothing will ever replace the sight, sound, and feel one can have as the choir marches down the center aisle, rocking, clapping, and praising God amid scores, hundreds, or thousands of parishioners, there are formats, settings, shapes, and forms that can re-create aspects of the gospel sound and allow us to glimpse some of our favorite gospel artists until Sunday comes around again.

Gospel music can be heard on mainstream local radio, ensconced between everything from R&B classics to hip hop, on more than fourteen hundred local radio broadcasts. But it is also served to the public through individually syndicated programs like *The BeBe Winans Show* and through entire gospel networks, including Rejoice! Musical Soul Food and SGN, the Light. There are satellite programs and Internet stations that solely offer gospel and inspirational music. Audiences have made *Bobby Jones Gospel*, hosted by Ambassador Bobby Jones, which has been on the air for more than a quarter century, and *Lift Every Voice* with Gerard Henry the most watched regular programs on Black Entertainment Television (BET), while the cable network's *Celebration of Gospel* is a regular blockbuster in terms of audience and the artists who participate. Dr. Bobby Cartwright Jr.'s *Gospel Superfest*, an independently produced series of syndicated television specials that airs quarterly on major network affiliates (ABC, NBC, CBS), is reportedly the cumulative ratings leader among such gospel programs. His shows also air on the world's largest Christian Network, TBN (Trinity Broadcasting Network), which is carried by over two billion television households worldwide. TV One, TBN, the Christian Television Network (CTN), the Word, and the Gospel Music Channel are part of a ever-expanding list of television and basic cable outlets that feature or cover gospel artists and their diverse sounds daily.

Internet sites, such as GospelFlava.com, GospelCity.com, and Blackgospel.com, are major resources for news, interviews, and reviews, while newsletters like the *Gospel News Update*, the *Belle Report*, the *Gospel Electronic Urban Report*, and the *Gospel Zone* deliver daily or weekly news from and about the gospel music industry and related fields.

Since the mid-1990s, gospel music has helped a number of successful theatrical releases to earn millions of dollars with some of the projects even debuting in the top five at the box office. Among the most commercially successful thus far are *Tyler Perry's Diary of a Mad Black Woman* and *Tyler Perry's Madea's Family Reunion*, as well as *Woman, Thou Art Loosed* from Bishop T. D. Jakes. *The Fighting Temptations* and *Kingdom Come* both produced soundtracks that found receptive audiences. *The Gospel*, which was released in October 2005, generated strong box office and DVD sales. The film starred Boris Kodjoe and Idris Elba of HBO's *Soul Food* and *The Wire*, respectively. This "prodigal son" remake also featured such major gospel artists as Yolanda Adams, Hezekiah Walker, Martha Munizzi, and Fred Hammond, one of the film's executive producers, and resulted in a top-selling soundtrack. Another gospel-flavored film with a similar theme, *Preaching to the Choir*, was released in 2006 with Eartha Kitt, Tichina Arnold, Patti LaBelle, and Malik Yoba among its recognizable names. Though it created less buzz than its predecessor, *The Gospel*, the film has found a second life through cable television. Another theatrical release, *The Ladykillers* starring Tom Hanks, was only moderately successful at the box office. It is notable in this context because of its traditional gospel music soundtrack featuring songs by such artists as the Swan Silvertones, the Soul Stirrers, and Donnie McClurkin and because of the two inspirational hip hop tracks by the Nappy Roots.

Since the 1990s, gospel artists have also become increasingly visible in print media, including mainstream and targeted advertisements, newspaper features, and full-scale autobiographies. They have represented makeup companies (Trin-i-tee 5:7 and Mary Mary—Revlon), hair care products (Dottie Peoples—Gillette's LustraSilk), toothpaste (CeCe Winans—Crest), department and office supply stores (CeCe Winans—Kmart; Yolanda Adams—Office Depot), auto companies (Vickie Winans—Chrysler) and have been listed among the most beautiful black women (Yolanda Adams—*Essence*). Entertainment and lifestyle sections in such publications as the *New York Times* and the *Detroit Free Press,* as well as Christian lifestyle magazines, among them *Gospel Today, The Gospel Truth,* and *XII* (Twelve), make it possible for gospel music fans and those just interested in good music to read hundreds of stories about the music and its messengers. An impressive number of gospel artists have written autobiographies in recent years; the list includes Pastor Shirley Caesar, Kirk Franklin, Dr. Bobby Jones, Mary Mary, Pastor Donnie McClurkin, the Williams Brothers, and CeCe Winans.

Gospel music aficionados can also gather with thousands of others to enjoy the music they love in both festival and convention settings. Huge outdoor festivals (the Chicago Gospel Festival and the Motor City PraiseFest) have brought top artists to the community for free, artists from the surrounding area who want the exposure as well as the big names, who normally command impressive per ticket fees. Perhaps the biggest ticketed festival in the country is MegaFest, a combination of several events in one fast-paced week, produced by Bishop T. D. Jakes.

Conferences and conventions, such as the Gospel Music Workshop of America, Inc., the National Convention of Gospel Choirs and Choruses, Edwin Hawkins Music and Arts Seminar, I Hear Music in the Air, About My Father's Business, and the Gospel Heritage Foundation's Praise and Worship Conference attract thousands annually. Besides classes and new artist showcases, many of these also include recording sessions, midnight musicals, and in some cases, separate sessions for the various gospel formats: quartet, choir, and urban contemporary/holy hip hop.

Recreational activities and gospel music not only coexist but enhance one another in many scenarios. Skaters can pick up gospel skate mixes, that is, compilations of songs specially formatted for them and their favorite activity. In fact, while the skate mixes are new, gospel skating parties have existed for decades. Churches or groups rent a skating rink and hire a disc jockey who plays nothing but gospel music. Those who want to exercise to gospel music can find classes in local churches and centers or work out with videos featuring such experts as Donna Richardson (*Sweating in the Spirit*).

Christian light clubs, alternatives to night clubs, offer soft drinks and gospel music, without alcohol or smoking. Christian comedians, also called gospel comedians, have also emerged since the 1980s with names like Jonathan Slocumb, Akintunde, Broderick Rice, Small Fire (formerly Small Frie), and Sister Cantaloupe among the most recognized. Their CDs, DVDs, and live appearances poke fun at everything from long-winded preachers to dating mishaps and thus allow those who want to laugh outloud to do so without having to fast forward through racy material that has to be hidden from the children or the pastor.

When we consider that gospel music emerged just over one hundred years ago in small, virtually invisible storefront churches, the list of the new applications and forms through which the artists can share the good news and fans can receive it seems quite impressive. As these examples demonstrate, the music is no longer just for Sunday morning worship or aimed solely at the faithful. It is also clear that before the twenty-second century turns, there will be ample opportunities for scholars to focus on these emerging trends and further enlighten us on their history, development, and place within gospel music and black culture.

APPENDIX A

Beyond the term "praise and worship," there are a number of other words from the Old Testament of the Bible that have also found their way into the vocabulary of those involved in praise and worship, including its leaders, teams, and participants.

Barak—to bless the Lord by remembering all He has done.

Halal—to praise the Lord with abandon (as one would a sports team). It is found in the word "hallelujah," which can be translated "Praise Yahweh."

Shabach—to praise God with a loud, exuberant voice.

Tehillah—to sing praises to the Lord.

Towdah—to offer God a sacrifice of praise, rejoicing in something before it has even happened (such as healing).

Yadah—to acknowledge publicly with extended hand or with raised hands.

Zamar—to "touch the strings," to use musical instruments in praise.[1]

APPENDIX B

Morning service, including praise and worship

December 12, 2002

Bishop Carl B. Holland, pastor

Consuella Smith, praise and worship leader

Praise and worship team consists of five members, one man and four women, including the praise team leader, who all stand in a single line across the pulpit area of the church

11:30 Prayer

11:42 Praise and worship team enters and gets in place during last part of the prayer; approximately one hundred members of the congregation are in their seats by the time the sermon begins

Song: "O Come Let Us Adore Him" (tune: "O Come All Ye Faithful")

Verses: For He alone is worthy . . .

O Come and Lift Him Higher . . .

O Come let us adore Him . . .

11:50 Drummer and saxophonist join guitarist (some congregants have tambourines)

11:51 Song: "With my Hands Lifted Up (and My Mouth Filled with Praise)"
Most of congregation is standing

11:53 Choir enters choir stand
Congregation participates, sings with hands uplifted

11:54 Psalm 37 is read ("Fret not thyself because of evil doers")

11:55 Song: "Lord, I Lift Your Name on High" (led by Consuella Smith)
Congregation is seated
Song: "Jesus, I'll Never Forget" (old devotional song)
Most of audience is still seated
Song: "There's a Storm out on the Ocean" (old devotional song)
Song: "None Like You"
Congregation is asked to stand

12:02 Song: "Can't [Cain't] Nobody Do Me Like Jesus" (old devotional/gospel song)
Male singer takes the lead
Song: "Living, He Loved Me (Dying, He Saved Me)" (congregational song)
Song: "I Won't Let His Name Go Down" (congregational song)
Praise and worship ends

12:10 Announcements

12:15 Song: "You Can't Hurry God" (led by Kyra Edwards)

12:25 Bishop Holland comes to the podium and makes pastoral announcements

12:44 Offering
Song: "Just Want to Praise You"

12:51 Announcements

12:56 Song: "Nobody Like Jesus" (choir sings)

1:10 Bishop Holland returns to the podium

2:12 Sermon ends/altar call begins
Song: "Jesus Saves" (choir sings)

2:20 Final words from Bishop Holland
Church is dismissed.

171

APPENDIX C

Watch Night service, including a praise and worship segment
December 31, 2002–January 1, 2003
James A. Jennings Jr., pastor
Marcus Jennings, praise and worship leader

9:07 Seven praise team members, four women and three men, including
the praise leader; leader is in front; six across behind him; band consists
of organist and drummer; hundreds of congregation members are in the
pews by the time the sermon begins
Song: "God Is Good" (praise and worship)
Song: "Let Jesus Fill This Place" (praise and worship)
Song: "Wonderful (Yes He Is)" (chant)

9:22 Minister of music Jimmy Dowell ("J. D.") greets the audience with
"Praise the Lord, everybody!" and introduces the praise and worship
dancers
Song: "Jesus Be a Fence" (performed by Fred Hammond and Radical for
Christ on CD)

Six children dance, the audience claps along, and some stand
Song: "O Give Thanks unto the Lord"
The audience is exhorted to get on their feet; some also rock from side to side

9:40 Prayer by praise team leader Marcus Jennings

9:45 Praise team divides and goes to two different sides to be seated
Rev. Retha Glover recites two scriptures: Psalm 34:1–2 ("I will bless the Lord at all times") and Psalm 100 ("Make a joyful noise unto the Lord")

9:47 Song: "Praise Him"

9:52 Welcome is officially offered
Song: "Welcome" (praise and worship song). Congregation gives one another hugs and handshakes
Scripture: Psalm 150
Praise and worship team leaves

10:00 Jimmy Dowell introduces choir segments
Song (congregational): "What a Mighty God We Serve"
Two adult praise and worship dancers perform
Song: "O, To Be Kept" (hymn)

10:15 Dowell exhorts audience
Song: "This Morning When I Rose" (congregational song)

10:20 Stewardship report for 2002
Christmas ministries report

10:30 Song: "Down through the Years" (Pastor Jennings leads)
Song: "Fellowship Song" (congregational song)

10:42 Song: "Bless the Lord, O My Soul" (praise and worship song)

11:30 Sermon by Pastor Jennings begins

1:00 Service ends

APPENDIX D

Bible study, including praise and worship
August 12, 2003
Marvin L. Winans, pastor
Randy Short, praise and worship leader
Praise and worship team consists of eight women, including the leader,
and one man; six band members; hundreds of congregation members are
in their seats by the time the lesson begins

7:00 Prayer (individual, silent)

8:00 Song: "I Love You Lord" (one verse led by Pastor Winans)

8:01 Exhortation from the praise and worship leader

8:02 Song: "Hallelujah You're Worthy"

8:06 Exhortation from the praise and worship leader

8:07 Song: "Shout unto God with the Voices of Triumph (Clap Those Hands, O Ye People)"
The team leads the audience in gestures on "We lift you high . . . we clap our hands . . ."

8:12 Prayer by Pastor Winans that signals that Bible study is about to begin (including the sentence he uses each week: "May they be blessed by Thee but never impressed by me . . .")

8:13 Announcement of the beginning Scripture for the study: Romans 11:20
Song: "Great Is Thy Faithfulness" (led by Pastor Winans)

8:16 Song: "Great Is Thy Mercy" (led by Pastor Winans)

8:18 Praise team is seated; lesson begins

9:10 Song: "We Fall Down" (led by Pastor Winans)

9:30 Bible study ends

APPENDIX E

SURVEY REGARDING PRAISE AND WORSHIP
IN DETROIT AREA CHURCHES

This survey was initially distributed September 10, 2004, during the annual Detroit Musicians' Fellowship Dinner held at Hope United Methodist Church in Southfield, Michigan. The musicians who responded work for churches that they categorized under the following headings: Apostolic, Baptist, Church of God in Christ, Disciples of Christ, Methodist (African Methodist Episcopal and United Methodist), Pentecostal, United Church of Christ, Spiritual, and nondenominational. The questions and responses for each question are presented in the following table.

Question	Choices	Responses	Percentage
Praise and worship music is part of the worship experience at the church where I am employed:	A. At every service	26	70.27

Question	Choices	Responses	Percentage
	B. At most services	6	16.22
	C. Occasionally	4	10.81
	D. Never	1	2.70
Total responses received		37	100.00
This same church includes traditional devotional service songs:	A. At every service	27	72.9
	B. At most services	6	16.2
	C. Occasionally	3	8
	D. Never	1	3
Total responses received		37	100.00
Our praise and worship segment consists of:	A. Only music designated as "praise and worship"	7	18.92
	B. A combination of music forms	30	81.08
Total responses received		37	100.00
This church uses:	A. A praise and worship leader	5	13.51
	B. A praise and worship team	21	56.76
	C. Both a leader and a team	11	29.73
Total responses received		37	100.00

Question	Choices	Responses	Percentage
The time allotted for praise and worship is:	A. Open-ended	15	40.54
	B. Limited	22	59.46
Total responses received		37	100.00

NOTES

Introduction

1. Crawford, "Jazzin' God," 45; Morris, "I'll Be a Servant," 337–38.
2. For an overview of this period when gospel realized its first commercial successes, see Boyer, *How Sweet the Sound*, 49–184.
3. Tim Sinclair, "Hollywood Takes Notice of Christian Tunes," *Huntsville Times*, August 26, 2005, http://www.al.com/huntsvilletimes/.
4. Hendricks, "Holy Dope Dealer," 583.
5. GospelCity.com, "2003 Farmer Jack PraiseFest in Detroit," June 5, 2003, http://www.gospelcity.com/dynamic/news-articles/events/23.
6. Horace C. Boyer includes a section on Detroit and gospel during its formative years in *How Sweet the Sound*, 123–34.
7. National Convention of Gospel Choirs and Choruses, "Our History," http://www.ncgccinc.com/; Elon Eloni (Mary) Wilks, personal interview, May 1, 2002.
8. Charles E. Simmons, "King Solomon Baptist Church/NW Goldberg," *Michigan Citizen* (Detroit), July 10–16, 2005, Faith and Community section.
9. In 2005, 2006, and 2007 Aretha Franklin underwrote a standing-room-only, three-day musical/preaching revival at Greater Emmanuel Institutional Church of God in Christ in Detroit. See Susan Whitall, "Aretha's Taking Detroit to Church," *Detroit News*, July 24, 2005, http://www.indystar.com/.

10. Read more about Bill Moss and the Celestials, the Clark Sisters, and Mattie Moss Clark in Heilbut, *Gospel Sound*, 249–50. Also see Boyer, *How Sweet the Sound*, 125–27, for a discussion of Mattie Moss Clark and the Clark Sisters.
11. Stan North, "Kierra 'KiKi' Sheard," review of *I Owe You*, by Kierra Sheard, Gospelflava.com, September 7, 2004, http://www.gospelflava.com/reviews/kierrasheard.html.
12. In late 2005 St. James was renamed Shield of Faith International Ministries. However, without any intention of disregarding or disrespecting this new designation, it will be referred to as St. James Baptist Church within this text since the national recording history that drew me to investigate it as well as the research referenced here was completed while it was known as St. James.
13. My partner in producing the Motor City PraiseFest since 1991 has been Mike Watts of Watts-Up, Inc.

Chapter 1

1. Dorgan Needom, telephone interview, August 25, 2004. Paul Allen raised the question of whether the spate of praise and worship projects might be a case of "bandwagoning." PAJAM, personal interview, January 21, 2004.
2. Carl B. Phillips, telephone interview, February 16, 2005.
3. Munroe, *Purpose and Power*, 62, 145.
4. See appendix A for a list of some of the terminology and behaviors associated with praise and worship.
5. Marcus Jennings, personal interview, January 2, 2003.
6. Law, *Power of Praise and Worship*, 140.
7. Munroe, *Purpose and Power*, 61. For extensive discussions of praise and worship from a religious rather than academic standpoint, see Law, *Power of Praise and Worship*, and Munroe, *Purpose and Power*.
8. Consuella Smith, personal interview, January 6, 2003.
9. A. Williams, "Byron Cage Interview."
10. E.g., Leah praises God when she gives birth to a third son, Judah, whom she can present to her husband, Jacob (Genesis 29:35). The Psalms contain examples of the praises offered to God by David (Psalm 30), the descendants of Korah (Psalm 47), and even anonymous individuals (Psalm 92). And in the New Testament book of Luke, the crowds praise God for the miracles they had seen Jesus perform on the day of his triumphal entry into Jerusalem (Luke 19:36).

    The point at which Abraham prepares to sacrifice his son Isaac is one of the earliest mentions of the word "worship" in the Old Testament (Genesis 22:5). That act was, for the patriarch, a moment of worship in that he willingly submitted to what he believed was the will of God (Kenoly and Bernal, 88). The three young men who refused to bow down to the golden image made by King Nebuchadnezzar, usually called the Hebrew Boys within the Christian Church, demonstrated their unwillingness to worship anything or anyone other than their own God despite the threat of being thrown into a fiery furnace (Daniel 3). In the New Testament, the references to worship include the description of the twenty-four elders who were seated on the throne and then fell on their faces and worshipped God during John's revelation (Revelation 11:16).

11. See appendix A for a list of Hebrew words associated with contemporary praise and worship.

12. Munroe, *Purpose and Power*, 114.

13. "Shabach," written by Tobias Fox, was recorded by the Full Gospel Baptist Fellowship (*A New Thing*, 1995). It has also been recorded by Walt Whitman and the Soul Children of Chicago (*Growing Up*, 1996) and Byron Cage (*Prince of Praise*, 2003).

14. Blue Letter Bible, "The Names of God in the Old Testament," April 1, 2002, http://www.blueletterbible.org/study/misc/name_god.html (accessed May 30, 2006). Besides Munizzi, others who have recorded this praise and worship classic include Vicki Yohe, Judy Jacobs, and Juanita Bynum.

15. Certainly, the religions practiced by people of African descent throughout the diaspora are vast and encompass a variety of praise and worship rituals as well. Those, however, are outside of the focus of this chapter.

16. Among the many and varied scholarly arguments concerning the existence of African retentions within black American culture is the well-known "debate" between Melville Herskovits and E. Franklin Frazier. A concise summary of the two sides is provided by Albert J. Raboteau in *Slave Religion*, 48–55. Pearl Williams-Jones provides a list of African characteristics within gospel music in "Afro-American Gospel Music."

17. Hall, "African Religious Retentions."

18. Jackie Patillo, telephone interview, June 14, 2004.

19. Lincoln and Mamiya, *Black Church*, 1.

20. Paris, *Black Pentacostalism*, 54.

21. Pitts, *Old Ship of Zion*, 91–131.

22. Paris, *Black Pentacostalism*, 51.

23. Much of Pitts's research, especially the early chapters of his book, covers the devotional services he witnessed. For a detailed accounting of how these devotional services flow, see *Old Ship of Zion*.

24. An individual metered hymn that is performed in this style is also referred to as a "Dr. Watts," even if it was not written by Dr. Isaac Watts, the prolific English hymn writer of the eighteenth century. The label came to refer to the style, not the composer. See http://www.negrospirituals.com/song.htm.

25. Southern, *Music of Black Americans*, 29.

26. Pitts, *Old Ship of Zion*, 11.

27. Jennings, personal interview.

28. Needom, telephone interview.

29. For one example, listen to Rice, "The Deacon's Prayer."

30. Redman, "Worship Awakening," 369–70.

31. Redman explains that while the seeker service is marked by technological advances, the term goes back to the camp meetings of the early 1800s, revivalists such as Charles G. Finney, and the early Methodists, who used the label "seeker" to describe anyone interested in joining their ranks and becoming converted. He cites Aimee Semple McPherson and Robert Schuller, who used

"illustrated sermons"and "star-studded musical entertainment," respectively, as twentieth-century forerunners of the current seeker service proponents (ibid., 376–77).

32. Ibid., 376.

33. Redman describes singing in the Spirit this way: "The last phrase or line of the song may be repeated several times as a way of setting up what follows, then one musician (often the keyboardist) will repeat a two or three chord progression, creating a drone-like musical effect. The congregation takes over singing freely either in tongues or repeating a phrase in English. This can last for a few minutes or until the worship leaders feel led to end it" (ibid., 376–77).

34. Hamilton, "Triumph," 29.

35. Ibid., 31. This tendency to select a place of worship because of the music has been documented by other researchers who discuss various periods in U.S. church history. For example, Portia Maultsby notes that the Black Church of the nineteenth century pulled congregants in at least two different directions, one with services and music shaped by an African-centered aesthetic, the other with a European mode of worship. Maultsby, "Afro-American Religious Music."

36. Marvin L. Winans, personal interview, January 14, 2004.

37. The list of the artists who have won the Dove (now GMA) Award for Praise and Worship Album of the Year can be found on the GMA website: http://www.gmamusicawards.com.

38. Among them are the Winans family, Kirk Franklin, Yolanda Adams, Donnie McClurkin, Nicole C. Mullen, Martha Munizzi, and Vicki Yohe, all of whom have styles that have allowed them to reach beyond their expected constituencies with new musical sounds.

39. Taylor, "Breaking Barriers."

40. Maranatha! Music's history comes from the company's website: http://www.maranathamusic.com.

41. Promotional materials for Integrity Media, 2003–4.

42. Patillo, telephone interview, June 14, 2004. Also see the biographies section of the Integrity Music website, http://www.integritymusic.com/artists/index.html?target=/worship/artist/archives.html.

43. "We Worship You," released by holy hip hop artist the Ambassador on the CD *The Thesis,* would exemplify a praise and worship song recorded by an artist some might not readily associate with that specific genre. The Verity Records–issued, Grammy-nominated title *The Praise and Worship Songs of Richard Smallwood* contains all previously recorded songs by the acclaimed composer and singer.

44. John Leland, "Christian Music's New Wave Caters to an Audience of One," *New York Times,* April 17, 2004, late edition, A8.

45. Rachinski qtd. in ibid.; Paul Herman, personal interview, June 12, 2006.

46. I extend my gratitude to Larry Berkove, a long-time mentor and colleague, who explained this interpretation of Judaism to me and first suggested it as a way of viewing the shifts within gospel music.

47. Paul Allen, personal interview, January 21, 2004.

48. "Rhythm and praise" is a term attributed to urban contemporary gospel com-

posers and performers Anson and Eric Dawkins, known to fans as Dawkins and Dawkins. They explain the need for the label: "Gospel rhythm and blues is an oxymoron. To say that you have good news and then you're going to sing the blues about it makes no sense. So we wanted to have rhythm and praise. It fits our music, and it fits a lot of things that folks like Jimmy (J. Moss), Kirk (Franklin), Trin-i-tee 5:7 and other groups with a hip hop, R&B, urban flavor are doing." R&P integrates urban musical influences and yet can be used for worship within and beyond the walls of the traditional church. Dawkins and Dawkins, interview.

49. Carr, "Kurt Carr's One Church."
50. Taylor, "Breaking Barriers."
51. Gospelflava.com, review of *In His Presence—Live,* by Judith Christie McAllister, http://www.gospelflava.com/articles/judithchristiemcallisterpresenceaudio.html.
52. See also Taylor, review of *Live from Another Level.*
53. In fact, when asked about the number of white artists being supported by black consumers, gospel music veteran and Music World Entertainment Vice President Telisa Stinson responded by email:

> It's the most EVER! I think it has a lot to do with certain white artists having a real gospel sound and the popularity of praise and worship. However, black gospel artists that sing praise and worship don't sell nearly as well. My theory is [that it is] because the gospel community actually purchases praise and worship music by those from the Christian market, but that the Christian market doesn't buy praise and worship by gospel artists to the same extent.

A second industry professional concurred with her assessment. As a research topic, this is an area ripe for future inquiry.
54. Alliance Agency, Martha Munizzi biography, http://www.theallianceagency.com/artists/martha.htm.
55. Capital Entertainment, Vicki Yohe biography, http://www.capitalentertainment.com (accessed September 19, 2005).
56. Qtd. in Lockett, review of *I Just Want You.*
57. Radio and Records, "Gospel National Airplay," March 29, 2006, http://www.radioandrecords.com.
58. See Heilbut, "Secularization," 106.
59. While most Americans still worship among those who look like them, a number of churches, including such megachurches as Church without Walls (Tampa, FL), pastored by Paula White; Solid Rock (Monroe, OH), where Darlene Bishop is pastor; World Harvest Church (Columbus, OH), headed by Rod Parsley; and Lakewood Church (Houston, TX), led by Joel Osteen, have huge multicultural congregations. Praise and worship music and charismatic preaching are just two of the elements these churches have in common.
60. In 2006 One in Worship was held in Greensboro, North Carolina.
61. Qtd. in Nichole M. Christian, "'Spiritual Super Bowl' Puts Faith and Detroit in Spotlight," *Detroit Free Press,* June 6, 2005, available online at http://www.freep.com/voices/columnists/echristian6e_20050606.htm. Visit the One in Worship website, http://www.oneinworship.com, to read more about the event and its history.

62. Cummings, "Cross-Cultural Worship."
63. Ibid.
64. Lindsey, interview.
65. Israel and New Breed, "I Hear the Sound" (*Live from Another Level*, 2004).
66. The Reverend Edgar L. Vann Jr., telephone conversation with the author, December 31, 2002.
67. Lacy, "Fred Hammond Concert Recap."
68. Taylor, review of *Byron Cage*.
69. The Detroit Musicians' Fellowship Dinner is held annually in the fall. On September 10, 2004, the cofounder, Carolyn Cole, allowed me to distribute my survey on the use of praise and worship music. Although almost half of those who completed my survey were serving at Baptist churches, the balance represented a range of churches—Apostolic, Church of God in Christ, Disciples of Christ, Methodist (African Methodist Episcopal and United Methodist), Pentecostal, United Church of Christ, Spiritual, and nondenominational. Because of that diversity and the age range of those present (early twenties to over seventy), the results are another means of assessing the extent to which praise and worship music is used in Detroit's black churches. Appendix E presents the numbers and percentages for each of the questions the survey posed.
70. Appendices B, C, and D provide a chronological timeline for the praise and worship services observed for this study at Greater Christ Temple Church, St. James Baptist Church (aka Shield of Faith Ministries), and Perfecting Church, respectively.
71. More about Phillips and his gospel music–related service is on the Detroit Gospel.com website: http://www.detroitgospel.com.
72. Phillips, personal interview.
73. Smith, telephone interview.
74. Though one specific service is discussed for each of these churches, I have attended other services and events at these churches and at many others in the area that mirror what is reported here.
75. Smith, telephone interview.
76. Phillips, personal interview.
77. Read more about Reverend Nicks, St. James Baptist Church, and their contributions to gospel music at the Michigan State Museum's Lest We Forget: Legends of Detroit Gospel virtual exhibit, http://www.museum.msu.edu/museum/tes/gospel/nicks.htm.
78. Jennings, personal interview.
79. Watch Night services are held in black churches across the country on December 31, as believers praise God for seeing them through the year and ask for protection in the new one. The United Methodist Church traces the roots of Watch Night services to John Wesley, whom they believe held the first service in 1755 to encourage Christians to "reaffirm their covenant with God." See Waltz, *Dictionary for United Methodists*, s.v. "Watch Night Service." Snopes .com, a website dedicated to investigating urban legends, old wives' tales, etc., places the start of these services in North America in 1750 but situates the earliest Watch Night services in 1733 in what is now the Czech Republic. Snopes also debunks the legend that had been circulating since 2001 that Watch Night

began in 1862 with black slaves awaiting the enactment of the Emancipation Proclamation in 1863: http.www.snopes.com/holidays/newyears/watchnight .asp (accessed June 28, 2007).

80. Jennings, personal interview.
81. A biography of the Winans with recommended songs can be found at Soul-Tracks.com: http://www.soultracks.com/the_winans.htm.
82. M. Winans, personal interview. The Perfecting Church's website with more information on the church is http://www.perfectingchurch.org.
83. Beverly Ferguson (aka "Squeeze"), telephone interview, March 9, 2005. As the member auxiliary coordinator for Perfecting Church, Ferguson's duties include coordinating the annual Praise and Worship Weekend.
84. Randy Short, e-mail message to the author, May 5, 2004.
85. Ibid.
86. M. Winans, personal interview.
87. Short, e-mail message.
88. Needom, telephone interview.
89. Ibid.
90. Heron, "Call to Worship."
91. Carolyn Cole, telephone interview, June 18, 2007.
92. Heron, "Call to Worship."
93. Carolyn Cole, telephone interview, June 18, 2007.
94. Dorgan Needom also raised this point in a telephone interview, August 25, 2004.
95. Carolyn Cole, telephone interview, June 18, 2007.
96. Murphy, interview.
97. Marvin L. Winans, personal interview, January 14, 2004.

Chapter 2

1. Talbert, "Play by Play."
2. In "The Gospel Musical and Its Place in the Black American Theater," an updated version of his original article, "Let the Theatre Say 'Amen'" (*Black American Literature Forum* 25 [Spring 1991]: 73–82), Burdine uses the last two pages to revisit the prediction he made of the impending death of the gospel musical stage play in 1991. He writes: "How wrong I was." See Burdine, "Gospel Musical."
3. For criticism of the plays, see, e.g., Sandra Davis, "'Come out of the Rain'— Only If You Like Gospel," *Detroit Free Press*, October 3, 1991; Sandra Davis, "'Only the Strong' Delivers a Powerful Message," *Detroit Free Press*, November 22, 1992, 6D; and R. Johnson, "Songs for Salvation." For praise of the musicals, see, e.g., Pamela Sommers, "'I've Been Changed': Amen to All That," *Washington Post*, April 2, 1999, Style section, final edition; and Steve Holsey, "Momma Don't: Gospel Musical with a Message," clipping from the *Michigan Chronicle*, n.d.
4. E.g., Burdine, "Gospel Musical"; and McLaren, "From Protest to Soul Fest." Gates, "Chitlin Circuit," examines contemporary black theater, and while gospel musical plays are included, they are not the major focus of that piece. In

a much briefer article, my late colleague and fellow black theater aficionado Beverly Robinson arrived at some of the same conclusions I reached. Her article and the original version of this chapter were in press simultaneously and were published within months of one another. See Robinson, "Ticket to Heaven."

5. See, e.g., Wiggins, "In the Rapture"; Wiggins, "William Herbert Brewster"; Fletcher, "Witnessing a Miracle"; and Sugg, "Heaven Bound."

6. While Henry Louis Gates, in "The Chitlin Circuit," writes that plays like *Mama I Want to Sing* "are better regarded as pageants, or revues, than stage plays," he nevertheless describes this groundbreaking production as among the "far more respectable and well-groomed versions of gospel drama."

7. McLaren, "From Protest to Soul Fest," 50.

8. Snyder, "Serious Business," 32.

9. It has been difficult establishing the actual production dates for Matthews's plays. While the reviews for his first productions are dated 1989–91, Vanessa Williams Snyder ("Serious Business," 32) places his first production in 1983. Attempts to confirm dates with Matthews were fruitless.

10. Davis, "'Come out of the Rain'—Only If You Like Gospel"; Holsey, "Momma Don't: Gospel Musical with a Message."

11. Gates, "Chitlin Circuit," 958; Kelley L. Carter, "The Circuit Is in Town." *Detroit Free Press,* February 14, 1999, 1F, 5F.

12. Promotional materials for *Momma Don't,* May 1989.

13. Qtd. in Snyder, "Serious Business," 32.

14. Bob Davis, "Jamie Foxx and Theater Phenom David E. Talbert Behind NBC Television Special," *Soul-Patrol Times,* January 25, 2006, http://www.davisind.com/wc/view_entry.php?id=1807&date=20060127&friendly=1 (accessed June 30, 2000).

15. Angela Barrow-Dunlap, telephone interview, June 9, 2004.

16. Ibid.

17. Souvenir tour booklet for *If These Hips Could Talk,* 2004.

18. Bishop T. D. Jakes, called "America's Best Preacher" by *Time* and CNN in 2001, is a prolific author who was also one of the first to take a gospel musical play to the big screen. *Woman Thou Art Loosed* is a virtual franchise that includes a book, a series of large conferences for women, a CD, a stage play, and, finally, the movie. The film opened at number 6 or number 7 at the box office, depending on which reports one reads, and grossed $2 million that initial weekend (October 4, 2004), the amount for which it was reportedly made. "News for Shaun of the Dead 2004," Internet Movie Database, http://www.imdb.com/title/tt0365748/news; "Film Forum: Woman, Thou Art a Box Office Hit!" *Christianity Today,* http://www.christianitytoday.com/movies/filmforum/041007.html.

19. "Tyler Perry," 60–62.

20. Tony Brown, "'Mad Black Woman' Draws from Gospel 'Chitlin' Circuit,'" *San Diego Union Tribune,* March 24, 2005, http://www.signonsandiego.com/uniontrib/20050324/news_1c24black.html.

21. Raboteau, *Slave Religion,* 245; Levine, *Black Culture,* 38–41.

22. Edmonds, "Negro Little Theatre Movement," 82.
23. Qtd. in Wiggins, "William Herbert Brewster," 246.
24. Hay, "African-American Drama," 5–8.
25. See Burroughs, *Slabtown Convention*, 3, 7; Sugg, "Heaven Bound," 249; Wiggins, "William Herbert Brewster."
26. Twining, "Heaven Bound," 347–51.
27. Wiggins, "William Herbert Brewster," 245–46, 249; Heilbut, *Gospel Sound*, 60.
28. Sarah Haygood, telephone interview, March 13, 1999.
29. Snyder, "Serious Business," 33–34.
30. Larry Robinson, telephone interview, July 1, 1999.
31. R. Jones, "Orderly and Disorderly," 43–51.
32. Burdine, "Gospel Musical," 81.
33. Qtd. in Farmer, "Melodramas of Soul," 34.
34. Raboteau, *Slave Religion*, 211–88.
35. Wilson, "Ground on Which I Stand." This is the text of a speech the playwright delivered June 26, 1996, at the eleventh bienniel Theatre Communications Group national conference at Princeton University.
36. DuBois, "Krigwa Players," 134.
37. Burnim, "Symbol of Ethnicity," 170.
38. For a compelling look at Dorsey's life and the social context in which gospel developed, see M. Harris, *Rise of Gospel Blues*.
39. Maultsby, "Impact of Gospel Music," 19–33; Reagon, "Gospel Music Composers," 10–18.
40. Williams-Jones, "Afro-American Gospel Music," 376; Burnim, "Symbol of Ethnicity," 135.
41. Gates, "Chitlin Circuit," 955.
42. Al Hobbs, personal interview, April 11, 1991.
43. Burnim, "Functional Dimensions," 113.
44. A 2005 version, "Jesus Can Work It Out (Remix)," became a national hit on both gospel and secular stations.
45. E.g., Vickie Winans added Williams's special chorus to her song "Work It Out," which has a very similar message.
46. Davis, *I Got the Word*, 55–56.
47. Larry Robinson, telephone interview, July 1, 1999.
48. Comment left at http://www.davidetalbert.com.
49. Wiggins, "In the Rapture," 17.
50. E.g., there are these lyrics from the Negro spiritual "Elijah Rock": "Satan is a liar and a conjurer, too; if you don't watch out, he'll conjure you."
51. Wiggins, "In the Rapture," 16–17.
52. Ibid.
53. The Negro spiritual that comes to mind is "And He Never Said a Mumblin' Word."
54. Wiggins, "In the Rapture," 16–17.
55. Gates, "Chitlin Circuit," 953.
56. Snyder, "Serious Business," 33–34.
57. Gates, "Ghitlin Circuit," 954–55.

58. DuBois, "Negro Art," 310–11.
59. Watkins, *On the Real Side*, 30–33.
60. Tony Mayberry, telephone interview, June 2, 1999.
61. Keil, *Urban Blues*, 15.
62. Snyder, "Serious Business," 33.

Chapter 3

1. For an accessible, readable history of the relationship African Americans have had with clothing, including church attire, see White and White, *Stylin'*.
2. Lurie, *Language of Clothes*, 3–4.
3. "Fashionably correct" is a phrase attributed to Tina Campbell. Terrell, "An Inspiriting Few Minutes," 21.
4. Lerson Tanasugarn, "Buddhist Monk and Novice Summer Ordainment Program," May 20, 2003, http://www.lerson.org/social/Ordain.html (accessed September 9, 2005).
5. "Amish: General Information," Believe Religious Information Source, http://mb-soft.com/believe/txn/amish.htm (accessed September 9, 2005).
6. See Cole, *Vows*.
7. See White and White, *Stylin'*, 5–36; O'Neal, "African American Church," 125–26.
8. Ibid.
9. "But every woman that prayeth or prophesieth with her head uncovered dishonoureth her head. It is just as though her head were shaved. If a woman does not cover her head, she should have her hair cut off; and if it is a disgrace for a woman to have her hair cut or shaved off, she should cover her head." I Corinthians 11:5–6.
10. Rubenstein, *Dress Codes*, 91, 104.
11. Qtd. in ibid., 104.
12. Ibid., 104–5.
13. This is an ironic preoccupation given that in the West African world from which the enslaved were brought, there was no perceived separation between the so-called sacred and secular since God was seen as part of every aspect of life. It was only upon being brought to the New World that the enslaved Africans encountered, and many eventually adopted, the Western perspective, which often placed them at odds with those artists and others who, for cultural and personal reasons, saw no need to draw the sacred/secular dividing line in dress, music, or any other part of life. A number of scholars have examined this important aspect of African, and later African American, culture. See, e.g., Teresa L. Reed's discussion in *The Holy Profane*.
14. O'Neal, "African American Church," 125–28.
15. Ibid., 128.
16. Gwen Morton, telephone interview, April 11, 2000.
17. Morton, telephone interview, May 29, 2006.
18. This is the congregation to which I have belonged since 1984. The pastor is Dr. Charles G. Adams.

19. Nkenge Abi, telephone interview, August 11, 2006.
20. This was transcribed from listener phone calls to FM 98 WJLB taken by my intern, Sonia Green, April 23, 2006.
21. A typical yet poignant story regarding women being prohibited from entering certain sanctuaries with trousers on involves the colleagues of a deceased woman. They traveled a half hour one way to pay their respects at her church, only to find the pastor standing at the door, requiring each woman to open her coat. Women who revealed that they were wearing pants were turned away.
22. Some of the most memorable lines about the necessity of keeping feminine laps covered in church are attributed to Shirley Gaither, an evangelist and pastor's wife: "Sometimes, for example, women will wear those short skirts to church. If they sit on the front row, I tell the nurse to go put a scarf over their legs. I mean, my husband's up there trying to preach and some woman's sitting on the front row with the gates of hell wide open." Qtd. in Cunningham and Marberry, *Crowns*, 107.
23. Da'Dra Crawford Greathouse, telephone interview, June 30, 2005.
24. Calvin Terrell lists several of the items that were in the GMWA dress code as of 2003. See Terrell, "Stomps and Shouts." My favorite story about someone "skirting" the law, so to speak, centers around Sylvia Holyfield, minister of music at Detroit's St. Stephen AME Church. After being turned away from the GMWA mass choir rehearsal because she had on pants, she went to her room, put on one of the oversized T-shirts one buys while vacationing—and generally wears for sleeping—and was admitted to the rehearsal.
25. C. Phillips, telephone interview.
26. O'Neal, "African American Church," 129.
27. "Glamour Girl of Gospel Music," 24.
28. Joe Ligon, telephone interview, March 10, 1985.
29. Boyer, *How Sweet the Sound*, 226–39; Darden, *People Get Ready*, 263, 266.
30. Ernestine Rundless, one of the founding members of the Detroit-based Meditation Singers, from which Della Reese emerged, always contended that they, not the Ward Singers, sang in Las Vegas first and that their performances were in the main room while the Wards performed in the lounges. Ernestine Rundless, personal interview, Detroit, Michigan, May 12, 1985.
31. Boyer, "African American Gospel Music," 484.
32. The "Hosanna" video was released to television and cable outlets in support of the platinum-selling CD *The Rebirth of Kirk Franklin* (2003). The "Looking for You" video was released in support of *Hero* (2005).
33. See chapter 5 for a description of the various types of attire Franklin wears in the video for "The Revolution."
34. Horace C. Boyer, e-mail message to the author, August 31, 2004.
35. Pastor Shirley Caesar, the Caravans, the Coonton Spirituals, Lee Williams and the Spiritual QC's, and Evelyn Turrentine Agee are among those who are popular, award-winning traditional gospel performers as of this writing.
36. Qtd. in Light, "Say Amen, Somebody!" 92.
37. Qtd. in "Fashion Revival," 15.
38. Clark, "Being Who They Are."

39. Terrell, "Inspiring Few Minutes," 20.
40. Adams qtd. in "Fashion Revival," 15. The "Barbie" remark was made during the taping of the 2005 Stellar Awards.
41. Larry Berkove, telephone interview, September 23, 2004.
42. During my own interview with holy hip hop producer Maji, he mentioned the fact that he no longer wears fitted shirts or tank tops in public because of the disconcerting responses he received from some women, including "Wow! Look at that . . ." Rather than place himself in line to be tempted, he has removed these items from his public wardrobe. Jason Wilson, personal interview, November 3, 2003.
43. Lowe, "Put on Some Clothes." The group chose to disband in late 2006.
44. See Burnim, "Black Gospel Music Tradition," 154–55.
45. Examples of Tonex's varied techniques can be found on the CD titled *Pronounced Toe-Nay* as well as on *Out the Box.*
46. Sweet Finesse Entertainment, "Tonex Spills a Piece from the Past during Dove Awards: Don't Judge a Book by Its Cover," press release, June 15, 2005.
47. Ibid.
48. Ibid.
49. Cusic, *Sound of Light,* 365.
50. Jeff Grant, telephone interview, September 5, 2003.
51. Tracey Artis, telephone interview, July 7, 2005.
52. Eady, "Is Image Really Everything?" 11. Other handpicked groups who did perform or are still performing gospel are Ramiyah and 2103, both produced by PAJAM. The Righteous Riders, who broke up after several years of performing holy hip hop together, became a group after performing individually for a compilation produced by Tyscot Records.
53. Artis, telephone interview, July 7, 2005.
54. Eady, "Is Image Really Everything?" 10.
55. Three album covers featuring gospel artists in leather include the Winans, *Let My People Go;* the Mighty Clouds of Joy, *Night Song;* and Izzy, *In Awe of You.*
56. Also see Burnim, "Women in African American Music," 506.
57. Heilbut, *Gospel Sound,* 62. My colleague Dr. Gloria House (Aneb Kgositsile) has pointed out to me that this is a response West African women often give when moved by the music.
58. Boyer, *How Sweet the Sound,* 198; Heilbut, *Gospel Sound,* 75–77.
59. L. Jones, "Kirk Franklin," 65.
60. Heilbut, *Gospel Sound,* 248; Carpenter, *Uncloudy Days,* 182–84.
61. B. Johnson, "Fashion Revival," 15.
62. Harris, "Mirror Mirror," 12–16.
63. Eady, "Is Image Really Everything?" 11.
64. Lines from Thomas A. Dorsey's classic "The Lord Will Make a Way Somehow" as well as from Cleavant Derricks's "Have A Little Talk with Jesus" are included in the verses; Gene Maclellan's "Put Your Hand in the Hand" provides key lines in the chorus and the song's title. The R&B song "Back in Love Again," recorded by Love, Tenderness, and Devotion (LTD), is the source for other lines in the chorus.

65. Clark and North, review of *Spiritual Love*.
66. The feedback interview panel consisted of Portia Dye, choir member; Timothy Dye, choir director, praise leader, and youth leader; Kyra Edwards, choir, usher board, and nurses' guild member; Sean Mosley, praise team and youth choir member; Carl Phillips, minister of music and gospel radio announcer; Consuella Smith, praise leader and evangelist; and DeRonae Smith, choir director and minister.
67. Feedback interviews, February 3, 2000. Another factor worth investigating in the future would be how much their prior knowledge of an artist like CeCe Winans and her family's major place in gospel music history factored into their assessment of her attire and demeanor.
68. Trin-i-tee 5:7, "Spiritual Impact."
69. Dr. Esther Coleman, telephone interview, August 1, 2005.
70. Da'Dra Crawford Greathouse, telephone interview, June 30, 2005.
71. Vickie Winans, e.g., dropped seventy-five pounds through a modified version of the Atkins diet along with exercise as she discusses in a feature story in *Ebony* magazine ("Vickie Winans," 140–46). Dorinda Clark Cole talks about exercise as a regular part of her life in an interview for GospelCity.com (http://www.gospelcity.com/dynamic/artist-articles/interviews/33). Others, however, have chosen gastric bypass route for both health and cosmetic reasons. And one group of already petite singers allegedly is restricted from snacks, red meat, and anything that would move them from thin to average size.
72. To view almost two dozen generally trim gospel artists in their awards-night finery, see Brother Steve, "2006 Stellar Awards," 69–73.
73. M. Winans, personal interview.
74. The men who created the group and produced Ramiyah explained that two outfits were being shipped in for the young ladies to try on for the Stellar Awards televised ceremony. However, the first ensemble simply "did not work at all," while the second was quite form fitting. Since it was so close to performance time, the decision was made that the group would perform the best they could despite the fit of the garments; although they performed well, Ramiyah did indeed become the talk of much of the gospel music industry. PAJAM, personal interview, January 21, 2004.
75. Grant, telephone interview.
76. Qtd. in Barney, "Going through Changes," 42.
77. Teresa Hairston, telephone interview, September 7, 2005.
78. Qtd. in Barney, "Going through Changes," 42.
79. Ibid.

Chapter 4

1. Verna Green, personal interview, May 24, 2000.
2. I am indebted to the work of Rosalie Riegle Troester and Patricia Hill Collins for the theoretical foundation for this chapter. "Othermothers" is a word Riegle Troester coined to describe those women who contribute to the maturation and acculturation of children and young people other than their own. See Riegle

Troester, "Turbulence and Tenderness." Much of Collins's work on mother-hood and othermothers celebrates black women who transform the lives of children who are not their own but who also bring about positive changes in the political conditions in their cities and who confront issues of gender, class, and racial equality in the workplace. See P. Collins, Black Feminist Thought, 173–200.

3. The term "gospel announcers" is used throughout this chapter to refer to any individual who presents gospel music on radio; in most instances these indi-viduals are also asked to host in live settings as well, due to the notoriety they attain through their work on-air. Gospel announcers are also known as reli-gious announcers, gospel radio personalities, gospel disc jockeys, or DJs. "Gospel announcer" is used here because it is the name used by the Gospel Announcers Guild (GAG) of the GMWA. The guild originally referred to its members as religious announcers. The GAG is an auxiliary to the GMWA, the largest gospel music convention in the world with ten to twenty thousand del-egates attending the annual convention each August. According to Bishop Samuel Williams of New York, the vice chair of the GAG, the guild's mem-bership as of June 2005 was more than nine hundred announcers, a figure he estimates to be approximately 25 percent of those who play gospel music on ra-dio in the United States.

4. Maultsby, "Afro-American Religious Music," 12–14; Reagon, "Gospel Music Composers," 13–15.

5. Boyer, "Take My Hand," 142–43; M. Harris, "Thomas A. Dorsey," 176–79.

6. Heilbut, *Gospel Sound,* xxix; Maultsby "Impact of Gospel Music," 26; Lornell, *"Happy in the Service,"* 23.

7. Spaulding, "History of Black-Oriented Radio," 102–4; Lornell, *"Happy in the Service,"* 22–33.

8. Cantor, *Wheelin' on Beale,* 89.

9. Spaulding, "History of Black-Oriented Radio," 93.

10. Barlow, *Making of Black Radio,* 57.

11. Here, I am referring to works that cover many decades of radio history or that focus specifically in one or more sections on gospel radio. E.g., in *Legendary Pi-oneers of Black Radio,* Gilbert A. Williams lists some of the men and women of the 1950s and 1960s, including Martha Jean "the Queen" Steinberg, who be-came "cultural heroes" because of their on-air style and community deeds (16). Yet, while the work of many of the men he cites is documented through the personal interview chapters presented in his book, not one woman, let alone any woman gospel announcer, receives this analysis. In *Woke Me Up This Morn-ing,* Alan Young presents three separate interviews with gospel announcers; not one of them is female. David Carson, in *Rockin' Down the Dial,* breaks this mold by devoting a chapter to Steinberg; however, his work stops at the 1970s and, thus, does not allow for a discussion of her switch from R&B to gospel music. Horace Boyer's article "Gospel Music" names five important women an-nouncers and the cities from which they broadcast: Mary Mason (Philadel-phia), Mary Dee (Baltimore), Mary Holt (Cleveland), June McCray (Miami), and Irene Joseph [*sic*] Ware (Mobile).

12. Barlow, *Making of Black Radio*, 35–46, 93–95.
13. Cantor, *Wheelin' on Beale*, 86; Allen, *Singing in the Spirit*, 35.
14. Spaulding, "History of Black-Oriented Radio," 116–17.
15. Mother Mattie Davis, telephone interview, August 18, 1993.
16. Cantor, *Wheelin' on Beale*, 89.
17. John Phillips and Vermya Phillips, personal interview, August 13, 1991. Also see Consolidated Productions, biography of Vermya H. Phillips, http://www.cosdtd.com/vermyaphillips_bio.htm.
18. Pauline Wells Lewis, personal interview, August 14, 1991.
19. Anthony Heilbut writes, "On many sepia stations, the most community-minded people are the gospel d.j.'s." *Gospel Sound*, 268.
20. DjeDje, "Gospel Music," 52.
21. The list includes Albertina Walker, founder in 1952 of the Caravans, one of gospel's most popular and star-studded groups ever, who worked in radio on Chicago's WMPP from 1980–85. In 2000 Vickie Winans, award-winning gospel recording artist, television host and commercial spokesperson, was named announcer for two weekend programs on WYBA 106.3 FM, Chicago, *Music in the Air* and *Churchin' with Vickie*. Another Stellar Award winner, Evelyn Turrentine-Agee, was cohost of a program called *War on Sin* in Detroit for five years. She and her cohosts played music, introduced live performances, and, because of their day jobs in various community service agencies, also dispensed information on legal matters, social services, food programs, etc. In 2007 Yolanda Adams began hosting a nationally syndicated daily radio program based in Houston, Texas, her hometown.
22. Martha Jean Steinberg, personal interview, October 13, 1993.
23. Ibid. See also Cantor, *Wheelin' on Beale*, 91–92; Carson, *Rockin' Down the Dial*, 198. A record label was named Premium Stuff in Steinberg's honor in the 1960s; three recordings were made on that label. Soulful Detroit.com, "The Mike Hanks Story: 1967: Premium Stuff and Wee 3." http://www.soulfuldetroit.com/web11-mike%20hanks/mike%20hanks%20text/14-mh-1967%20premium%20etc.htm.
24. Steinberg, personal interview.
25. Carson, *Rockin' Down the Dial*, 198–99.
26. Williams, *Legendary Pioneers of Black Radio*, 16.
27. Steinberg, personal interview.
28. Program book for the seventeenth annual King of Kings Palm Sunday Gospel Service, Fisher Theater, Detroit, Michigan, April 16, 2000.
29. Qtd. in ibid.
30. Ibid.
31. Steinberg, personal interview; Tim Kiska and Charles Hurt, "Martha Jean Was First in the Hearts of Her Fans," *Detroit News*, January 2000, http://www.detnews.com/ 2000/metro/0001/30/01300017.htm; King of Kings Palm Sunday program book.
32. V. Green, personal interview.
33. King of Kings Palm Sunday program book.
34. Irene Johnson Ware, telephone interview, June 2, 2000.

35. Every one of the more than forty-five announcers I have interviewed for my research has described his or her work as constituting or being an extension of ministry.

36. Ware, telephone interview, June 16, 2000. Ware remembers that Katherine Delcambre was the first Miss Mandy; she could not recall the name of the second but states that neither stayed longer than two years.

37. Several colleagues with whom I shared these names were taken aback. They came to the same conclusion I did: "Mandy" sounds very much like "Mammy," who was the alleged keeper of the master's kitchen and children during slavery. "Topsy Turvy" brings to mind Topsy, the "star" of what Patricia A. Turner calls the semi-humorous/semi-tragic subplot of the wild slave child in *Uncle Tom's Cabin*. See *Ceramic Uncles*, 13–14 and 24–25, for her reading of these images within American culture.

38. Ware, telephone interview, June 2, 2000.

39. Ware, telephone interview, February 12, 2006.

40. McAdams, "WGOK GM," 92.

41. Paris, *Black Pentecostalism*, 54. Paris calls the song and testimony services, the sermon, and the altar call the "major subsegments" of the service. For an extended look at how several gospel announcers, including Steinberg, incorporate these elements into commercial radio programs, see Pollard, "Gospel Announcers."

42. Steinberg, personal interview.

43. Ware, telephone interview, June 28, 2000.

44. Vails, "Let's Have Church."

45. King of Kings Palm Sunday program book.

46. Tim Kiska, "Martha Jean 'the Queen': Radio Voice of the 'Forgotten Man,'" *Detroit News*, March 10, 1996, http://www.detnews.com/michig/pages/ steinber/steinber.html.

47. Justin Hyde, "Detroit's First Casino Set to Open Today," *Las Vegas Sun*, July 29, 1999, http://www.lasvegassun.com (accessed May 18, 2000).

48. V. Green, personal interview.

49. Steinberg, personal interview.

50. Ibid.

51. Ware, telephone interview, June 16, 2000.

52. Ibid. and Ware, telephone interview, June 2, 2000.

53. Ware used to write national columns for both *Record World* and *Black Radio Exclusive*. An extensive yet partial list of her awards and achievements can be found in the online Sheroes Archives of the National Association of Black Female Executives in Music and Entertainment, Inc.: http://www.nabfeme .org/html/ware-irene.htm.

54. Ware, telephone interview, June 2, 2000.

55. Ibid.; McAdams, "WGOK GM"; website for NABFEME, the National Association of Black Female Executives in Music and Entertainment: http:// www.womenet.org.

56. King of Kings Palm Sunday program book.

57. Jay Butler, telephone interview, June 14, 2000; Carol Cruickshank, telephone interview, June 16, 2000; Ware, telephone interview, June 2, 2000.

58. Butler, telephone interview; V. Green, personal interview, 2000.
59. H. LeBaron Taylor, telephone interview, May 26, 2000. Taylor also included on his list of noteworthy women gospel announcers Louise Williams Bishop of Philadelphia.
60. Detroit Regional Chamber, "Chamber History: Chronology—Part 2 (1954–2003)," http://www.detroitchamber.com/detroiter/articles.asp?cid=103&detcid=83 (accessed June 26, 2006).
61. George Stewart, telephone interview, June 16, 2000.
62. Ware, telephone interview, June 16, 2000.
63. Stewart, telephone interview.
64. Sam Williams, telephone interview, June 12, 2000.
65. Ware, telephone interview, February 12, 2006. Though not currently in broadcast radio, Ware remains a presence in both the local and national radio and gospel music worlds and has received two more heritage awards since her departure from the airwaves. After being appointed to and completing a three-and-a-half-year term on the Mobile County Personnel Board, Ware was elected to the post, where she is scheduled to remain through 2010.
66. Ojay, "A Woman's Touch"; Jerry Boulding, telephone interview, May 25, 2000.
67. Teresa Hairston, telephone interview, September 7, 2005.
68. Lisa Collins, telephone interview, June 16, 2000.
69. The website can be found at http://www.musicalsoulfood.com/home.asp.
70. Juandolyn Stokes, personal interview, February 2006.
71. L. Collins, *Gospel Music Industry Roundup*, 56.
72. Ibid., 48–57.
73. Louversey Green, telephone interview, February 2006.
74. Students in my first Introduction to Gospel Music course at the University of Michigan–Dearborn (fall 2004) monitored Pender's program and were asked to comment on what they heard in terms of the criteria we had discussed for gospel announcers. Many of them wrote moving tributes to Pender's ability to "sound as if I could tell her anything without being judged" and to "play something for every taste." Pender herself was so touched by what was written that she asked the students' permission to run their essays in her obituary.

Chapter 5

1. Holy hip hop artists are also known as Christian rappers and Christian emcees. However, there are others who prefer to be known as hip hop artists who are Christians or rappers with a Christ-centered message. In this chapter and book, I use "holy hip hop" (HHH) to refer to all the artists who use hip hop as a vehicle for disseminating the gospel message.
2. One of the most vocal in his attacks against hip hop in general, including HHH, is Elder G. Craige Lewis, who has traveled the country for more than a dozen years denouncing the genre as a tool of Satan. See his website at http://www.exministries.com to read his extensive arguments.
3. A handful of academic articles investigate the hip hop–gospel music connection. In "Facing Truth and Resisting It," Garth Kasimu Baker-Fletcher examines and categorizes the rhymes of African American Christian rappers

using the theory that "the Christian message is expressed in rap music through the polarities of oppugnancy [creative forms of resisting oppression] and/or opacity [the tendency of oppressed people to simultaneously live with negativity and oppose it] using religious symbols and language" (30). In "Santa Claus Ain't Got Nothing on This!" Guthrie P. Ramsey Jr. explores the broader hip hop aesthetic in the performances of such gospel artists as Karen Clark Sheard and Kirk Franklin. In "Rappin' for the Lord," Cheryl Renee Gooch looks at the fact that some Black Church leaders view the use of gospel rap as a complement to other religious music forms. In "Rap Culture, the Church, and American Society," Michael Eric Dyson states that rap mirrors the weaknesses and strengths of society; examining it more critically would allow the church and others to identify their own shortcomings. This chapter differs from these works in that I argue that a close textual analysis of the testimonies and rhymes of holy hip hoppers reveals their commitment to delivering the gospel message of their forefathers in a package for their contemporaries.

4. Smitherman, *Talkin' and Testifyin'*, 76.
5. Paris, *Black Pentacostalism*, 54.
6. Raboteau, *Slave Religion*, 237.
7. One classic story told by Shirley Caesar is "Hold My Mule" found on *Live in Chicago with Rev. Milton Brunson and the Thompson Community Singers*. Among the best-known stories performed by Dorothy Norwood is "The Denied Mother" recorded on Dorothy Norwood and the Combined Choir of Atlanta, Georgia, *The Denied Mother*.
8. Smitherman, *Talkin' and Testifyin'*, 42–43.
9. Boyer, "African American Gospel Music," 486.
10. Tim Smith, personal interview, September 25, 2003.
11. Cummings, "America's Holy Hip Hop." Allmusic.com presents a one-sentence critique of Wiley, whom it calls "the original gospel rapper" at http://www.allmusic.com/cg/amg.dll?p=amg&sql=11:cyec97u7krkt. An equally brief mention of Michael Peace, whom Allmusic.com says debuted in 1987, can be found at http://www.allmusic.com/cg/amg.dll?p=amg&sql=11:kifyxqq5ldke. Lisa B. Deaderick also calls Wiley, Peace, and D-Boy Rodriguez the ones who were the first Christian rap artists. See "Two Turntables . . . and the Son of God," *Daily Press*, March 4, 2006, http://www.dailypress.com/features/religion/ (accessed June 26, 2007).
12. Carpenter, *Uncloudy Days*, s.v. "Wiley, Stephen."
13. T. Smith, personal interview.
14. Carpenter, *Uncloudy Days*, s.v. "Wiley, Stephen."
15. T. Smith, personal interview.
16. Southern, *Music of Black Americans*, 463–64; Boyer, *How Sweet the Sound*, 12–29.
17. See Smith and Jackson, *Hip Hop Church;* John Leland, "Rappers Are Raising Their Churches' Roofs.," *New York Times*, September 13, 2004; Gaines, "More Churches Getting in Step"; and Kay S. Pedrotti, "Holy Hip-Hop: Saturday Night Gathering Captures Teen Talent, emotions," http://www.thelutheran.org/.
18. Dr. D, telephone interview, January 22, 2005.

19. Campo-Flores, "Get Your Praise On." In this article, Campo-Flores covers Club 3 Degrees in Memphis.
20. The Edwin Hawkins Music and Arts Seminar, the Gospel Heritage Praise and Worship Conference, and the Bobby Jones Retreat have included urban contemporary artists, including those who perform holy hip hop, as panelists and performers.
21. For a look at rap with references to Islam, Rastafarianism, humanism, and Christianity, see Pinn, *Noise and Spirit*. See also Reed, *Holy Profane*, 149–60.
22. *College Drop Out* was briefly nominated in 2004 for a gospel Stellar Award in the category of Rap/Hip Hop CD of the Year until it was pointed out that West's CD contains several songs with sexually explicit lyrics and profanity and was, therefore, an unsuitable candidate for such a nomination. See Gospel City.com, "Kanye West Removed from Stellars Ballot," September 27, 2004, http://www.gospelcity.com/dynamic/industry-articles/industry_news/103. In May 2005 West was nominated in the Best Gospel Artist category by Black Entertainment Television (BET). See Jawn Murray, "Straight Talk," AOL Black Voices, May 23, 2005, http://bv.channel.aol.com/entmain/buzz_canvas?id=20050520181209990001.
23. Kia Jones-Glenn, e-mail message to the author, December 10, 2004.
24. See Light, "Say Amen, Somebody!"
25. K. Franklin, *Church Boy*.
26. Kim Williams listed the names Tonex uses for his various incarnations, including Tonex-singing, T.boy-production, T.Bizzy-hip-hop, O'ryn-rock/experimental/abstract, and Anthony C. Williams II-preaching/speaking. E-mail message to the author, December 24, 2004.
27. Ibid. Also see Cunningham, "America's Holy Hip-Hop."
28. This designation does not include artists such as Aretha Franklin and Amy Grant who sing both secular and gospel. GospoCentric Records vice president Tracey Artis explains that Franklin had sold twelve million units as of February 2005. E-mail message to the author, December 24, 2004.
29. Batdorf, review of *Nu Nation Project*.
30. I conducted feedback interviews in 2000 by showing "The Revolution" and several other videos to seven gospel music fans, twenty to thirty-five years in age, who also serve as choir members, ministers, and/or praise and worship leaders in their churches.
31. The symbol of the cross is a prevalent, if not ubiquitous, presence in urban contemporary gospel videos serving as a framing device in videos by Hezekiah Walker ("Let's Dance"), Trin-i-tee 5:7 ("Put Your Hand in the Hand . . ."), and the Cross Movement ("When I Flow") to name a few.
32. Qtd. from the Cross Movement website, http://www.crossmovement.com.
33. This information and much more can be found on the Cross Movement's website: http://www.crossmovement.com.
34. ChristianHipHopper.com, 2006, http://www.christ-in-a-hip-hopper.com/pages.asp?pageid=38574 (accessed June 29, 2006).
35. Dockett, "The Cross Movement."
36. Corbin, review of *Human Emergency*.

37. Kim Williams, e-mail message to the author, December 24, 2004; Corbin, *review of Human Emergency.*
38. Kia Jones-Glenn, e-mail message to the author, December 10, 2004. Another group whose name is known to those who do not see themselves as HHH fans is Grits, having both toured and recorded with gospel icon CeCe Winans, performing such songs as "Anybody Wanna Pray?" (*The Throne Room,* 2003) and "A Place Like This" (*Purified,* 2005).
39. E.g., Tonic of the Cross Movement recounted being caught off guard amid the positive responses that followed a performance in 1990, when a young lady said to him, "What you're doing is of Satan." David Segal, "The Rap That MTV Won't Play," *Washington Post,* October 22, 2000. Other artists and even pioneering HHH radio announcer Tim Smith recalled similar charges from those who were not fans of Christian rap during my personal interviews with them.
40. The Quest (Reginald and Eboni Dockery), personal interview, August 2, 2004.
41. Ward, *How I Got Over,* 1.
42. The Ambassador (William Branch), personal interview, October 25, 2003.
43. Vanessa Bell Armstrong qtd. in B. Jones, *Touched by God,* 201.
44. Jason Wilson (Maji), personal interview, November 3, 2003. He has served as executive producer or producer on such Christian-themed rap projects as *The Yunion: H.E.R. Project* (2004) and *The Yuinon: Genocide* (2005).
45. Segal, "The Rap That MTV Won't Play."
46. Genesis 3:15 forecasts this confrontation when God says to Satan, "I will put enmity between thee and the woman, and between thy seed and her SEED. It shall bruise thy head, and thou shall bruise His heel." It is also to be found in many of the eschatological (end time) scriptures found in Revelation that the Cross Movement and other HHH groups reference frequently.
47. Shannon Gaston (Vessel), e-mail message to the author, November 25, 2004. He and his coproducers expect to rerelease their documentary on Christians who use rap to evangelize on DVD. *The Next Level,* Team Elohim (Vessel— Shannon Gaston, Greg Zonca, and Korey L. Campbell), producers, 2001.
48. See, e.g., Revelation 21:1: "And I saw a new heaven and a new earth: for the first heaven and the first earth were passed away; and there was no more sea."
49. E.g., it is the mode of escape used by the slaves in the folktale retold in Hamilton, *The People Could Fly.* The song, "I'll Fly Away," a congregational song that has also been performed in traditional and contemporary gospel forms, contains the words:
    One glad morning when this life is over, I'll fly away
    To a land on God's celestial shore, I'll fly away . . .
    Just a few more weary days and then, I'll fly away
    When I die, Hallelujah by and by, I'll fly away.
50. In the book of Job, chapters 26, 28, and 31, as well as in Psalm 88 and Proverbs 15 and 27, Abaddon appears to be a term for the dwelling place of the dead. But in Revelation 9:11 it is a person, the angel who reigns over the abyss. See Youngblood, *Nelson's New Illustrated Bible Dictionary,* 2. For an extensive look at this word, see Huie, "Who Is the Destroyer?" The scripture references for this dense set of lines include Isaiah 27:1 and Revelation 12:3, 17:1–14, 19:20, and 21:1.

51. E.g., the Ambassador of the Cross Movement holds a bachelor of science degree in Bible from Lancaster Bible College as well as a master's degree in theology from Dallas Theological Seminary. His master's thesis is titled "Theological Implications of Hip-Hop Culture." The Ambassador Online, "About the Ambassador," http://www.theambassadoronline.com/pages.asp?pageid=25110. Da'T.R.U.T.H. is a graduate of both Philadelphia Biblical University and the Institute of Jewish Studies, http://www.datruth.net/default2.asp.
52. The phrase "weak in the knees" is an old description of an individual's response to his or her beloved as well as the title of a song made popular in 1992 by the R&B girl group SWV (Sisters with Voices), which, along with the group, is referenced in the lyrics.
53. For a highly satirical look at how difficult to decipher some Christian rap lyrics have been deemed by some, see "Christian Hip-Hop Artist's Lyrics Too Theologically Complex for Rap Fans," *Holy Observer,* May 15, 2004, http://www.holyobserver.com/detail.php?isu=v02i01&art=dawgma (accessed May 5, 2005).
54. Capulong and North, review of *Higher Definition.*
55. Marvin Winans, lecture titled "Detroit, Gospel Music, and the Winans," University of Michigan–Dearborn, November 10, 2004.

Epilogue

1. Lisa Collins lists the top gospel releases as well as the projects released by the major and independent labels in each issue of *The Gospel Music Industry Roundup.* See, e.g., the 2007 edition, pp. 8, 19–20.

Appendix A

1. See Munroe, *Purpose and Power,* 114–25; and Law, *Power of Praise and Worship,* 130–35.

WORKS CITED

Recordings

The Ambassador. "I Love You Jesus." *Christology in Laymen's Terms.* Seventh Street
  Records/Diamante, 2000.
————. "My Clothes, My Hair." *The Thesis.* Cross Movement Records, 2005.
————. "We Worship You." *The Thesis.* Cross Movement Records, 2005.
BB Jay. "His Love." *Universal Concussion.* Jive Records, 2001.
Caesar, Shirley. "Hold My Mule." *Live in Chicago with Rev. Milton Brunson and the
  Thompson Community Singers.* Rejoice Records, 1988.
Caesar, Shirley, with Tonex. "I Know the Truth." *I Know the Truth.* Shu-Bel Records,
  2005.
Carr, Kurt. "If I Tell God." *One Church.* Gospo Centric/Zomba Records, 2005.
Corey Red and Precise. "The Answer." *Street Prophecy Volume II.* 2004. http://www
  .coreyred.net.
Cosmopolitan Church of Prayer Choir. "Jesus Can Work It Out." *1600 AM WWRL
  Presents Inspirational and Gospel Classics.* Savoy, 1986.
The Cross Movement. "Blood Spilla." *Heaven's Mentality.* Cross Movement Records,
  1997.
————. "Cry No More." *Holy Culture.* Cross Movement Records, 2003.
————. "Rise Up." *Holy Culture.* Cross Movement Records, 2003.
————. "When I Flow." *Holy Culture.* Cross Movement Records, 2003.
Da' T.R.U.T.H. "My Story." *Moment of Truth.* CMR Records, 2004.

Franklin, Kirk. "Hosanna" video. *The Rebirth of Kirk Franklin*. GospoCentric, 2003.
———. "Looking for You" video. *Hero*. GospoCentric, 2005.
———. "Now Behold the Lamb." *Kirk Franklin: Christmas*. GospoCentric Records, 1995.
———. "The Revolution" video. *The Nu Nation Project*. GospoCentric, 1998.
———. "Stomp." *God's Property from Kirk Franklin's Nu Nation*. GospoCentric Records, 1997.
Gospel Gangstaz. "Once Was Blind." *I Can See Clearly Now*. GospoCentric Records, 2001.
Hayes, Charles. "Jesus Can Work It Out (Remix)." Icee Records, 2005.
Israel and New Breed. "Come in from the Outside." *Live from Another Level*. Integrity Gospel, 2004.
———. "Friend of God." *Live from Another Level*. Integrity Gospel, 2004.
———. "I Hear the Sound." *Live from Another Level*. Integrity Gospel, 2004.
Kiwi (Kimberly Williams). "Pure Flave." *Pure Gospel, Pure Flava*. Crystal Rose Records, 2002.
———. Tired." *The Window*. Jordan River's Pen, 2007.
McAllister, Judith Christie. "Because of Who You Are." *Say the Name*. Sony, 2005.
———. "Expressions from My Soul." *In His Presence Live*. Artemis Strategic, 2006.
———. "Praise Jam." *In His Presence Live*. Artemis Strategic, 2006.
———. "This Is The Day." *Send Judah First*. Judah Music Records, 2001.
Norwood, Dorothy. "The Denied Mother." *Dorothy Norwood and the Combined Choir of Atlanta, Georgia: "The Denied Mother."* Savoy Records, n.d.
Papa San (Tyrone Thompson). "Step Pon Di Enemy." *God & I*. GospoCentric Records, 2003.
Rice, Broderick. "The Deacon's Prayer." *Tommy Ford Presents Broderick E. Rice*. Born Again Records, 1996.
"Shabach." Recorded by the Full Gospel Baptist Fellowship Mass Choir. *A New Thing: Experience the Fullness*. GospoCentric, 1995.
———. Recorded by Walt Whitman and the Soul Children of Chicago. *Growing Up*. CGI Records, 1991.
Tonex. *Out the Box*. Verity Records, 2004.
———. *Pronounced Toe-Nay*. Jive Records, 2000.
Trin-i-tee 5:7. "My Body," *Spiritual Love*. B-Rite Music, 1999.
———. "Put Your Hand." *Spiritual Love*. B-Rite Music, 1999.
The Winans. "It's Time." *Return*. Warner Brothers, 1990.
Winans, CeCe, with Grits. "Anybody Wanna Pray?" *The Throne Room*. Pure Springs Records, 2003
———. "A Place Like This." *Purified*. Pure Springs Records, 2005.
Winans, Marvin L. *Marvin L. Winans Presents Perfected Praise*. Sparrow Star Song, 1992.
Winans, Marvin L., and the Perfected Praise Choir. *Friends*. Against the Flow Records, 2001.
Winans, Vickie. "The Diet Medley." *Share the Laughter*. CGI Records 5339, 1999.
———. "Work It Out." *Vickie Winans*. Light Records, 1994.

Yohe, Vicki. *I Just Want You.* Pure Springs Records, 2003.
————. *He's Been Faithful.* Pure Springs Records, 2005.

Published Sources

Allen, Ray. *Singing in the Spirit.* Philadelphia: University of Pennsylvania Press, 1991.
Baker-Fletcher, Garth Kasimu. "Facing Truth and Resisting It." In *Noise and Spirit: The Religious and Spiritual Sensibilities of Rap Music,* ed. Anthony B. Pinn, 29–48. New York: New York University Press, 2003.
Barlow, William. *The Making of Black Radio.* Philadelphia: Temple, 1999.
Barney, Deborah Smith. "Going through Changes." *Gospel Today,* April–May 1996.
Batdorf, Rodney. Review of *Nu Nation Project,* by Kirk Franklin. All Music Guide. http://www.mp3.com/albums/322381/reviews.html (accessed June 28, 2006).
Boyer, Horace C. "African American Gospel Music." In *African Americans and the Bible,* ed. Vincent L. Winbush, 464–88. New York: Continuum, 2000.
————. "Gospel Music." In *Black Women in America: An Historical Encylopedia,* ed. Darlene Clark Hine, 495–97. Brooklyn: Carlson, 1993.
————. *How Sweet the Sound: The Golden Age of Gospel.* Washington, DC: Elliott and Clark, 1995.
————. "Take My Hand, Precious Lord, Lead Me On." In Reagon, *We'll Understand It Better By and By,* 141–63.
Brother Steve. "2006 Stellar Awards: Gospel's Glitziest Affair!" *Gospel Today,* March–April 2006.
Burdine, Warren R. "The Gospel Musical and Its Place in the Black American Theater." In *A Sourcebook of African-American Performance: Plays, People, Movements,* ed. Annemarie Bean, 190–203. London: Routledge, 1999.
Burnim, Mellonee. "The Black Gospel Music Tradition: A Complex of Ideology, Aesthetic, and Behavior." In *More Than Dancing,* ed. Irene V. Jackson, 147–67. Westport, CT: Greenwood, 1985.
————. "The Black Gospel Music Tradition: Symbol of Ethnicity." PhD diss. Indiana University, 1980.
————. "Functional Dimensions of Gospel Music Performance." *The Western Journal of Black Studies* 12 (1988): 112–21.
————. "Women in African American Music: Gospel." In *African American Music,* ed. Mellonee Burnim and Portia Maultsby, 493–508. New York: Routledge, 2006.
Burroughs, Nannie Helen. *The Slabtown Convention.* 23rd ed. Washington, DC: Nannie H. Burroughs, 1988.
Carpenter, Bil. *Uncloudy Days: The Gospel Music Encyclopedia.* San Francisco: Backbeat Books, 2005.
Campo-Flores, Arian. "Get Your Praise On." *Newsweek,* April 19, 2004.
Cantor, Louis. *Wheelin' on Beale.* New York: Pharos, 1992.
Capulong, Maria, and Stan North. Review of *Higher Definition,* by the Cross Movement. http://www.gospelflava.com/reviews/crossmovementdefinition.html (accessed March 19, 2004).

Carr, Kurt. "Kurt Carr's One Church." Interview by Rene Williams. GospelCity.com, April 21, 2005. http://www.gospelcity.com/dynamic/artist-articles/interviews/191 (accessed June 12, 2006).

Carson, David. *Rockin' Down the Dial.* Troy: Momentum Books, 2000.

Clark, Melanie. "Being Who They Are: Interview with Mary Mary." Gospelflava.com. 2000. http://www.gospelflava.com/articles/marymary2.html (accessed May 9, 2004).

Clark, Melanie, and Stan North. Review of *Spiritual Love,* by Trin-i-tee 5:7. Gospelflava.com. 1999. http://www.gospelflava.com/reviews/spirituallove.html.

Cole, Dorinda Clark. Interview by Christopher Heron. Gospelcity.com. January 3, 2003. http://www.gospelcity.com/dynamic/artist-articles/interviews/33 (accessed May 29, 2006).

Cole, Harriet. *Vows: The African-American Couples' Guide to Designing a Sacred Ceremony.* New York: Simon and Schuster, 2004.

Collins, Lisa, ed. *Gospel Music Industry Roundup 2007.* Los Angeles: Eye on Gospel, 2007.

Collins, Patricia Hill. *Black Feminist Thought: Knowledge, Consciousness, and the Politics of Empowerment.* Boston: Unwin Hyman, 1990.

Corbin, Jon. Review of *Human Emergency,* by the Cross Movement. April 12, 2005. http://cmusicweb.com/hiphop/crossmovement/humanemergency.shtml.

Crawford, George W. "Jazzin' God." *The Crisis* 36, no. 2 (February 1929): 45.

Cummings, Tony. "America's Holy Hip Hop." *Cross Rhythms,* January 7, 2003. http://www.crossrhythms.co.uk/articles/print.php?Article_ID=7033 (accessed June 26, 2007).

———. "Cross-Cultural Worship Is the Name of the Game for Pioneering Israel Houghton." *Cross Rhythms,* April 26, 2006. http://www.crossrhythms.co.uk/articles/music/Israel_Houghton/21248/p1/ (accessed June 13, 2007).

Cunningham, Michael, and Craig Marberry. *Crowns: Portraits of Black Women in Church Hats.* New York: Doubleday, 2000.

Cusic, Don. *The Sound of Light: A History of Gospel and Christian Music.* Milwaukee: Hal Leonard, 2002.

Darden, Robert. *People Get Ready.* New York: Continuum, 2004.

Davis, Gerald L. *I Got the Word in Me and I Can Sing It, You Know.* Philadelphia: University of Pennsylvania Press, 1985.

Dawkins and Dawkins. Interview by Mark Christian Tilles. Gospelflava.com. 1999. http://www.gospelflava.com/articles/dawkins.html (accessed April 24, 2005).

DjeDje, Jacqueline Cogdell. "Gospel Music in the Los Angeles Black Community: A Historical Overview." *Black Music Research Journal* 9, no. 1 (Spring 1989): 35–79.

Dockett, Kymo. "The Cross Movement: Making Some Major Moves!!" *What's the Word.* June 27, 2005. http://www.wtwmagazine.com.

DuBois, W. E. B. "Negro Art." *The Crisis* 22 (June 1921). Reprinted in *The Oxford W. E. B. Du Bois Reader,* ed. Eric J. Sundquist, 310–11. New York: Oxford University Press, 1996.

———. "Krigwa Players Little Negro Theater." *Crisis* 32 (July 1926): 134.

Dyson, Michael Eric. "Rap Culture, the Church, and American Society." *Black Sacred Music: A Journal of Theomusicology* 6, no. 1 (1992): 268–73.

Eady, Saul, Jr., "Is Image Really Everything?" *Gospel Industry Today.* March 2000.

Edmonds, Randolph. "The Negro Little Theatre Movement." *The Negro History Bulletin* 12 (1949): 82–86, 92–94.

"Film Forum: Woman, Thou Art a Box Office Hit!" *ChristianityToday.com.* www.christianitytoday.com/movies/filmforum/041007.html.

Franklin, Kirk, with Jim Nelson Black. *Church Boy.* Nashville: Word Publishing, 1998.

Fletcher, Winona L. "Witnessing a 'Miracle': Sixty Years of *Heaven Bound* at Big Bethel in Atlanta." *Black American Literature Forum* 25 (Spring 1991): 83–92.

Gaines, Adrienne S. "More Churches Getting in Step with Hip-Hop Music." *Charisma.* August 2003.

Gates, Henry Louis, Jr. "The Chitlin Circuit." *New Yorker.* February 3, 1997, 44–50. Reprinted in Walter Levy, ed., *Modern Drama: Selected Plays from 1879 to the Present* (Upper Saddle River: Prentice Hall, 1999), 945–59.

"Glamour Girl of Gospel Music." *Ebony.* October 1957.

Gooch, Cheryl Renee. "Rappin' for the Lord: The Uses of Gospel Rap and Contemporary Music in Black *Religious* Communities." In *Religion and Mass Media: Audiences and Adaptations,* ed. Daniel A. Stout and Judith M. Buddenbaum, 228–42. Thousand Oaks: Sage Publications, 1996.

Hall, Robert L. "African Religious Retentions in Florida." In *Africanisms in American Culture,* ed. Joseph E. Holloway, 107–11. Bloomington: Indiana University Press, 1990.

Hamilton, Michael S. "The Triumph of the Praise Songs." *Christianity Today* 43, no. 8 (July 12, 1999): 28–35.

Hamilton, Virginia. *The People Could Fly.* Illustrations by Leo and Diane Dillon. New York: Knopf, 2004.

Harris, Michael W. *The Rise of Gospel Blues: The Music of Thomas Andrew Dorsey in the Urban Church.* New York: Oxford University Press, 1992.

———. "Thomas A. Dorsey: Conflict and Resolution." In Reagon, *We'll Understand It Better By and By,* 165–82.

Harris, Teresa, with Fred Steen, Jr. "Mirror Mirror on the Wall." *Gospel Industry Today.* June 2000.

Hay, Samuel A. "African-American Drama, 1950–1970." *Negro History Bulletin* 36 (1973): 5–8

Heilbut, Anthony. *The Gospel Sound.* 1971. Reprint, New York: Limelight, 1997.

———. "The Secularization of Black Gospel Music." In *Folk Music and Modern Sound,* ed. William Ferris and M. L. Hart, 101–15. Jackson: University of Mississippi Press, 1982.

Hendricks, Obery M., Jr. "'I Am the Holy Dope Dealer': The Problem with Gospel Music Today." In *Readings in African American Church Music and Worship,* ed. James Abbington, 553–89. Chicago: GIA Publications, 2001.

Heron, Christopher. "The Call to Worship: The Titans of Today's Worship Teams Speak." GospelCity.com, March 25, 2003. http://www.gospelcity.com/dynamic/artist-articles/interviews/152 (accessed June 20, 2007).

Holt, Grace Sims. "Stylin' outta the Black Pulpit." In *Rappin' and Stylin' Out: Communication in Urban Black America,* ed. Thomas Kochman, 189–204. Urbana: University of Illinois Press, 1972.

Huie, Bryan T. "Who Is the Destroyer?" December 1997. http://users.aristotle.net/~bhuie/abaddon.htm (accessed June 29, 2006).

Johnson, Billy, Jr. "Fashion Revival." *Entertainment Weekly,* May 26, 2000, 15.

Johnson, James Weldon. *God's Trombones.* 1927. Reprint, New York: Viking Press, 1976.

Johnson, Reed. "Songs for Salvation." *American Theatre* 13, no. 2 (February 1999): 18+.

Jones, Bobby. *Touched by God.* New York: Pocket Books, 1998.

Jones, Lisa C. "Kirk Franklin: New Gospel Sensation–Gospel Musician." *Ebony.* October 1995.

Jones, Rhett S. "Orderly and Disorderly Structures: Why Church and Sports Appeal to Black Americans and Theatre Does Not." *Black American Literature Forum* 25 (Spring 1991): 43–52.

Keil, Charles. *Urban Blues.* Chicago: University of Chicago Press, 1966.

Kenoly, Ron, and Dick Bernal. *Lifting Him Up: How You Can Enter into Spirit-led Praise and Worship.* Lake Mary, FL: Creation House, 1995.

Lacy, Dwayne. "Fred Hammond Worship Alive Concert Recap, October 10, 2004, in Houston, Texas." Gospelflava.com. http://www.gospelflava.com/articles/fredhammondworshipaliveconcert2004.html.

Law, Terry. *The Power of Praise and Worship.* Tulsa: Victory House, 1985.

Levine, Lawrence W. *Black Culture and Black Consciousness.* 1977. Reprint, Oxford: Oxford University Press. 1978.

Light, Alan. "Say Amen, Somebody! Kirk Franklin Puts the 'Go' Back into Gospel." *Vibe.* October 1997.

Lincoln, C. Eric, and Lawrence Mamiya. *The Black Church in the African American Experience.* Durham: Duke University Press, 1990.

Lindsey, Aaron. Interview by Christopher Heron. GospelCity.com, July 2003. http://www.gospelcity.com/dynamic/artist-articles/interviews/1.

Lockett, DeAngella. Review of *I Just Want You,* by Vicki Yohe. GospelCity.com, October 1, 2003. http://www.gospelcity.com/dynamic/music-articles/reviews/61 (accessed March 5, 2005).

Lornell, Kip. *"Happy in the Service of the Lord": African-American Sacred Vocal Harmony Quartets in Memphis.* 1988. Reprint, Knoxville: University of Tennessee Press, 1995.

Lowe, Valerie G. "Put on Some Clothes." *Charisma,* August 2004. http://www.charismamag.com/a.php?ArticleID=9441 (accessed September 9, 2006).

Lurie, Alison. *The Language of Clothes.* 1989. Reprint, New York: Owl, 2000.

McAdams, Janine. "WGOK GM Johnson-Ware Keeps Priorities Focused." *Billboard* 108, no. 47 (November 23, 1996): 92.

McLaren, Joseph. "From Protest to Soul Fest: Langston Hughes' Gospel Plays." *Langston Hughes Review* 15 (1997): 49–51.

Maultsby, Portia. "Afro-American Religious Music: A Study in Musical Diversity." Papers of the Hymn Society of America 35. Springfield, OH: The Hymn Society of America, 1981.

———. "The Impact of Gospel Music on the Secular Music Industry." In Reagon, *We'll Understand It Better By and By,* 19–33.

Morris, Kenneth. "I'll Be a Servant for the Lord." Interview with Bernice Johnson Reagon in Reagon, *We'll Understand It Better By and By,* 337–38. Washington: Smithsonian Institution Press, 1992.

Murphy, William, III. Interview by Rene Williams. GospelCity.com, September 24, 2004. http://www.gospelcity.com/dynamic/artist-articles/interviews/134.

Munroe, Myles. *The Purpose and Power of Praise and Worship.* Shippensburg: Destiny Image, 2000.

The Next Level. Holy Hip Hop Documentary. Team Elohim (Vessel—Shannon Gaston; Greg Zonca, and Korey L. Campbell), producers. 2001.

Ojay, Eddie. "A Woman's Touch." Interview. Program #7. *Black Radio: Telling It Like It Was.* Produced by Jacquie Gales Webb, Lex Gillespie, Sonja Williams. Radio Smithsonian. 1996. Transcript.

O'Neal, Gwendolyn S. "The African American Church, Its Sacred Cosmos and Dress." In *Religion, Dress and the Body,* ed. Linda B. Arthur, 117–34. Oxford: Berg, 2000.

Paris, Arthur. *Black Pentecostalism: Southern Religion in an Urban World.* Amherst: University of Massachusetts Press, 1982.

Pinn, Anthony B., ed. *Noise and Spirit: The Religious and Spiritual Sensibilities of Rap Music.* New York: New York University Press, 2003.

Pitts, Walter F., Jr. *Old Ship of Zion: The Afro-Baptist Ritual in the African Diaspora.* 1993. Reprint, New York: Oxford University Press, 1996.

Pollard, Deborah Smith. "Gospel Announcers (Disc Jockeys): What They Do and Why It Matters," *Arkansas Review: A Journal of Delta Studies* 31, no. 2 (August 2000): 87–101.

Raboteau, Albert J. *Slave Religion.* 1978. Reprint, Oxford: Oxford University Press, 1980.

Ramsey, Guthrie P., Jr. "Santa Claus Ain't Got Nothing on This! Hip Hop Hybridity and the Black Church Muse." *Race Music: Black Culture from Bebop to Hip-Hop.* 2003. Reprint, Berkeley: Center for Black Music Research, 2004. 190–215.

Reagon, Bernice. "Pioneering Gospel Music Composers." In Reagon, *We'll Understand It Better By and By,* 10–18.

———, ed. *We'll Understand It Better By and By.* Washington, D.C.: Smithsonian, 1992.

Redman, Robert R. "Welcome to the Worship Awakening." *Theology Today* 58, no. 3 (October 2001): 369–83.

Reed, Teresa L. *The Holy Profane.* Lexington: University Press of Kentucky, 2003.

Robinson, Beverly. "Ticket to Heaven." *American Theatre* 16, no. 9 (November 1999): 22+.

Riegle Troester, Rosalie. "Turbulence and Tenderness: Mothers, Daughters, and 'Othermothers' in Paule Marshall's *Brown Girl, Brownstones.*" In *Double Stitch,* ed. Patricia Bell-Scott et al., 163–72. New York: HarperPerennial, 1993.

Rubenstein, Ruth P. *Dress Codes.* Boulder: Westview, 1995.

Smith, Efrem, and Phil Jackson. *The Hip Hop Church: Connecting with the Movement Shaping Our Culture.* Downer's Grove, IL: InterVarsity Press, 2005.

Smitherman, Geneva. *Talkin' and Testifyin': The Language of Black America.* Boston: Houghton Mifflin, 1977.

Snyder, Vanessa Williams. "The Serious Business of Gospel Plays." *Gospel Today* 10, no. 6 (August 1999): 32–34.

Southern, Eileen. *The Music of Black Americans: A History.* 1971. Third Edition. New York: Norton, 1997.

Spaulding, Norman W. "History of Black-Oriented Radio in Chicago, 1929–1963." PhD diss. University of Illinois at Urbana-Champaign, 1981.

Sugg, Redding S., Jr., ed. and comp. "Heaven Bound." *Southern Folklore Quarterly* 27 (December 1963): 249–66.

Talbert, David E. "Play by Play." GospelCity.com, July 24, 2000. http://www.gospelcity.com/dynamic/industry-articles/articles/14.

Taylor, LaTonya. "Breaking Barriers." *Christianity Today*, January 19, 2004. http://www.christianitytoday.com/music/interviews/2004/byroncage-0104.html (accessed March 4, 2005).

———. Review of *Byron Cage*, by Byron Cage. *Christianity Today*, January 19, 2004. http://www.christianitytoday.com/music/reviews/2003/byroncage.html (accessed August 25, 2005).

———. Review of *Live from Another Level*, by Israel and New Breed. http://www.christianitytoday.com/music/reviews/2004/livefromanotherlevel.html.

Terrell, Calvin. "An Inspiriting Few Minutes with Mary Mary." *Sister 2 Sister.* November 2002.

———. "Stomps and Shouts: GMWA Celebrates 36th Anniversary in Tampa." *Sister 2 Sister.* November 2003. http://www.s2smagazine.com/content/content.asp?issueid=200311&listid=09 (accessed June 26, 2006).

Trin-i-tee 5:7. "Spiritual Impact." Interview by Willie Gary. Black Family Channel (formerly the MBC Network). Original airdate May 31, 2002.

Turner, Patricia A. *Ceramic Uncles and Celluloid Mammies.* New York: Anchor, 1994.

Twining, Mary A. "'Heaven Bound' or 'the Devil Play.'" *CLA Journal* 14 (1976): 347+.

"Tyler Perry: Meet the Man behind the Urban Theatre Character Madea." *Jet*, December 1, 2003, 60–64.

Vails, Donald R. "Let's Have Church." Interview. Program #10. *Black Radio: Telling It Like It Was.* Produced by Jacquie Gales Webb, Lex Gillespie, Sonja Williams. Radio Smithsonian. 1996. Transcript.

Van Biema, David. "America's Best Spirit Raiser." *Time.* September 17, 2001.

"Vickie Winans: At Home with the Gospel Star Who Lost 75 Pounds and Reenergized Her Career." *Ebony.* August 2003.

Waltz, Alan K. *A Dictionary for United Methodists.* Nashville: Abingdon Press, 1991.

Ward-Royster, Willa, with Toni Rose. *How I Got Over: Clara Ward and the World-Famous Ward Singers.* Philadelphia: Temple University Press, 1997.

Watkins, Mel. *On the Real Side.* New York: Simon and Schuster, 1994.

White, Shane, and Graham White. *Stylin': African American Expressive Culture.* Ithaca, NY: Cornell University Press, 1998.

Wiggins, William H., Jr. "In the Rapture." In the Festival of American Folklife program booklet. Washington, DC: Smithsonian Institution and the National Park Service, 1976: 16–17.

———. "William Herbert Brewster." In *We'll Understand It Better By and By*, ed. Reagon, 245–51.

Williams, Andrea R. "The Byron Cage Interview." *Gospel News Update*, August 25, 2003.

Williams, Gilbert A. *Legendary Pioneers of Black Radio.* Westport, CT: Praeger, 1998.

Williams-Jones, Pearl. "Afro-American Gospel Music: A Cyrstallization of the Black Aesthetic." *Journal for the Society of Ethnomusicology* 19, no. 3 (September 1975): 373–85.

Wilson, August. "The Ground on Which I Stand." *American Theatre* (September 1996): 14+.

Winans, CeCe with Renita Weems. *On a Positive Note.* New York: Atria, 1999.

Young, Alan. *Woke Me Up This Morning: Black Gospel Singers and the Gospel Life.* Jackson: University of Mississippi Press, 1997.

Youngblood, Ronald F., general ed. *Nelson's New Illustrated Bible Dictionary.* Nashville: Nelson, 1995.

Interviews

Abi, Nkenge. Telephone interview. August 11, 2006.

Allen, Paul. Personal interview. Detroit, MI. January 21, 2004.

The Ambassador (William Branch). Personal interview. Detroit, MI. October 25, 2003.

Artis, Tracey. Telephone interview. May 11, 2004.

———. Telephone interview. July 7, 2005.

Barrow-Dunlap, Angela. Telephone interview. June 9, 2004.

Berkove, Larry. Telephone interview. September 23, 2004.

Boulding, Jerry. Telephone interview. May 25, 2000.

Butler, Jay. Telephone interview. June 14, 2000.

Cole, Carolyn. Telephone interview, June 18, 2007.

Coleman, Esther. Telephone interview. August 1, 2005.

Collins, Lisa. Telephone interview. June 16, 2000.

Cruickshank, Carol. Telephone interview. June 16, 2000.

Davis, Mattie. Telephone interview. August 18, 1993.

Dr. D (Duane A. Knight). Telephone interview. January 22, 2005.

Feedback interviews. Detroit, MI. February 3, 2000. Respondents: Portia J. Dye, Timothy Dye, Kyra D. Edwards, Sean C. Mosley, Carl Phillips, Consuella Smith, and DeRonae K. Smith.

Ferguson, Beverly. Telephone interview. March 9, 2005.

Grant, Jeff. Telephone interview. September 5, 2003.

Greathouse, Da'Dra Crawford. Telephone interview. June 30, 2005.

Green, Louversey. Telephone interview. February 2006.

Green, Verna. Personal interview. Troy, MI. May 24, 2000.

Hairston, Teresa. Telephone interview. September 7, 2005.

Harris, Bertha. Telephone interview. June 12, 1995.

Haygood, Sarah. Telephone interview. March 13, 1999.

Hobbs, Al. Personal interview. Indianapolis, IN. April 11, 1991.

Jennings, Marcus. Personal interview. Detroit, MI. January 2, 2003.

Lewis, Pauline Wells. Personal interview. Salt Lake City, UT. August 14, 1991.

Ligon, Joe. Telephone interview. March 10, 1985.

Manners, Claudette. Personal interview. Oak Park, MI. February 16, 1995.

Mayberry, Tony. Telephone interview. June 2, 1999.

Morton, Gwen. Telephone interview. April 11, 2000.

———. Telephone interview, May 29, 2006.

Needom, Dorgan. Telephone interview. August 25, 2004.

PAJAM (J. Moss, Walter Kearney, and Paul Allen). Personal interview. Detroit, MI. January 21, 2004.

Patillo, Jackie. Telephone interview. June 14, 2004.

Phillips, Carl B. Personal interview. Detroit, MI. January 6, 2003.

———. Telephone interview. October 22, 2004.

Phillips, John, and Vermya Phillips. Personal interview. August 13, 1991.

The Quest (Reginald Dockery and Ebony Dockery). Personal Interview. Detroit, MI. August 2, 2004.

Robinson, Larry. Telephone interview. July 1, 1999.

Smith, Consuella. Personal interview. January 6, 2003.

———. Telephone interview. February 16, 2005.

———. Telephone interview. March 9, 2005.

———. Telephone interview. June 16, 2005.

Smith, Tim. Personal Interview, September 25, 2003.

Steinberg, Martha Jean. Personal interview, Detroit, MI. October 13, 1993.

Stewart, George. Telephone interview. June 16, 2000.

Stokes, Juandolyn. Personal interview. Atlanta, GA. February 2006.

Taylor, LeBaron. Telephone interview. May 26, 2000.

Ware, Irene Johnson. Telephone interview. June 2, 2000.

———. Telephone interview. June 16, 2000.

———. Telephone interview. June 28, 2000.

———. Telephone interview. February 12, 2006.

Wilks, Elon Eloni. Personal interview. Detroit, MI. May 1, 2002.

Williams, Sam. Telephone interview, June 12, 2000.

Wilson, Jason (Maji). Personal interview. Detroit, MI. November 3, 2003.

Winans, Marvin L. Personal interview. Detroit, MI. January 14, 2004.

Winans, Vickie. Telephone interview. June 12, 1995.

———. Telephone interview. June 20, 2005.

INDEX

Note: Italicized page numbers refer to illustrations.